The English Lan~~~~~~
Poetry of South

The English Language Poetry of South Asians

A CRITICAL STUDY

Mitali Pati Wong

with Syed Khwaja Moinul Hassan

McFarland & Company, Inc., Publishers

Jefferson, North Carolina, and London

ALSO OF INTEREST

The Fiction of South Asians in North America and the Caribbean: A Critical Study of English-Language Works Since 1950, by Mitali P. Wong and Zia Hasan (McFarland, 2004)

ISBN 978-0-7864-3622-4
softcover : acid free paper ∞

LIBRARY OF CONGRESS CATALOGUING DATA ARE AVAILABLE

BRITISH LIBRARY CATALOGUING DATA ARE AVAILABLE

Cover photograph © 2013 Shutterstock

Manufactured in the United States of America

McFarland & Company, Inc., Publishers
Box 611, Jefferson, North Carolina 28640
www.mcfarlandpub.com

To the memory of the late
Syed Khwaja Moinul Hassan,
who collaborated with the author in the
early stages of research on this project. — M.P.W.

Acknowledgments

Many thanks are in order for Mrs. Labiba Hassan for her support of this project following the death of her husband, Syed Hassan. I also wish to thank Claflin University's Center for Excellence in Teaching for a summer research grant that helped me to acquire a significant amount of materials, and one semester of sabbatical leave in 2010 that facilitated the completion of this project. Special thanks go to the librarians at the Claflin University library for their assistance with acquisitions as well as interlibrary loans. I am grateful to my colleague Dr. Mohammed Yousuf, associate professor of politics and justice studies at Claflin University, for assisting me with the acquisition of collections of poetry from different countries. Thanks are also due to Ms. Lisa Young, who served as a research intern in 2009 and assisted with the review of literature for several chapters.

The completion of this manuscript would not have been possible without the support of my family. I am very grateful for my daughter Sumitra's very generous assistance with typing several chapters, and my daughter Paramita's assistance with locating publishers of many little-known first editions of poetry when Syed and I first began this project. Finally, there are no words to express my gratitude for husband Dr. Eugene Wong's continuous encouragement and support with the daily grind of actual composition as I devoted all my spare time to this manuscript.

Table of Contents

Preface

While studying the types of English-language fiction composed by writers of the South Asian diaspora for *The Fiction of South Asians in North America and the Caribbean* (2004), I was struck by the fact that some of the authors had also published volumes of poetry. Upon discussion with my colleague Dr. Syed Hassan (now deceased), who was himself a diasporic South Asian poet as well as a critic of postcolonial poetry, we commenced exploratory research and found that there was very limited scholarship on the poetry of the South Asian diaspora, and definitely much less than scholarship on South Asian fiction. We realized that there was a major need for a critical study of South Asian poetry that established connections in time, place, themes, motifs, and methodology in the context of the growing body of scholarship on postcolonial theory. We envisioned a critical study that would lay the foundation for systematic future studies in the academy of the English-language poetry of South Asians.

Living in the twenty-first century, in which South Asians often emigrate from continent to continent, setting narrow boundaries in terms of taxonomy (such as "Indian Poetry in English," "Indian Poetry," "Caribbean Poetry," "Canadian Poetry," "Sri Lankan Poetry," "Poetry from Fiji") constricts scholarship in finding common literary devices and common experiences in the English-language poetry of the South Asian diaspora. Even the editors who work within national boundaries, as is the case with *Indivisible: An Anthology of Contemporary South Asian American Poetry* (2010), comprehend the need to recognize contemporary English-language poets of South Asian descent in the United States at a level comparable to the recognition given to fiction writers (Banerjee et al. xv). Syed did not live to read Jahan Ramazani's *A Transnational Poetics* (2009), a work of scholarship that has significantly influenced this volume. Nor did Syed have the opportunity to read the poems anthologized in *Indivisible* (2010), which takes a transnational approach to the poetry of the South Asian diaspora in the United States.

1

While in the area of contemporary postcolonial literary criticism there is more emphasis on theorizing literature, almost at the expense of the text, the lack of a study that maps or surveys (an unfashionable term) English-language South Asian poetry to render this body of poetry accessible to educators and students is evident. Anthologies are compiled by poets both in the Indian subcontinent and in the United States offering selections according to the editors' preferences for certain types of poetry over others. Despite the increasing geopolitical importance of the region in the second decade of the twenty-first century, commonly used anthologies of world literature and Asian literature provide very little or no exposure to this body of poetry. This volume seeks to close the gap by providing ten chapters and a closing piece, arranged in a work that critically surveys the English-language poetry of South Asians in terms of time, place, themes, and poetic methodologies. The transnational perspective taken in this study seeks to reach transnational audiences. To this end, selective notes have been provided at the end of chapters to keep the content accessible to readers whose backgrounds in history and critical theory may be quite diverse. Due to copyright restrictions, only two lines have been quoted per poem discussed. Working with this limitation, I have used numerous paraphrases, hoping that readers will be encouraged to seek the full text of the poems analyzed in the chapters.

While readers and scholars in the Indian subcontinent may be familiar with the colonial and postcolonial English-language poets of that region, they may not be as familiar with the poetry of the old and new South Asian diaspora. Similarly, those familiar with the poetry of the diaspora may not be as familiar with the poetry of the subcontinent. Hence, this study seeks to establish connections between colonial and postcolonial South Asian poetry in English as well as between the poetry of the old and new diaspora and the subcontinent, which can be done by adopting a transnational perspective. Jeet's recent anthology titled *The Bloodaxe Book of Contemporary Indian Poets* (2008) presents poets whose audience is Indian even though several of the poets currently live and work abroad. Poets as editors can be uncomfortable with chronological and thematic clustering (Banerjee et al., *Indivisible* xvi), but critical studies cannot ignore chronology, themes, and poetic methodology. This study recognizes the need for flexibility and therefore seeks throughout to point out "much of the exciting resonances *between* poets" (*Indivisible* xvi) of South Asian ancestry through place and time. The resonances are transnational and may be appreciated in the context of the poetry of the Indian subcontinent as well as the poetry of the old and new South Asian diaspora. To this end, I hope that I have fulfilled the goals set by my deceased collaborator.

My colleague and friend Syed always maintained that as an English-language South Asian poet from Bangladesh, he was "a citizen of the world." He also often observed that diasporic South Asian poetry in English could be published from any country in any continent, transcend specific ethnic connotations, and engage a diverse reading public. With Syed's serious illness in February 2008, and his untimely death while he was on the road to recovery on April 3, 2009, this research project suffered serious setbacks. At the time, I was waiting to combine Syed's drafts with my work, and I had composed chapters five, six, seven, and nine, and part of chapter one. When Syed was hospitalized in 2008, I was unable to acquire any of his drafts or notes. After his death in 2009, I received permission from both Syed's widow and the publisher of this volume to compose the chapters that were his share of this project. The road has been long and difficult. Aside from the overarching philosophy of this work that combines both Syed's views and my own, and his vision that the English-language poetry of South Asians would continue to grow and flourish in the twenty-first century, the discussions presented in all eleven chapters of this volume present my own work.

Syed was a popular English professor among both his students and colleagues. By the time I took up Syed's unfinished work, I observed that Syed's former students and colleagues were often quoting from Syed's published poetry. And none of these admiring readers were of South Asian heritage! It was as if after Syed's death, Syed's poetry demonstrated his hypothesis regarding the widespread appeal of South Asian poetry — its passion, its protests, its *angst*. Syed often stated with flippancy that he had spent a lifetime "trying to be human" and "learning to be human." Indeed, the central motifs of South Asian poetry in English are about the human condition itself. Shortly before his death, while discussing my efforts to continue this project over the telephone, Syed quoted passages from Shakespeare's *King Lear* from memory to me: "unaccommodated man is no more but such a poor, bare, fork'd animal." The two hundred years of English-language poetry composed by South Asians return us again and again to the elemental condition of being frail and human in the universe.

Mitali Pati Wong

ONE

Locating South Asian Voices: The Transnational Case for South Asian Poetry in English

South Asian poetry in English began in the Indian subcontinent in the early nineteenth century, lost momentum during the independence movement of the early decades of the twentieth century, and in the post–World War II era has continued to develop and flourish across national boundaries as literary artists of the South Asian diaspora spread into different continents. In the late twentieth and early twenty-first centuries, South Asian poetry in English presents both transnational and specific national paradigms. In *Clio Unbound* (1979), Arthur B. Ferguson interprets the term "paradigm" as "denot[ing] a pattern of shared ideas, values, and assumptions that provides the generally accepted language for the discussion of a given issue affecting the life of a society" (258). Also appropriate is an earlier application of the term "paradigm" by Renaissance historian J.G.A. Pocock, who writes in *Politics, Language, and Time* (1971) that

> paradigms controlling concepts and theories — so satisfactorily discharge the intellectual functions expected of them that they authoritatively indicate not merely the solutions to problems, but the kinds of problems which are to be conceptualized as requiring solution [13].

The purpose of this study is to explore the transnational poetics of English-language South Asian poetry while at the same time grouping poets flexibly according to regions, time periods, literary movements, and poetic methodologies. The term "transnational poetics" is adapted from Jahan Ramazani's *A Transnational Poetics* (2009). Ramazani states:

> The main reasons why mononational constructions of modern and contemporary poetry do not suffice should be obvious. That many of the key modernists were expatriates is frequently rehearsed. "Modern Western culture," summarizes

Edward Said, "is in large part the work of exiles, émigrés, refugees,"[1] Yet the implications of such human displacement for nation-based literary histories have not been fully absorbed within institutions of literary instruction, dissemination, and criticism, which remain largely nation-centric. Whether these migrant writers left home compelled by politics or lured by economics, whether in search of cultural traditions or freedom from the burden of such traditions, whether for publishing opportunities, educational advancement, or new cultural horizons, they produced works that cannot always be read as emblematic of single national cultures [24–25].

In his essay titled "Contemporary Postcolonial Poetry," Jahan Ramazani notes that "postcolonial studies has also been surprisingly unreceptive to postcolonial poetry" (*A Companion to Twentieth Century Poetry* 597). Ramazani's view is that "since poetry mediates experience through a language of exceptional figural and formal density, it is a less transparent medium by which to recuperate the history, politics and sociology of postcolonial societies" (597). Ramazani reminds us that the genre of poetry "also demands specifically literary modes of response and recognition — of figurative devices, generic codes, stanzaic patterns, prosodic twists and allusive turns" (597).

This critical study seeks to establish parameters for over one hundred and fifty years of English-language poetry by South Asians with regard to poetics, canon, genre, and ultimately the inner anxiety (*angst*) expressed in the poetry that relates the self of the poet to the unrest and injustices of the temporal and spatial world that the artist inhabits. These correspondences are discernible in both the much-maligned poetry of colonial times and the modernist and postmodernist postcolonial poetry from the Indian subcontinent as well as the diaspora. In addition to focusing upon poetic methodology, the analysis of poems in the following chapters covers the relevance of historical allusions as well as underlying concerns of gender, race, and class. Comparisons are offered between poets of different places and time periods, although due to the diversity of the poets, the sociopolitical paradigms that surface in the poetry vary according to the temporal and spatial contexts. Overall, South Asian poets are perceptive of injustice and oppression as evidenced in their writings. It is interesting to note that the perception of injustice in the colonial poetry has been succeeded by an awareness of inequities of gender and class in the postcolonial poetry of the Indian subcontinent, and the awareness of inequities of race, class, and gender in the poetry of the diaspora. Hence, to the formidable body of poetry discussed in this study one might apply Octavio Paz's comment: "Poetry is knowledge, salvation, power, abandonment. An operation capable of changing the world, poetic activity is revolutionary by nature; a spiritual exercise, it is a means of interior liberation. Poetry reveals this world, it creates another" (*The Bow and the Lyre* 3). This application of Octavio Paz's definition also serves as a reminder of Paz's close association with avant-garde Indian poetry circles in both English and vernacular Indian languages such as Bangla/Bengali during Paz's term as Mexican ambassador to India during the 1960s.

While critical studies of a few individual poets are being published in the Indian subcontinent, these studies seem to be used by academics mainly within specific national boundaries. According to Vinay Dharwadkar, "Viewed as a whole at the beginning of the twenty-first century, the map of subcontinental poetry in English looks larger, more crowded, and more diverse than its map at any time in the first one hundred and fifty years of its existence" (264). Dharwadkar has aptly diagnosed the malaise that has continued to afflict the systematic (and unbiased) study of South Asian poetry in English, especially in the Indian subcontinent:

> What is equally remarkable is that, consciously or unconsciously, they also continue to engage in the dialectic of critique, counter-critique and self-reflexive critique launched by early nineteenth-century prose writers, even though the objects of their critical-poetic imagination are now very different: ethnic identities rather than racial divisions, male dominance rather than European colonization, civil war rather than religious conversion, separatism rather than balkanization, and self-contained nations rather than expanding empires" [279].

In comparison, criticism on South Asian fiction continues to proliferate across the world, and university curricula for courses on South Asian literature in English mostly emphasize contemporary fiction with limited attention to poetry.[2] It is interesting to note that not one of the chapters of *Modern South Asian Literature in English* (2003) by Paul Brians, otherwise a valuable introduction for university courses on South Asian writers, examines the contributions of a modern or postmodern English-language poet of South Asian origin. From the 1970s to the 1990s a number of influential anthologies were published by Oxford University Press, and these anthologies have made some poets more accessible than others. The poets of the Indian subcontinent have been anthologized somewhat more systematically than the poets of the diaspora. Bruce King's exhaustive landmark study *Modern Indian Poetry in English* (first edition 1987, second edition 2001), complete with charts of biographies and the histories of publishing houses and literary journals, has provided a valuable beginning toward establishing of a canon of Indian English poetry after 1947. However, King's focus on poets from the national boundaries of the Indian republic leads to limited discussions of diasporic poets and poets from other countries of the subcontinent. Also, after the publication of the first edition of King's book, two of the Indian poets discussed in that edition relocated to the United States on a long-term basis, a phenomenon that makes a strong case for the application of the methodology of transnational poetics in analyzing the major paradigms of the English-language poetry of South

Asians. With regard to poets of the South Asian diaspora, the very recent publication of *Indivisible: An Anthology of Contemporary South Asian American Poetry* (2010), with its inclusion of forty-nine diasporic South Asian poets, suggests that the mapping continues. Even as editors of anthologies seek to preserve the works of poets whose slim volumes may not have survived beyond single editions with limited circulation, the relative neglect of English-language South Asian poetry can be related to the absence of a critical study that examines the major paradigms of colonial and postcolonial South Asian poetry from a transnational (and global) perspective.

For a transnational approach to South Asian poetry, it is important to define the South Asian diaspora that is spread across the world. Exploring the literature of indenture, Mariam Pirbhai writes:

> When we speak of diasporic South Asians today we are referring to people — be they descendants of the oldest diasporic communities or part of more recent migrations — who now occupy a common position away from the Indian subcontinent, a distance that is experienced, to differing degrees, in geographic, national, linguistic, political, socioeconomic, ethnocultural, religious, and gendered terms. Of course, the diversity and complexity of South Asian identity can be traced to the Indian subcontinent itself, a densely populated region whose cultural fabric is as ancient as it is changing, and as cohesive as it is fragmented. On the other hand, South Asian identity continues to be shaped within the equally complex framework of multiple cultural and national affiliations that stretch from East to South Africa, West to South-East Asia, the Caribbean region, North America, Europe, Australia, New Zealand, and the islands of the Indian Ocean and the Pacific Rim [13].

Pirbhai points out that in the nineteenth century, the South Asian diaspora was represented by the indentured workers brought to the British colonies to replace slaves on plantations (3–5). This "old diaspora" was followed by a new diaspora in the twentieth century as there developed a need for technical and other professionals:

> South Asian immigration to North America, Europe, and Britain's settler colonies mainly brings to view a second wave of migration of which the initial catalysts were the interrelated factors of the world wars and the decolonization of the British Empire. For instance, the period between the 1960s and 1980s witnessed a substantial increase in South Asian migration as a response to Europe and North America's shortage of industrial, skilled, and professional labour, resulting in the subsequent lifting of their racially discriminatory immigration policies [6].

Hence, the poetry of the South Asian diaspora includes the voices of the immigrant professionals writing of lost homelands, as in the poems of Agha Shahid Ali, Zulfikar Ghose, Sasenarine Persaud and the late A.K. Ramanujan, as well as poets such as Fiji-born Sudesh Mishra and Guyana-born Cyril

Dabydeen and David Dabydeen, who often allude to the histories of indenture of ancestral memory.

Transnational Poetics and Postcolonial Theory

One of the most challenging tasks faced by the individual who seeks to study the approximately one hundred and eighty years' worth of published English-language poetry by South Asians is envisioning the vast circumference of a theoretical umbrella[3] that can include the earliest nineteenth-century English-language poets from Kolkata such as Kasiprasad Ghose as well as the contemporary South Asian American poets published in the 2010 anthology *Indivisible*. This is where it becomes helpful to view the almost two centuries of South Asian English-language poetry as a historical continuum that begins with nationalism and the poetry of resistance, stagnates under overpowering nationalism, and is reinvented under late modernism, postmodernism, confessionalism, existentialism, and surrealism to become a vehicle of the late twentieth and early twenty-first centuries' transnational poetics.

It is necessary to explain the application of Jahan Ramazani's theory of transnational poetics in the context of this study. According to Ramazani, poetry seems like "an improbable genre to consider within transnational contexts" (*A Transnational Poetics* 3). He writes, "While prose fiction's interdiscursive and intercultural porosity is frequently rehearsed, lyric poetry especially is seen as a genre of culturally and psychologically inward turns and returns, formally embodied in canonical attributes such as brevity, self-reflexivity, sonic density, repetition, affectivity, and subtlety" (*A Transnational Poetics* 3). Ramazani also refers to Mikhail Bakhtin's theories:

> Although many transnational poems are "lyric" in being compressed, self-aware, and sonically rich, they also evince Bakhtin's dialogism, heteroglossia, and hybridization — the latter a term Bakhtin uses for the literary mixture of "utterances, styles, languages, belief systems." From Eliot and Sterling Brown to Braithwaite, Muldoon and Grace Nichols, cross-cultural poems cannot be reduced to Bakhtin's putative lyric homogeneity: instead, they switch codes between dialect and standard, cross between the oral and the literary, interanimate foreign and indigenous genres, span distances between far-flung locales, frame discourses within one another, and indigenize borrowed forms to serve antithetical ends [*A Transnational Poetics* 4].

Using the example of A.K. Ramanujan's lyric "Chicago Zen," Ramazani also points out that "among the hybridizing literary strategies of postcolonial poetry that can be traced in part to modernist bricolage are translocalism, mythical syncretism, heteroglossia, and apocalypticism" (*A Transnational Poetics* 101). Most of these strategies are discernible in the representative body of South Asian English-language poetry examined in this study.

With regard to theorizing postcolonial poetry, Jahan Ramazani's comments in *The Hybrid Muse* are validated in this study by combining theory with literary analysis:

> Postcolonial theory has been entirely preoccupied with continually interrogating itself, rehearsing questions about its complicity in European discourses, the (non) representability of "other" cultures, and the definition of its primary terms, including "nation," "hybridity," "the other," and "postcolonial" itself. While theoretical inquiry is not necessarily inimical to poetry ... the genre also demands specifically literary modes of response and recognition — of figurative devices, generic codes, stanzaic patterns, prosodic twists, and allusive turns [4].

Ramazani also states that

> poetics helps to reveal the literary energies of these texts, which aesthetically embody the postcolonial condition in particular linguistic and formal structures. The best postcolonial poems are resonant and compelling in no small part because of their figurative reach, verbal dexterity, tonal complexity, and their imaginative transformation of inherited genres, forms, and dramatic characters [*The Hybrid Muse* 4].

Discussing the poetry of A.K. Ramanujan, Ramazani also refers to theories of the Russian formalist Victor Shklovsky:

> Complete integration within the new discursive or cultural field produces dead metaphors and overassimilated art. In order for the newly hybridized discourse to reorient perception, a tension must remain between the native and foreign, tenor and vehicle, focus and frame. Metaphorical or poetic discourse, as Victor Shklovsky famously argued, renews perception by "defamiliarizing" the world [*The Hybrid Muse* 74].

In addition to explaining the applications of Ramazani's theories of transnational poetics and the hybridization of postcolonial poetry, it is important to frame the discussions in this study within the larger context of major trends in postcolonial theory. In *Postcolonial Theory: A Critical Introduction* (1998) Leela Gandhi has connected the theoretical contributions of Gayatri Spivak, Homi Bhabha, Franz Fanon, and Edward Said with poststructuralist theorists. Gandhi emphasizes the contributions of Edward Said as well as those of the earlier theorists that postcolonial theories build upon:

> While the publication of Said's *Orientalism* in 1978 is commonly regarded as the principal catalyst and reference point for postcolonial theory, insufficient attention is given to the fact that this ur-text (and its followers) evolved within a distinctly poststructuralist climate, dominated in the Anglo-American academy by the figures of Foucault and Derrida. Indeed, Said's own work draws upon

a variety of Foucauldian paradigms. In particular, Foucault's notion of a discourse, as elaborated in *The Archaeology of Knowledge* and in *Discipline and Punish*, informs Said's attempt to isolate the principle and workings of Orientalism. In addition, Gayatri Spivak first gained admission to the literary pantheon through her celebrated translation of Derrida's *Of Grammatology* in 1977. And much of her subsequent work has been preoccupied with the task of dialogue and negotiation with and between Derrida and Foucault. Arguably, then, it is through poststructuralism and postmodernism — and their deeply fraught and ambivalent relationship with Marxism — that postcolonialism starts to distil its particular provenance [25].

Gandhi also points out the location of postcolonial theory in the field of contemporary literary criticism:

> It could be said that postcolonialism is caught between the politics of structure and totality on the one hand, and the politics of the fragment on the other. This is one way of suggesting that postcolonial theory is situated somewhere in the interstices between Marxism and postmodernism/poststructuralism. It is, in a sense, but one of the many discursive fields upon which the mutual antagonism between these competing bodies of thought is played out [167].

Following the precedents of contemporary postcolonial criticism, this study uses Homi Bhabha's application of Bakhtin's hybridity. In *The Location of Culture*, Bhabha emphasizes that

> to grasp the ambivalence of hybridity, it must be distinguished from an inversion that would suggest that the originary is, really, only an effect. Hybridity has no such perspective of depth or truth ... it is not a third term that resolves the tension between two cultures ... in a dialectical play of "recognition." ... What is irremediably estranging in the presence of the hybrid — in the revaluation of the symbol of national authority as the sign of colonial difference — is that the difference of cultures can no longer be identified or evaluated as objects of epistemological or moral contemplation: cultural differences are not simply there to be seen or appropriated [113–14].

Bhabha states elsewhere:

> I have developed the concept of hybridity to describe the construction of cultural authority within conditions of political antagonism or inequity. Strategies of hybridization reveal an estranging movement in the "authoritative," even authoritarian inscription of the cultural sign. At the point at which the precept attempts to objectify itself as a generalized knowledge or a normalizing, hegemonic practice, the hybrid strategy or discourse opens up a space of negotiation where power is *unequal* but its articulation may be *equivocal*. Such negotiation is neither assimilation nor collaboration. It makes possible the emergence of an "interstitial" agency that refuses the binary representation of social antagonism. Hybrid agencies find their voice in a dialectic that does not seek cultural supremacy or sovereignty. They deploy the partial culture from which they emerge to construct visions of community, and versions of historic memory, that

give narrative form to the minority positions they occupy: the outside of the inside; the part in the whole ["Culture's in Between" 212].

Bhabha's critical terminology, such as "ambivalence," "cultural translation" (also the "poetics of translation"), "cultural difference" and "the location of culture" as well as "unhomeliness," which have become established terms in postcolonial theory, are referenced in the following chapters.

Beginning with Bhabha's theories, Ashok Bery, in *Cultural Translation and Postcolonial Poetry* (2007), has developed a poetics of cultural translation that can be applied to postcolonial poetry across continents. Bery writes, "All translation is a use and appropriation, all translation involves hegemonic relationships; consequently all translation is ethically compromised, including intracultural translation, such as that between the past and the present" (18). Bery also explains that poets can both foreignize and domesticate imagery (11–13). Bery's theory of cultural translation is applicable to the works of diasporic and immigrant poets who often tend to "foreignize" their experiences and moods. Some of the diasporic poets encapsulate transnational experiences in their relocations across continents.

Bery concedes the great complexity of translation theories as used in feminist criticism and postcolonial studies: "particularly in feminist and postcolonial perspectives on translation, there is an awareness that these issues in turn need to be related to power differentials between nations, languages and cultures" (7–8). In keeping with the theory of cultural translation, this study recognizes women's subaltern voices in South Asian English-language poetry. The term "subaltern" is derived from Gayatri Spivak's well-known question, regarding which Leela Gandhi comments, "In 1985 Gayatri Spivak threw a challenge to the race and class blindness of the Western academy, asking 'Can the subaltern speak?'" (1). Gandhi explains that "by 'subaltern' Spivak meant the oppressed subject, the members of Antonio Gramsci's 'subaltern classes' ... or more generally those 'of inferior rank,' and her question followed on the work begun in the early 1980s by a collective of intellectuals now known as the Subaltern Studies group" (1).

In poem after poem by South Asian women poets in the subcontinent as well as the women poets of the South Asian diaspora, the images of the female body draw attention to women's subaltern status in South Asian culture. Second- and third-wave feminist scholarship (as in the writings of American poet Adrienne Rich) has reiterated that poetic language used by women has specific characteristics. While such views may seem to border upon essentialism, this study avoids essentialism by examining the poetics of each woman poet separately while drawing methodological and thematic parallels for analytical purposes. Specific sections of this study focus upon the need to locate women's voices in the context of the poetics of women's poetry in South Asia and in diasporic South Asian communities.

Just as postcolonial theory incorporates some of the tenets of both Marxism and postmodernism, two philosophies that are in some ways poles apart, South Asian poetry inhabits a middle space that is between the poetry of protest and resistance and the deeply subjective or introspective lyric. While the canon of much of this South Asian English-language poetry is still unmapped and the poems to some extent occupy a subaltern and somewhat neglected position in academic circles, the voices of the speakers in a majority of the poems are recognizably bourgeois. Transnationalism has been present from the beginnings of English-language poetry. This aspect emerged in the nineteenth century, when European forms and models were "domesticated" and hybridized. The speakers' viewpoints in the early poems of the colonial era inevitably raise the question of whether the poems present hybridized and Europeanized perspectives or the perspectives of the Indian elite upon the subalterns of India. Often the social backgrounds of the poets link them to the *zamindari* or feudal landlord class who had oppressed the lower classes and then joined with the colonial elite. From 1978, there has been an ongoing (and unresolved) debate with regard to the "orientalist" gaze of these early Indian English poets first brought into focus by Homi K. Bhabha and R. Parthasarathy.

The Major Paradigms of South Asian Poetry in English

While studying the English-language poetry of South Asians, the reader's journey through time, place, and literary history uncovers aspects of Romanticism, Victorian realism, influences of European classics and the history of empires, pastoralism, modernism, confessionalism, surrealism, and existentialism, eventually reaching a condition of permanent dislocation. Ramabai Espinet's "nowhere place" becomes a recurring trope of the condition of the speakers/personae in English-language poetry by South Asians. In studying tropes, the following chapters examine what J. Hillis Miller terms "the tropological dimension of literary language, to the way figures of speech turn aside the telling of a story or the presentation of a lyrical theme" (ix).

The immigrant poet's world is a nowhere place, as is the world of the colonial poet. These voices speak of alienation and anxiety. Contemporary South Asian poetry collections published by diasporic poets tend to present heteroglossias of immigrant experiences, of being caught between cultures, seeking to translate the experiences of one culture into another. The post–1947 era witnesses the poetry of immigrant experiences among the poets of the South Asian diaspora. Many of the immigrant poets write with nostalgia about lost homelands in both space and time (King 209–10). These memory poems often have a dreamlike quality where there is a need to escape from the reality of a new land of adoption into the memory of one's lost homeland, which is sometimes depicted with arcadian imagery, as in A.K. Ramanujan's and Meena Alexander's memories of southern India, and the memories of Guyana or Trinidad in the poetry of Caribbean poets Mahadai Das, Ramabai Espinet, David Dabydeen, Cyril Dabydeen, Arnold Itwaru, and Sasenarine Persaud. Also, sometimes the space/place occupied by the immigrant poet is viewed as a "nowhere place," as in one of Ramabai Espinet's poems (*Nuclear Seasons* 30–37). These nowhere places and memories of lost homelands are identifiably examples of pastoralism and resistance. The imaginary homelands emphasize the homelessness of diasporic artists, suggesting that when one leaves, one can never return because the place one left is changed forever by time. Romanticizing the past or one's early life often ignores the negatives of the past, such as oppression and poverty, although some poets (including Espinet) can depict both aspects.

There is also a recognizable blending of indigeneity with pastoral elements. Pastoralism is evident in the rural images and metaphors found throughout the colonial and postcolonial era in both the poetry from the subcontinent and the poems of the diasporic South Asian poets. Pastoralism can be viewed as both resistance and escape as the pastoral scenes of the lost homeland re-surface in the memory of the immigrant poet who seeks an escape in moments of stress when he/she faces the challenges of the land of adoption. The connection of pastoralism and resistance in this chapter is indebted to Sidney Burris's *The Poetry of Resistance: Seamus Heaney and the Pastoral Tradition*. Burris writes that "Heaney's verse has responded to the complex alignments of his homeland by renovating the authoritative techniques of pastoral literature, a literature that has traditionally entailed political resistance" (viii). Burris also emphasizes the word "rural," asserting that this word "leads directly to pastoral writing, the provenance of that exotic combination of country affairs and literary art" (ix).

Locating temporal and spatial dimensions of poems and speakers is important but not in the same way as in the study of a work of fiction. Often images of place and time are combined in images of houses that encapsulate generations of family history and sometimes the histories of nations, as in the poems of Agha Shahid Ali set in Kashmir. Another characteristic element, reflexivity (as well as self-reflexivity), is very significant in this body of poetry, in both the colonial and postcolonial periods. Self-reflexivity is recognizably a modernist trait. Mirrors are often used as images in which seeing the reflection of one's self returns one to the quest for self-identity. In the post–1947 era, the poetry from the Indian subcontinent as well as the poetry of the South Asian diaspora reiterates the image of the fragmented self of the modern/post-modern artist. Many of the poems discussed in this study are between East and West, occupying a position for which Ramazani's adaptation of Bhabha's "interstitial" space may be used (*A Transnational Poetics* 17). Bhabha's original use of the term becomes a precursor to transnational interpretations of post-colonial writing when he states:

> It is in the emergence of the interstices — the overlap and displacement of domains of difference — that the intersubjective and collective experiences of *nationness*, community interest, or cultural value are negotiated…. Terms of cultural engagement, whether antagonistic or affiliative, are produced performatively. The representation of difference must not be hastily read as the reflection of *pre-given* ethnic or cultural traits set in the fixed tablet of tradition. The social articulation of difference, from the minority perspective, is a complex, on-going negotiation that seeks to authorize cultural hybridities that emerge in moments of historical transformation [*The Location of Culture* 2].

Another element of English-language poetry by South Asians is the discernible influence of classics of both Europe and the Indian subcontinent. Barbara Goff points out that the cultural analysis of postcolonialism is connected with colonialism and empire (9). Colonial British education placed emphasis on the classics, a characteristic retained in African and South Asian curricula. Historically interesting parallels exist between European literatures that developed after the fall of the Roman Empire and the increased publication of English-language postcolonial literature with the decline of British colonialism.

The Language of South Asian Poetry

The term "South Asian" as used in this study refers to poets "who can trace their cultural ties to the region known as South Asia which includes India, Pakistan, Bangladesh, Nepal, Sikkim, Bhutan, Sri Lanka, and perhaps peripherally, Afghanistan and Myanmar (Burma)" (Wong and Hasan 1). While the present study uses the term "South Asian" to refer to the poetry of the Indian subcontinent as well as the poetry of the South Asian diaspora, it differentiates between these two large bodies of poetry in terms of their literary history and evolution. Unlike the fiction of South Asians, which has significant debts to Western literary models, the poetry of South Asians developed as a cultural hybrid in the nineteenth century with many poets who either continue to publish bilingually or are heavily indebted to poetry in South Asian classical and modern languages. For the purposes of this study, poetry in classical

Sanskrit, medieval and modern Hindi, medieval and modern Bangla/Bengali, modern Urdu, and modern Oriya have been examined and compared to Indian English poems, and it now appears that the so-called "orientalism" and florid language and imagery of pre–1947 English-language poetry has close parallels in the ornate metaphors and flowery language of poetry in vernacular Indian languages.[4] The debate on this subject has been ongoing since 1978, when Homi Bhabha critiqued the flowery language of colonial Indian English poetry and R. Parthasarathy responded with greater understanding of the language and forms.[5]

From the nineteenth century onward, South Asian poets writing in English have made attempts to appropriate the language of the colonizer as a language of their own. Among contemporary poets, the choice of idioms and metaphors tends to differ between those poets who use the British standard and those who use the American standard. The influence of the metaphors and idioms of Indian vernacular languages is noted by poet and critic Arvind Krishna Mehrotra, who writes:

> Each poet's "continuous" language or idiolect is constituted differently: Ramanujan's is of English-Kannada-Tamil, Kolatkar's and Chitre's of English-Marathi, Ali's of English-Urdu, Mahapatra's of English-Oriya, and Jussawalla has in an interview spoken of "various languages crawling around inside [his] head" [6].

This hybridization emerged from the beginnings of Indian English poetry in the nineteenth century. Bangladeshi scholar Kaiser Haq defends the hybridized early poetry of the colonial era when he points out that

> the earlier poetry generally is imitative of British models, and the influences on it are all too apparent. Byron and Scott were the dominant influences on two of the earliest poets ... these poets used their borrowed poetic modes to deal with Indian themes and problems [xvii].

It is evident that the characteristic of hybridizing European poetic forms with Indian themes and motifs was an early manifestation of transnationalism in English-language South Asian poetry.

In his introduction to *Contemporary Indian Poetry* (1990), Kaiser Haq offers valuable commentary on how Indians appropriated the English language to form a language of their own:

> Various forms of English coexist in the vast country. At one end there is what some linguists have called "Indian Standard English," which is a kind of "Modified Standard." At the opposite extreme is the practice, common even among illiterates, of interspersing speech in Indian languages with English words and phrases. Between the two extremes are several kinds of what Hugo Schuchardt in his seminal paper of 1891 terms "Indo-English" [xvi].

Haq also points out that the use of English opened the doors to Western culture, and that from the nineteenth century onward, the culture of the Indian subcontinent has been significantly hybridized:

> As a vehicle of Western culture, English had a quickening effect on the Indian intelligentsia analogous to that of Renaissance classical learning on the intelligentsia of Europe. The result was the syncretistic culture of the so-called Indian Renaissance, from which dates the subcontinent's modern cultural history. One literary repercussion of this has been the creation of a modern literature in the Indian languages, one radically different in form and sensibility from anything in the past: another has been the birth of Indian literature in English [xvi].

While regional variations/regional English dialects in India were recorded and studied in the late nineteenth and early twentieth centuries, only infrequently does regional English appear in the voices of the speakers of Indian English poetry. This preference for formal English contrasts with David Dabydeen's use of Guyanese Creole to bring to life the dramatic voices of his speakers. The bourgeois and even elite nature of Indian English poetry has been maintained by the use of formal English, which is readily accessible to a global reading public and does not need any translations. Sometimes, the dramatic voices of speakers in poems use community dialects or *patois* as in Ezekiel's "Miss Pushpa," but the examples are limited.

Toward a Canon

While Bruce King's *Modern Indian Poetry in English* and several other influential anthologies have provided a foundation for the selection of poets and poems from India and Pakistan for this study, the principle of selection has been the established reputations of poets that have lasted over several decades with continued productivity. Poets who have received major awards as well as nominations for awards are discussed. A few minor poets have been included because their work falls into the same genres as those of the major poets discussed in a specific group or cluster to show the prevalence of specific themes and techniques.

There is emphasis in the following chapters on the development of the poetics of women poets both in the subcontinent and within the diaspora. Traditionally, South Asian communities have displayed a tendency to segregate adults by gender since the late Middle Ages through the colonial period. Therefore, the worldview of the women poets is distinctly different from that of the male poets. Also, the traditional masculinities of South Asian communities in the subcontinent and within the diaspora display descent lines that can be traced to an ancient patriarchal tradition where patriarchy represented a form of social order. The socially constructed gender identities of male and female speakers emerge clearly in poem after poem. Hence, the poetry has been grouped by gender. It is significant to note that androgynous voices are not common in the English-language poetry of South Asians whereas flexible gender identities of speakers are often observed in the vernacular poetry of the subcontinent, especially in the Urdu and Hindi poetry from the Sufi mystical tradition.

The second chapter discusses a number of nineteenth-century poets whose ethnicity was Bengali but whose poems were composed and published in English. This cluster or group includes Kasiprasad Ghose, Henry Derozio, Michael Madhusudhan Dutt, the sisters Aru Dutt and Toru Dutt, and several other members of the Dutt family — Greece Chunder Dutt, Hur Chunder Dutt, Vires Chunder Dutt, Soshee Chunder Dutt — as well as Sri Aurobindo, Manmohan Ghosh, Nobokisson Ghosh, and Jotindra Mohan Tagore. The third chapter groups post–1947 poetry from the Indian subcontinent into three clusters: selected poets from Pakistan, women poets from India, and male poets from India. In focusing upon these three groups, one can identify the specific characteristics of each cluster. The fourth chapter analyzes the transnational and hybrid elements in contemporary postcolonial Indian poetry.

The fifth chapter analyzes the contributions of five poets of the South Asian diaspora. Four of these poets (the late Tambimuttu, David Dabydeen, Sudeep Sen, and Moniza Alvi) have published from the United Kingdom, while Fiji-born Australian poet Sudesh Mishra writes and publishes in Australia. All of these poets can be linked to the British and South Asian literary traditions. The sixth chapter covers English-language poetry published by writers of South Asian ancestry from Canada, analyzing poets as diverse as Michael Ondaatje, Rienzi Crusz, Cyril Dabydeen, Arnold Itwaru, and Sasenarine Persaud. The seventh chapter examines a number of immigrant male poets of South Asian descent in North America. This earlier group of immigrants who were also well-established poets in their countries of origin includes the late A.K. Ramanujan, the late G.S. Sharat Chandra, the late Agha Shahid Ali, the late Syed K.M. Hassan (deceased co-author of this volume), and academicians Zulfikar Ghose, Waqas Khwaja, and Darius Cooper. The eighth chapter discusses the major trends in the poetry of contemporary male poets of South Asian origin in the United States.

The ninth chapter analyzes the poetics of South Asian women's poetry in North America, focusing on the poetry of Meena Alexander, Sujata Bhatt, Chitra Divakaruni, Mahadai Das, and Ramabai Espinet as representatives of first-generation immigrant poets. The tenth chapter discusses the major trends in the poetry of contemporary women poets of South Asian origin in the United States. The final chapter is a closing piece or coda rather than a traditional "conclusion" because a large amount of the writing discussed is contemporary and still evolving.

Inclusions and exclusions are explained in each chapter. Very limited amounts of biographical information have been used for the purpose of locating specific poets in terms of time, space, cultural and social environments. In the absence of official biographies, and given the unavailability of records of births and deaths from different countries, information has been screened carefully. There are considerable discrepancies in reported information. Where scholarly sources were unavailable, only established newspapers and reputable Web-based materials have been used.

This study uses the phrase "the English-language poetry of South Asians" both to convey a transnational approach over space and time and to remain clear of the number of confusing names given to South Asian literature in English, as noted in *The Fiction of South Asians in North America and the Caribbean* (2004): "Confused and confusing literary taxonomies surround the English-language fiction of writers" from South Asia (Wong and Hasan 1). In this earlier study on fiction, the authors also point out that

> it is evident that we have a problem with the superficial packaging and labeling of writers and their texts. In the global culture of the twenty-first century, we are not always able to see beyond groups and group identities as we examine issues in literature. While the temporal and spatial dimensions of all art remain significant, we have probably reached a Babel-like situation in generating labels and taxonomies for authors and texts originating from the South Asian diaspora [2].

Taking a transnational approach in the present study includes demonstrating an unbiased perspective on scholarship. With the growth of postcolonial theory, there has developed a tendency to take a hegemonied view of scholarly writing, as in K.D. Verma's *The Indian Imagination: Critical Essays on Indian Writing in English*:

> It is this principle of synthesis, and not of blind imitation of the West, that was to pave the road to progress in India. Indeed, one of the most troublesome philosophical irresolvabilities in the discourse on India and in the development of postcolonial critical theory is the fundamental conception of synthesis. The cruel irony is that most western-educated Indians, other Asians and Africans are now questioning the very truth and universality of the European intellectual tradition that at one time shaped their thinking. This is also largely true of the writers and scholars of the diaspora who are confronted with the question of psychosociological identity, since like Yeats they cannot settle the puzzle of national or racial identity. Can East-West synthesis be achieved by an increased focus on the truth of history and human civilization? [28–29].

While steering clear of the epistemological debate that underlies Verma's comments, this study recognizes the scholarly contributions of both diasporic and Western scholarship as well as scholarship from the Indian subcontinent.

Throughout the study, the emphasis remains on objectivity and relevant methodology. When using the term "methodology," extended discussions of the theoretical genesis and ramifications of critical methodology have been avoided. There is a contemporary proliferation of studies that demonstrate a preference for theory over poems. This study concedes that the primary focus is on understanding the poems and the cultural contexts of the poetry with the purpose of mapping a somewhat neglected area of South Asian writing. By using this strategy, the present study hopes to avoid the pitfalls of several anthologists who do not explain either their selections or their exclusions, leaving the reader to conclude that the decision to include certain poets could be based on taste, ideology, favoritism, or a combination of all three elements. Most influential anthologies have been compiled by editors who are themselves poets. (However, in this case, the co-author of this book who was a poet passed away before completing his chapters.) Finally, the theoretical umbrella used for this study hopes to cover ground for a canon of almost two centuries' worth of English-language poetry by South Asians from a transnational perspective.

NOTES

1. Endnote numbers within quotations have been deleted throughout this study.

2. A number of professors of large universities in India and the United States were contacted regarding the percentages of fiction, poetry, and drama used in their courses on colonial and postcolonial South Asian literature. Fiction was well represented, with poetry lagging behind, and drama almost absent from recent curricula.

3. The term "theoretical umbrella" is adapted from its current use by physicists.

4. The late Syed Hassan studied comparisons of English-language poetry with Urdu and Bangla/Bengali poetry, and Mitali Wong has compared images and metaphors of Sanskrit, Hindi, Bangla/Bengali, and Oriya poetry to arrive at this conclusion.

5. For the debate beginning with Bhabha and Parthasarathy, see Homi K. Bhabha, "Indo-Anglian Attitudes," *TLS: Times Literary Supplement* (February 3, 1978), 3958:136; R. Parthasarathy, "Indo-Anglian Attitudes" (Letter), *TLS: Times Literary Supplement* (March 10, 1978), 3963:285; and Homi Bhabha, "Indo-Anglian Attitudes" (Letter), *TLS: Times Literary Supplement* (April 21, 1978), 3968:445.

WORKS CITED

Banerjee, Neelanjana, et al., eds. *Indivisible: An Anthology of Contemporary South Asian American Poetry*. Fayetteville: University of Arkansas Press, 2010. Print.

Bery, Ashok. *Cultural Translation and Postcolonial Poetry*. Basingstoke, UK: Palgrave Macmillan, 2007. Print.

Bhabha, Homi K. "Culture's in Between." *Artforum* 32.1 (1993): 167–68, 211–12. Print.

_____. *The Location of Culture*. London: Routledge, 1994. Print.

Brians, Paul. *Modern South Asian Literature in English*. Westport, CT: Greenwood Press, 2003. Print.

Burris, Sidney. *The Poetry of Resistance: Seamus Heaney and the Pastoral Tradition*. Athens: Ohio University Press, 1990. Print.

Dharwadkar, Vinay. "Poetry of the Indian Subcontinent." In *A Companion to Twentieth Century Poetry*. Ed. Neil Roberts. Malden, MA: Blackwell, 2001: 264–80. Print.

Ferguson, Arthur B. *Clio Unbound: Perception of the Social and Cultural Past in Renaissance England*. Durham, NC: Duke University Press, 1979. Print.

Gandhi, Leela. Postcolonial Theory: A Critical Introduction. New York: Columbia University Press, 1998. Print.

Goff, Barbara. *Classics and Colonialism*. London: Duckworth, 2005. Print.

Haq, Kaiser. *Contemporary Indian Poetry*. Columbus: Ohio State University Press, 1990. Print.

Hillis Miller, J. *Tropes, Parables, Performatives: Essays in Twentieth Century Literature*. Durham, NC: Duke University Press, 1991. Print.

King, Bruce. *Modern Indian Poetry in English*. New Delhi: Oxford University Press, 2001. Print.

Mehrotra, Arvind Krishna. *The Oxford India Anthology of Twelve Modern Indian Poets*. Delhi: Oxford University Press, 1992. Print.

Paz, Octavio. *The Bow and the Lyre: The Poem, the Poetic Revelation, Poetry and History*. Austin: University of Texas Press, 1973. Print.

Pirbhai, Mariam. *Mythologies of Migration, Vocabularies of Indenture: Novels of the South Asian Diaspora in Africa, the Caribbean, and Asia-Pacific*. Toronto: University of Toronto Press, 2009. Print.

Pocock, J.G.A. *Politics, Language, and Time: Essays on Political Thought and History*. New York: Athenaeum, 1971. Print.

Ramazani, Jahan. "Contemporary Postcolonial Poetry." In *A Companion to Twentieth Century Poetry*. Ed. Neil Roberts. Malden, MA: Blackwell, 2001: 596–609. Print.

_____. *The Hybrid Muse: Postcolonial Poetry in English*. Chicago: University of Chicago Press, 2001. Print.

_____. *A Transnational Poetics*. Chicago: University of Chicago Press, 2009. Print.

Verma, K.D. *The Indian Imagination: Critical Essays on Indian Writing in English*. New York: St. Martin's Press, 2000. Print.

Wong, Mitali, and Zia Hasan. *The Fiction of South Asians in North America and the Caribbean*. Jefferson, NC: McFarland, 2004. Print.

• TWO •

The Beginnings of the English-Language Poetry of South Asians: The Colonial Era in the Indian Subcontinent

The earliest poems published in English by South Asians come from the undivided province of Bengal in the nineteenth century. Bengal was one of the earliest settlements of the British East India Company.[1] The city of Kolkata (founded as "Calcutta" by Job Charnock of the East India Company in the seventeenth century) developed an English-language literary culture in the nineteenth century around the various colleges of the University of Kolkata.

According to Kaiser Haq, the beginnings of English-language writing by Indians can be traced to the end of the eighteenth century:

> The first book in English by an Indian was published in 1794. It was by one Sake Deen Mahomed, and he was by no means a lone figure.... The first English autobiography by an Indian was published in 1820 by Ram Mohun Roy, ideologue of the Indian Renaissance.... The first volume of poems by Henry Louis Vivien Derozio ... was published in 1827. The first play, Krishna Mohun Banerjea's *The Persecuted* came out in 1831, and the first novel, Bankim Chandra Chatterjee's *Raj Mohun's Wife*, appeared in 1864 [xvii].

Haq has also to some extent defended these earlier poets from the disparaging comments made by Bhabha: "Homi Bhabha gives the argument a fresh twist by dubbing them 'Orientalists,' meaning that they were as much in thrall of the Western orientalists' view of India as an exotic culture as they were of British poetic models" (xviii).

Combining the influences of late eighteenth- and nineteenth-century British poetry and eighteenth-century Bangla/Bengali–language poetry, there flourished a number of nineteenth-century Bengali poets whose poems were composed and published in English. These early South Asian poets in English wrote eloquently of nature and the complexity of human experience. This chapter examines common themes and motifs in the poems of Kasiprasad Ghose (regarded as the first Indo-English poet), Henry Derozio, Michael Madhusudhan Dutt, the sisters Aru Dutt and Toru Dutt, and other members of the Dutt family — Greece Chunder Dutt, Hur Chunder Dutt, Govin Chunder Dutt, Vires Chunder Dutt, Soshee Chunder Dutt, Romesh Chunder Dutt — as well as Sri Aurobindo, Roby Dutt, Manmohan Ghosh, Nobokisson Ghosh (whose pen name was Ram Sharma), and Jotindra Mohan Tagore. In its discussion and analysis of this body of poetry, this chapter seeks to demonstrate that the nineteenth-century English-language poets from undivided Bengal were deeply influenced by their formal English-language education in colonial times and often modeled their writing on English Romantic and Victorian poetry (Haq xvii). There is a recurrence of landscape poetry. The images of nature celebrate the tropical landscape of Bengal. The poems often combine nature, regional folklore, and Hindu philosophy in a manner reminiscent of Bangla/Bengali–language poetry in the eighteenth and nineteenth centuries. The hybrid characteristics of this body of poetry are significant. There are metaphors and images that have been influenced by the vernacular Bengali literature of the medieval Bhakti movement.[2] A number of poets published parodies that were quite popular in both nineteenth-century Bangla/Bengali and English writing. There also existed a tradition of extempore performance poetry in rural Bengali culture that used both parody and satire, elements of which appear in the nineteenth-century English-language poems from Bengal.

This flowering of the literary arts is often termed the "Bengal Renaissance," following which the rising spirit of nationalism led some of the poets to change from writing in English to writing in Bangla/Bengali, their mother tongue. The most notable of the poets to change the language of composition was Michael Madhusudhan Dutt, who wrote a famous epic in the Bangla/Bengali language. Most significant contributions came from Nobel laureate Rabindranath Tagore, and later from Sarojini Naidu, whose poetry became quite unfashionable in 1947 after the newly formed countries of the subcontinent gained their independence from British colonial rule. Poets and critics of South Asian poetry from the 1950s onward have pointed out that there is almost a clean break between pre-independence poetry in English by South Asians and the modernist and postmodern poetry published from the 1950s to the present.

It is interesting to observe that while the well-known poets writing in English prior to 1947 were mostly from eastern India, in the post-independence era, literary arts in English began to flourish in western India, especially in the city of Mumbai. A smaller group of English-language writers continued to work in eastern India, facing strong competition from vernacular literatures for readers. It is very important to note the significant contributions of the late Purushottam Lal's Writers Workshop as a publishing house that has from its beginnings in 1958 preserved the works of numerous lesser-known Indian English writers. According to Bruce King, the Writers Workshop began to publish volumes of poetry in 1959 (17). Some of the poets discussed in this chapter have been carefully preserved in one neglected Writers Workshop anthology titled *Indo-English Poetry in Bengal* (1974), edited by K.C. Lahiri. Bruce King has summarized the contributions of the Writers Workshop from the early 1960s onward as a publishing house that brought into focus several talented English-language poets, including Nissim Ezekiel, R. Parthasarathy, Adil Jussawalla, and G.S. Sharat Chandra (17–19).

It was in the province of undivided Bengal in the nineteenth century that the British spread English-language education in schools and colleges. The high school and college curricula were modeled on then contemporary curricula in Britain with an emphasis on European classics and Victorian British literature. The study of literature in English for educated Indians was primarily the study of British literature with a focus upon the canon. The nineteenth-century English-language poets from Bengal allude quite frequently to Shakespeare and Milton, to the major English Romantic poets, and, of course, to the poets of mid- and late Victorian England who were their contemporaries.

The Early Poets from Bengal

In this chapter, the English-language poets before Rabindranath Tagore, Sarojini Naidu, and Harindranath Chattopadhyay have been classified into four groups:

(1) The pioneers Kasiprasad Ghose, Henry Derozio, and Michael Madhusudhan Dutt;
(2) The women poets Aru Dutt and Toru Dutt;
(3) The male poets of the talented Dutt family; and
(4) The later nineteenth-century poets such as Nobokisson Ghose (Ram Sharma), Jotindra Mohan Tagore, Roby Dutt, Swami Vivekananda, Manmohan Ghosh, and Sri Aurobindo.

Some of the nineteenth-century poets from Bengal have the same last names, and several poets were from the same family. Poets who are related by family ties are mentioned as such in this chapter. However, the same last name does not indicate family connections unless specifically mentioned. In some cases, very little biographical information is available, as is the case with Roby Dutt. However, in the writings of all four groups there are poetic forms common in Victorian poetry, such as sonnets, ballads, lyrics, and narrative poems on historical subjects. There is realism, the influences of romanticism, and the presence of landscape poetry as well as poems of city scenes in nineteenth-century Kolkata. In terms of hybridization and cultural translation, these poets attempt to "domesticate" the forms of nineteenth-century British poetry into an Indian setting. Some of the later nineteenth-century poems have elements of naturalism, and Sri Aurobindo even has a brief piece on surrealism titled " A Dream of Surreal Science."

In the historical transition during the late nineteenth century from feudalism to the modern era in the Indian subcontinent, it is important to recognize the important contributions to the literary arts of two Bengali extended families, the Dutt family of Rambagan and the Tagore family of Jorasanko, which both produced several generations of writers and artists. The name of Rabindranath Tagore, who founded Visva Bharati University in Santiniketan, West Bengal, India, is synonymous with revolutionizing the world of arts and letters in the modern Bangla/Bengali language. However, he was a bilingual writer whose English poetry in *Gitanjali* brought him the Nobel Prize for Literature in 1913. As Paul Brians points out, "Although he wrote in Bengali, like the other writers, the language in which he acquired his worldwide fame was English" (10).

Nineteenth-century Indian poetry in English displays an interesting hybrid combination of imagery focused on the landscape and culture of West Bengal in and around the city of Kolkata and expressed through the poetic forms and literary devices of Victorian English poetry. It is as if these poets have acquired a *double vision* combining that of the somewhat ethnocentric Bengali from Kolkata and the colonial English. The term "double vision" is used in this study to distinguish this characteristic from W.E.B. Du Bois's "double consciousness." In *The Souls of Black Folk* (1903), Du Bois writes, "It is a peculiar sensation, this double-consciousness, this sense of always looking at one's self through the eyes of others, of measuring one's soul by the tape of a world that looks on in amused contempt and pity" (Electronic Text).[3]

While "double consciousness" implies an awareness that is developed under oppression, most of these nineteenth-century Bengali poets came from either relatively wealthy or middle-class backgrounds and were part of a social class for which the Bangla/Bengali term used is "bhadralok" (literally, polite people), so as to distinguish this group from the working classes. The term "double vision" aligns this body of poetry to the concept of a transnational poetic lens where the vision of the poet encompasses poetics beyond national boundaries and hegemonied discourses. With regard to the double or "split vision" that is a characteristic of postcolonial poetry, Jahan Ramazani has observed that in Third World literatures, juxtapositions caused by colonization and migration throw into relief what habit normally conceals, defamiliarizing the cultures of the colonizer and the colonized. Split vision is characteristic of postcolonial literatures, a seeing of cultures in terms of another [*The Hybrid Muse* 74].

These nineteenth-century poets from eastern India transform the settings, speakers, and images of their poems in ways that are shaped by their English-language education, their status of relative social privilege among the indigenous elite in a colonial society, and their emotional ties to Bengal and India. While this chapter analyzes poems from K.C. Lahiri's anthology, some other Indian collections have also anthologized several poets discussed in this chapter. Among late twentieth-century Indian detractors of colonial South Asian poetry in English is the well-known Allahabad-based poet Arvind Krishna Mehrotra, who published an influential anthology with Oxford University Press titled *Twelve Modern Indian Poets* (1992). According to Mehrotra:

Indians have been writing in English at least since the 1820s and it goes under many ludicrous names—Indo-English, India-English, Indian English, Indo-Anglian, and even Anglo-Indian and Indo-Anglican. "Kill that nonsense term," Adil Jussawalla said of "Indo-Anglian," and "kill it quickly." The term may not be easy to destroy, but much of the poetry it describes, especially that written between 1825 and 1945, is truly dead. Later poets have found no use for it [1].

Mehrotra continues by stating that "Henry Derozio, Toru Dutt, Aurobindo Ghose, and Sarojini Naidu were courageous and perhaps charming men and women, but not those with whom you could today do business" (2).

The break between colonial and postcolonial Indian poetry in English is clearly traceable to the influence of late modernism and postmodernism in Indian poetry circles after 1947. What is most surprising is that nineteenth- and early twentieth-century techniques lasted in Indian English poetry almost to 1947 and the end of India's colonial era. There is not much significant English-language poetry in India preserved from the decades when the struggle for independence under Mohandas Gandhi was ongoing. Writing in vernacular Indian languages became the vehicle for expressing one's nationalism, and even though the English language in India had already become hybridized and appropriated by Indian poets, expressing one's sentiments in English poetry was not popular, just as wearing Western-style clothing was not popular among educated and nationalistic Indians at the height of the independence movement. To clothe one's physical body and one's thoughts and emotions in styles and language that originated with the colonial oppressor was associated with disloyalty to one's homeland. This association of the choice of language and rhetoric as an indication of character has been noted from the time of the Renaissance in England in a well-known taxonomy of tropes:

Therefore there be that have called stile, the image of man (mentis character) for man is but his minde, and as his minde is tempered and qualified, so are his speeches and language at large, and his inward conceits be the mettall of his minde, and his manner of utterance the very warp and woofe of his conceits, more plaine, or busie and intricate, or otherwise affected after the rate [Puttenham 160–61].[4]

Due to the greater emphasis on writing in vernacular Indian languages in the first half of the twentieth century, the influence of modernism was not evident in English-language poetry from the Indian subcontinent until the middle of the twentieth century. The few poets who continued to write in English during the independence movement continued to use themes and techniques drawn from nineteenth-century poetry. Some of this poetry is stilted, formal, and somewhat imitative of late Victorian and Edwardian British poetry. The best-known English-language poet of the era of India's freedom movement is Sarojini Naidu.

Arvind Krishna Mehrotra has also provided valuable insights into the persistence of certain ideas in Indian literary circles from the time of the freedom movement that esteem poetry in vernacular Indian languages above Indian poetry in English. Mehrotra states:

Even after two hundred years, the Indian poet who writes in English is looked upon with suspicion by other Indian writers, as though he did not belong either to the subcontinent of his birth or its literature. The romantic idea that poetic expression is possible only in the mother tongue has led to several misconceptions about him, one of which is that he writes for a foreign audience, and his readers are nor in Allahabad and Cuttack but Boston and London [7].

Working through several decades of misconceptions, this chapter presents a fresh evaluation of colonial Indian English poets. Only selective biographical information is included for background relevant to the discussion of the poetry. The first group of pioneers consists of Kasiprasad Ghose, Henry Derozio, and Michael Madhusudhan Dutt.

The earliest Indian poet publishing in English was Kasiprasad Ghose (1809–1873). According to K.R. Ramachandran Nair, Ghose studied at Hindu College in Kolkata until 1828, and then edited *The Hindu Intelligence*, an English-language weekly (7). He received recognition as a poet with the publication in 1830 of a volume titled *The Shair and Other Poems* (Nair 7). A.N. Dwivedi compares this volume to Sir Walter Scott's *Lay of the Last Minstrel* (43). Nair takes a negative view of Kasiprasad Ghose's poetry, writing that "in spite of occasional bright flashes, Kasiprasad Ghose's poetry is generally imitative and full of conventional descriptions and moralisings. He had a predilection for unhappy and unfortunate themes. He was one of the pioneers of Indo-Anglian poetry" (7).

Kasiprasad Ghose's twenty-two-line lyric "The Moon in September" is crafted in eleven couplets that celebrate the beauty of the moon in a clear autumn sky. In fact, the season of the harvest, clear night skies, and references to the moon in this season are abundant in vernacular Indian poetry. The celebration of the beauty of the moon at night and the song of the bird (Bulbul) in the background is reminiscent of English Romantic poetry, of poems such as John Keats's "Ode to a Nightingale." Even though detractors have dismissed Ghose for writing a Keatsian ode, hybridization is clearly evident in his method, as is the attempt to domesticate a classical European poetic genre. The song of the Bulbul as well as the harvest moon are images from vernacular Indian poetry and folk songs that have been hybridized by Ghose into an English-language poetic form adapted from British poetry. One may compare this poem of the "Bengal Renaissance" with poetry of the English Renaissance, in which English and European themes are expressed in poetic forms from Latin and Greek poetry without hegemonied discourses that devalue the artist's contributions, because Latin, after all, was imposed on Britain as a result of being colonized by the Roman Empire.

To some extent, this hybridization and domestication of European poetic genres and poetic language allows the imagery of vernacular Bengali poetry to be expressed in a language and form that is transnational. In Ghose's poem, there are images of the transitory nature of life as in "his withering love" and "a cloud / Hath wrapt the Moon like Beauty in a shroud" (*Indo-English Poetry in Bengal* 94). In closing, Ghose refers to the moon exerting "a healing power and calm control" on the speaker (*Indo-English Poetry in Bengal* 94). This view of the calming effect of the moon on the individual is prevalent in Bengali culture. Less successful in its appeal is "The Farewell Song," where the speaker resorts to the clichéd depiction of his homeland as the land where sacred River Ganga (sometimes anglicized as "Ganges") flows: "Where mighty Ganga's billows flow / And wander many a country by" (*Gathered Grace* 8).

Kasiprasad Ghose also tried his hand at the form of the elegy in his poem addressed "To a Dead Crow" (a common bird in India). The crow has an unattractive plumage, emits a harsh call, and eats garbage. The speaker combines both pity and realism in lamenting the dead crow. In the past, the speaker was disturbed by cawing in the early hours of the morning: "When thou didst sing in caw, caw numbers, / Vex'd I've awoke from my sweet slumbers" (*Gathered Grace* 9). There is a tone of regret as the speaker views the dead bird. The choice of the bird is unusual because the common crow is not a songbird. English Romantic poetry celebrated the skylark and nightingale, and Bangla/Bengali poetry presents the parrot, the bulbul, the kokil (Indian cuckoo), and even the mynah (a talking bird), but not the crow. Hence in this poem the elegiac form is borrowed but the subject is Ghose's own.

A contemporary of Kasiprasad Ghose, Henry Derozio (1808–1831) taught English at Hindu College, Kolkata. His complete poems have been published by Writers Workshop, and he appears in several more recent anthologies that attempt to compile works that represent a canon of Indian English poetry. Henry Louis Vivian Derozio was born to a Portuguese father and an English mother on April 18, 1809, in Kolkata. He died on December 26, 1831, of cholera (Nair 1) and was buried on the edge of the Park Street cemetery in Kolkata. Derozio wrote lyrics, sonnets, ballads, and other narrative poems. Themes of love and death recur in his poems. His best-known narrative poem is "The Fakeer of Jungheera," and other well-known poems include "The Bridal," "The Golden Vase," "Song of the Hindustanee Minstrel," "Night," "The Tomb," "The Poet's Habitation," and "Poetic Haunts." According to K. R. Ramachandran Nair, in his short life of nearly twenty-three years, Derozio fulfilled a number of roles as "clerk, teacher, poet, journalist, free thinker, and social reformer" (1). He served as an assistant master in Hindu College, Kolkata, from 1828 to 1831, resigning after accusations that he was "a rebel and an atheist" and was corrupting the minds of the young (Nair 1).

Derozio displays control of the traditional forms of nineteenth-century English poetry such as the sonnet, writing both Petrarchan and Shakespearean sonnets. In the Petrarchan sonnet addressed to his students titled "To the Pupils of the Hindu College," he writes of the job satisfaction that the speaker, a college professor, experiences when "Expanding like the petals of young flowers / I watch the gentle opening of your minds" (*Indo-English Poetry in Bengal* 26). It is this good feeling that makes the professor's life worthwhile. In fourteen lines, Derozio captures the educator's joy in being with highly motivated students. In yet another sonnet, "The Harp of India," we find Derozio's emerging nationalism. The harp of India is symbolic of India's past glory. It hangs without strings, silent in a period of colonial rule. The speaker's message of awakening nationalism is clear in this sonnet's closing lines: "May be by mortal wakened once again, / Harp of my country, let me strike the strain!" (*Indo-English Poetry in Bengal* 26).

In his poems, Derozio often writes of time passing swiftly and evokes images of death, as in the song supposedly representing a "Chorus of Brahmins" (Hindu priests) where the speakers chant and pray to the sun before it sets: "Who upon the funeral pyre / Shall, ere Surya sets, expire" (*Gathered Grace* 3). In the lyric "A Walk by Moonlight," a poem in quatrains, the speaker walking with three friends on a moonlit night finds peace amid nature, almost hearing voices of natural objects such as grass: "Ah no; the grass has then a voice, / Its heart — I hear it beat" (5). In "Morning After a Storm," Derozio's speaker celebrates nature's beauty in a manner reminiscent of English

Romantic poetry: "While I looked on the with extreme delight, / How leapt my young heart at the lovely sight!" (6).

Among this group of early poets, Michael Madhusudhan Dutt (1824–1873) first began writing in English before his growing nationalism motivated him to switch to writing in Bangla/Bengali. Michel Madhusudhan Dutta was a native speaker of Bangla/Bengali who converted from Hinduism to Christianity in 1843. He was related to the Dutt family of Rambagan, Kolkata. His first wife Rebecca was English and his second wife Henrietta was French. Michael Madhusudhan Dutt went to study in England and he qualified for the bar. According to K.R. Ramachandran Nair:

> After his return to India he moved to Madras where he edited an English newspaper. His most well-known work is *The Captive Ladie* (1849), a metrical romance centred round the legends about the Rajput king Prithviraj Chauhan and his captive princess Sanyogita. Another blank verse work is *Visions of the Past*. His Bengali epic *Meghnad-Badha* narrating the adventures of Indrajit, son of Ravana, earned him an immortal place among Bengali poets.
>
> Madhusudhan Dutt's English poems show the influence of the English romantics, especially that of Byron. Most of his poems deal with episodes and incidents from Indian history and legends [*Gathered Grace* 11].

A.N. Dwivedi mentions that Michael Madhusudhan Dutt died in great poverty (21). Madhusudhan Dutt is best known for his "Miltonic" epic in Bangla/Bengali titled *Meghnad Vadh Kabya* ("Ballad of the Demise of Meghnad"). He appears to have been gifted in working with a variety of poetic genres in both English and Bangla/Bengali. Writing both lyrical and narrative poetry, he composed odes, sonnets, and love poems in quatrains. The sonnet "Composed During an Evening Walk" is clearly a nineteenth-century landscape poem with an almost Wordsworthian final couplet: "All these, meek even, do belong to thee, / And all these are thy earthly doves here" (*Indo-English Poetry in Bengal* 46). One of his lyrics of lost love brings to mind the tone and mood of Wordsworth's Lucy poems: "Thine image everywhere I see — / Thy voice in every gale I hear" (*Indo-English Poetry in Bengal* 49). His work even engages with abolitionist views as he writes of New World slavery in a poem titled "The Slave." Michael Madhusudhan Dutt's English-language poetry is as strongly emotive and politically conscious as his poetry in Bangla/Bengali.

The next two groups of nineteenth-century poets from Bengal both came from the very talented Dutt, or Dutta, family (Dutt and Dutta are alternative spellings of the same Bengali last name). The literary reputation of two women poets, sisters who died young, lasted for several decades during the colonial period. The poems of Aru Dutt (1854–1874) and Toru Dutt (1856–1879) have been reprinted in the more comprehensive anthologies of Indian poetry in recent decades. Writers Workshop has published all of Toru Dutt's collected poems.

Aru Dutt died of consumption (tuberculosis), like her sister Toru Dutt. Her creative career was brief, although the English critic Sir Edmund Gosse praised her poem "Morning Serenade" (Dwivedi 62). She also translated French poetry. Eight translations from French appear in Toru Dutt's *A Sheaf Gleaned in French Fields* (1876).

Aru Dutt's poems exemplify the cultural translation and hybridization of nineteenth-century English-language poetry from Bengal. In the lyric "Morning Serenade (from Victor Hugo)," Aru Dutt's theme and mood are reminiscent of the romantic lyrics of Emily Brontë, in which the speaker is a woman awaiting a real or imaginary lover: "I wait and weep, / But where art thou?" (*Indo-English Poetry in Bengal* 29). This poem is also printed as a concrete poem with all three stanzas having the same shape. However, while a reader familiar with British poetry finds the influence of Emily Brontë, a reader familiar with Bengali-language poetry can clearly discern the influence of oral Bengali vernacular folk poetry, with its many songs of separation where women waited and cried in the absence of their men who were expected to return. One such example of Bengali folk poetry is the collection of seasonal laments attributed to a woman speaker named "Kamala" collected by Bangladeshi poet Jasimuddin ("Kamalar baromasi").

Toru Dutt lived in France, England, and Italy for four years, becoming proficient in French and English. Her poetry also received praise from Sir Edmund Gosse (Dwivedi 65), and her published volumes include *A Sheaf Gleaned in French Fields* and *Ancient Ballads and Legends of Hindustan* (1882). In contrast to her sister's poems, whose strength lies in their intensity of emotion, Toru Dutt's poems have specific images of the flora and fauna of Bengal. In the lyric "The Casuarina Tree," Toru Dutt alludes to a python, a gray baboon, and the songbird, or Kokil (an Indian cuckoo). One cannot dismiss these as instances of "orientalism" because these creatures can still be observed in rural Bengal despite the rapid urbanization and industrialization of the postcolonial era. In her sonnet "Baugmaree," Toru Dutt writes of palm trees, tamarind trees, mango trees, and the lush greenery of her surroundings, which she terms "a sea of foliage" (*Indo-English Poetry in Bengal* 82). In her poem "Sita," Toru Dutt refers to the heroine of the Indian epic the *Ramayana*, who waited for her husband to return only to encounter suspicion and rejection from him. Sita's patience, virtue, and devotion to her husband has been viewed as a model of womanhood in traditional and patriarchal Hindu culture. However, due to the contributions of the women's movement in South Asia in the late twentieth century, Sita has become significantly de-mythologized. Thus, in the speakers created by Aru and

Toru Dutt, readers hear some of the voices of women in nineteenth-century Bengal.

The male poets of the Dutt family are discussed as a separate group because of the themes and techniques in their poetry. These poets are no longer in favor with the majority of editors of Indian anthologies. Many of their poems were published from London in an 1870 anthology titled *The Dutt Family Album*. According to A.N. Dwivedi, *The Dutt Family Album* (1870) contains 197 pieces, 66 of which are by the editor Govin Chunder Dutt, with 73 poems by Omesh Chunder Dutt, 47 poems by Greece Chunder Dutt, and 11 poems by Hur Chunder Dutt (*Indian Poetry in English* 19). The male poets of the Dutt family include Greece Chunder Dutt (1831–1892), Hur Chunder Dutt (1831–1901), Omesh Chunder Dutt (1836–1912), Vires Chunder Dutt (least-known member of the Dutt family), Gooroo Churn Dutt, and Govin Chunder Dutt (1828–1884), the father of Aru and Toru Dutt. Sonnets and lyrics appear to have been popular forms with this group of poets. As these poets are discussed more as examples of early Indian English poets rather than as part of the canon of South Asian English-language poetry, only a few representative poems have been analyzed in this chapter.

The poems of the Dutt family men are numerous and sometimes of uneven quality. Vires Chunder Dutt's sonnet "Air Raid" is probably a World War I poem. Very little is known about this poet who writes of sirens and trenches during an air raid: "The wheel revolves: what if the stifled breath, / The gasp, the stink of flesh, the crunching bone" (*Indo-English Poetry in Bengal* 85). The vivid imagery may be compared to the images in the poems of the British World War I poet, Wilfred Owen. Greece Chunder Dutt's poetry emphasizes the importance of place. Location, setting, seasons, and landscapes are significant in his poetry, in which the theme and mood are often tied to a place where the poem's speakers are living at the time of composition. Greece Chunder Dutt's poems vividly describe specific houses in the old city of Kolkata, such as "No 13 Manicktolla Street" (*Indo-English Poetry in Bengal* 34) and "Sonnet Khan Sahib's House, near College Square" (*Indo-English Poetry in Bengal* 35). "No 13 Manicktolla Street" is pictured as "Its trim-kept lawns a mossy wall / Secures from envious eyes" (*Indo-English Poetry in Bengal* 34). Khan Sahib's house has ornate architecture and the speaker imagines veiled Muslim women inside: "But now through the lattice-work, with creepers hung, / Glanced now and then an arm, or lustrous eye" (35). In the narrative poem "Samarsi," Greece Chunder Dutt celebrates a Rajput Hindu warrior from the Middle Ages, and in "The Maid of Roopnagore" he narrates a Hindu princess's refusal of Mughal emperor Aurangzeb's offer of marriage. There are strong elements of Hindu nationalism in these poems.

The poet Hur Chunder Dutt also writes about Aurangzeb with the suggestion that the later Mughal emperors did not have much support from their subjects. In Hur Chunder Dutt's dramatic monologue, Aurangzeb is racked with remorse and guilt at his father's death: "Why did I barter peace of mind / For royal pomp and state?" (*Indo-English Poetry in Bengal* 42). The reader recalls the soliloquies of Shakespeare's *Macbeth* and *Richard III*.

Also, there appears to be a continuity of writings suggestive of the Hindu intelligentsia's culture of defeat during the later days of the Mughal empire, which slowly changed to nationalism with the beginnings of the freedom movement during British colonial rule. Another Dutt family poet, Gooroo Churn Dutt, writes, "If then amongst thy sons a fallen race / Alas! degraded low, (unhappy days!)" (*Indo-English Poetry in Bengal* 30). Yet another Dutt family poet, and the editor of *The Dutt Family Album*, Govin Chunder Dutt, creates a speaker who views the ruins of the ancient Bengali kingdom of Gaur (or Gour) in northern West Bengal, and has dreams of a glorious past with military power. In his "Sonnet: Gour (Under an Indian Tale by V. Tregear)," the speaker describes his vision: "Huge elephants forward urged by mace and thong, / And snorting steeds in trappings rich arrayed" (*Indo-English Poetry in Bengal* 31). Aware of the colonized condition of Bengal, the Dutt family poets romanticized the glory of the past through historical allusions to people and places in ancient and medieval India. A.N. Dwivedi finds Govin Chunder Dutt's poems to be full of Christian elements (*Indian Poetry in English* 19).

Omesh Chunder Dutt (1836–1912) had the largest number of poems in *The Dutt Family Album*. He favors Indian historical themes in his poetry, as in "The Chief of Pokurna," in which the chief is ambushed by his enemies when he is riding along: "And ere the chief could draw his blade, / They hemmed him darkly round" (*Indo-English Poetry in Bengal* 64). The chief is taken prisoner, and sentenced to death by the king of Marwar. His son and successor gathers an army to avenge his father's death. Such legends of warriors were collected in the eighteenth century in James Tod's *Annals and Antiquities of Rajasthan*.

In "Kala Pahar," Omesh Chunder Dutt describes a barren hill of black basaltic rock that villagers believed to be the home of evil spirits: "They speak the truth who say God's curse / Is on this barren hill!" (*Indo-English Poetry in Bengal* 61). His poetry shows the hybridization of Indian legends and myths with techniques of English Romantic poetry to create a Coleridgean "willing suspension of disbelief" in the reader.

A poet of a later generation, Romesh Chunder Dutt (1837–1909), also belonged to the Dutt family of Rambagan in Kolkata. He was educated at Presidency College (now Presidency University) in Kolkata and worked in the Indian Civil Service. After retirement, he devoted himself to his writing. According to A.N. Dwivedi, he held office with the Legislative Council at Kolkata, and served as the minister of revenue and the diwan of Baroda (*Indian Poetry in English* 56). Romesh Chunder Dutt also translated the two great Sanskrit epics, the *Ramayana* and the *Mahabharata*, into English and wrote novels in Bangla/Bengali. His original English-language poetry appears in *Lays of Ancient India* (1894). He also published *A History of Civilization in Ancient India* (1890), *Economic History of British India* (1902), and *India in the Victorian Age* (1904). Two of his Bangla/Bengali novels were translated into English with the titles *The Lake of Palms* and *The Slave-Girl of Agra* (Dwivedi 21).

Romesh Chunder Dutt's poems also celebrate the glory of ancient India, as in "Buddha's Death," a lyric that presents the Buddha imparting spiritual wisdom literally until his death: "Taught the law with dying accents, / Stopped, and never spoke again" (*Indian Poetry in English* 57). In "Sita Lost," Dutt takes one of the last episodes of the *Ramayana* and presents a dramatic scene. Sita is asked to step into fire to prove that she has been a chaste and faithful wife to Rama during her imprisonment by the lustful King Ravana. In mythology, Sita is the daughter of the Earth. Sita's prayers to her mother Earth are answered as the ground opens and a golden throne emerges for Sita to leave and return to a world under the ground: "Mother Earth! Relieve thy Sita from the burden of this life! / Then the earth was rent and parted, and a golden throne arose" (*Indian Poetry in English* 59).

In "Night of Slaughter: Duryodhan's Death," the poet dramatizes an episode from the ancient Hindu epic, the *Mahabharata*. The mighty warrior Bhima fights the usurper Duryodhana until he delivers a fatal blow. Dutt uses animal imagery to create this scene of violent hand-to-hand combat: "Like two bulls that fight in fury blind with wounds and oozing blood, / Like two wild and warring tuskers shaking all the echoing wood" (*Indian Poetry in English* 60). Dutt's use of details brings to life episodes of legend without romanticizing characters such as Rama, who orders Sita to undertake a trial by fire, and Bhima, who kills his cousin Duryodhana, the *Mahabharata*'s antagonist.

The fourth group of later nineteenth-century English-language poets in Bengal includes Roby Dutt (1883–1918), Swami Vivekananda (born Narendranath Dutt), Sri Aurobindo (Aurobindo Ghosh), Jotindra Mohan Tagore, Nobokisson Ghosh ("Ram Sharma"), and Manmohan Ghosh.

According to K. C. Lahiri, Roby Dutt "knew sixteen languages, including Icelandic and Friesian" (*Indo-English Poetry in Bengal* 168). Dutt composed poetry that displays the influences of English Romantic and Victorian Nature poetry as well as the hybridized figurative language of Indian English poet from nineteenth century Bengal. In some of Roby Dutt's nature poems, the setting and imagery are not specifically identifiable as that of the Indian sub-continent as in the lyric "Beside a Lake": "And yonder lake / With prattling noise doth flow" (*Indo-English Poetry in Bengal* 69).

Yet in other lyrics, Roby Dutt's attempt at the hybridization of nineteenth century English and Bangla/Bengali nature poetry is evident as in the couplets of the lyric "Nature's Tie" where "The pole-propt *jui* out there with new-blown stars is set — / The *sheuli*-leaves are gay with bloom not bursten yet" (*Indo-English Poetry in Bengal* 70). The fragrant jui (Indian jasmine) and the transient sheuli flower that sheds its petals very soon were common flowers in the gardens of Roby Dutt's native Bengal. Roby Dutt's interest in archaisms is evident in his use of the archaic word "bursten." The use of couplets in this lyric reminds readers that couplets were often used in pre-modern poetry in Indian vernacular languages. Dutt's interest in beast fables is reminiscent of Indian folk tales (sometimes composed in verse) and emerges in the narrative poem titled "The Gnat and the Lion (Leontomuiomachia)" in which after being stung many times, the lion swallows the gnat (*Indo-English Poetry in Bengal* 72–73).

Roby Dutt's interest in languages, dialects, and archaisms also emerges in his unusual attempt to write in the Scottish dialect in a poem that appears to be an imitation of Robert Burns titled "The Lover's Lay." This love song contains traditional images of moonlight as in: "Look aboon, look aboon, look aboon, dearie, / Where on high afore the eye comes the moon cheary:" (*Indo-English Poetry in Bengal* 73).

Swami Vivekananda is better known for his religious and philosophical writings and his explication of Hindu philosophy to the West in his famous "Chicago address." His poems use forms and techniques of late Victorian English poetry. Swami Vivekananda was much admired as a Hindu spiritual leader. In a sonnet titled "In Memory of Swami Vivekananda," Nobokisson Ghosh writes, "With burning zeal he preached. His soul was one / Of rarest grace, and like a star it shone" (*Indian Poetry in English* 52).

Narendranath Dutt (1863–1902) was the secular given name of Swami Vivekananda before he became a monk and a disciple of Sri Ramakrishna. He was well known for his powerful preaching both in India and abroad. Some of his poems are on Hindu religious topics, but in a secular poem titled "To the Fourth of July" he celebrates the idea of independence in describing sunrise on the free American republic: "Then thou, propitious, rose to shed / The light of *freedom* on mankind" (*Indo-English Poetry in Bengal* 60). Presumably in his travels abroad, he sees an early violet that becomes a symbol of renewal and virtue amid adversity: "What though thy bed be frozen earth, The cloak the chilling blast" (*Indo-English Poetry in Bengal* 59). Some of his poems contain the same messages as his preaching, and this element is a deterrent to lyricism, as in the poem "In Search of God," where the epiphany described by the speaker ends with the observation in the final lines that all religions praise God: "The Vedas, Bible, and Koran bold Sing Thee in harmony" (*Indo-English Poetry in Bengal* 53). Swami Vivekananda knew several languages and among his poems is at least one love song translated from the Farsi of Persian poet Sadi as an "Ode" (*Indo-English Poetry in Bengal* 52).

The poetry of Sri Aurobindo and his older brother Manmohan Ghosh clearly display the hybridization of British forms and Indian themes. However, the poems of philosopher and Hindu religious teacher Sri Aurobindo (Aurobindo Ghosh) have faded away from anthologies of Indian poetry. Manmohan Ghosh (1869–1924) was sent to England at age seven, educated at the Manchester Grammar School, St. Paul's School in London, and Oxford University (Dwivedi 80). He was a professor of English at Presidency College (earlier Hindu College, now Presidency University). His poetry was favorably reviewed by Oscar Wilde in the *Pall Mall Gazette* (Dwivedi 22). His first publication was a collaborative work titled *Primavera* (1890). Later publications were *Love Songs and Elegies* (1898) and *Songs of Love and Death* (1926). Ghosh cherished a lifelong attraction to England, where he spent his formative years. In "London," the speaker dreams of his days in England: "Oh, the rush, the rapture of life! Throngs, lights, houses. / This is London. I wake as a sentinel from sleep" (*Indian Poetry in English* 81). Ghose is skilled in the poetic forms that he selects for his subjects, as in the moving sonnet addressed to his mother that closes with the powerful image of birthing in its final couplet: "She, from whose tearing pangs in glory first / I and the infinite wide heavens burst" (*Indian Poetry in English* 80).

The poetry of Sri Aurobindo (1872–1950) is not as well known as his philosophical writings. Like his older brother, Manmohan Ghosh, Sri Aurobindo was educated in England. He passed the Indian Civil Services examination (but did not join the colonial government), taught for some time at Baroda College, became interested in the freedom struggle, and then became a yogi (Dwivedi 23). He mastered several languages, such as Greek, Latin, French, English, German, Italian, Sanskrit, and Bengali (Dwivedi 23). In 1910, Sri Aurobindo moved to Pondicherry, where he founded the Aurobindo Ashram. His most important philosophical work is *The Life Divine* (1939–1940). His volumes of poetry include *Songs to Myrtilla and Other Poems* (1895), *Urvasie* (1896), *Vikramaurvasie* (1911), *Ahana and Other Poems* (1915), *Love and Death* (1921), *Hymn to the Mystic Fire* (1946), *Savitri* (1950–1951), *Songs of Vidyapati* (1956), and *Ilion* (1957).

While many of his poems are on subjects from European and Indian classics and continue in the style of nineteenth-century Indian English Romanticism, an occasional piece is unusual in subject, such as the sonnet "A

Dream of Surreal Science," in which surrealist imagery combines allusions to literature, Buddhism, European history, human biology, and physics, ultimately coming to a gloomy ending: "A scientist played with atoms and blew out / The universe before God had time to shout" (*Indian Poetry in English* 88).

Jotindra Mohan Tagore (1831–1908) was a prominent citizen and a member of the well-known Tagore family, which has produced generations of artists. He was a wealthy landowner with several titles who contributed to charitable projects, and was included among twelve prominent citizens of Bengal whose biographies appear in *Twelve Men of Bengal in the Nineteenth Century* (1910), written by F. B. Bradley-Birt. Tagore published one volume of English poetry titled *Flight of Fancy* (1881). In "An Indian Wreath" he writes of the flowers native to Bengal and romanticizes the image of the Rajput soldier heading off to battle and saying goodbye to his love (*Indo-English Poetry in Bengal* 154). There is a hybridized mixture of the themes and images of vernacular Bengali poetry with the forms and structures of Victorian English poetry, the same cultural translation that has been observed in other poems discussed in this chapter.

Somewhat unusual is the verse of Nobokisson Ghosh (1837–1918), who also used the pen name of "Ram Sharma." Ghosh's complete poems were collected in *The Poetical Works*, edited by D.C. Mallick and published in 1919 (*Indian Poetry in English* 52). According to A.N. Dwivedi, Ghosh was

> a copious writer of English verse. He held many administrative posts, but retired from service when barely forty. He is said to have led a blameless life and won the affection of a large number of his friends and admirers, both Indian and European. He was somewhat of an impractical idealist. Among his published works are: *Willow Drops* (1873–1874), *The Last Day: A Poem* (1886) and *Miscellaneous Poems* (1903) [52].

Dwivedi also notes that Ghosh died in great poverty (21).

Ghosh's poems include satiric monologues that remind readers of parodies that were popular in both Bengali and English popular culture in the nineteenth century. There is a dramatic quality in the voices of this poet's speakers that brings to life images of nineteenth-century society in Bengal. The sonnet "To His Mother" is a tribute to the speaker's mother and the imagery is reminiscent of nineteenth-century vernacular Bengali poetry. "On Women" is a sonnet celebrating the role of the mother, the wife, and the daughter as caregivers in the life of the male speaker. Ghosh's debt to the canon of British literature and classical European literature is clearly evident in his imitations. There is a recognizable attempt at cultural translation or "domestication" of well-known works from the canon of English literature. One such example is a humorous soliloquy based on *Hamlet* in which an obese speaker/persona laments the eating habits that have led to his present physical appearance: "I have expanded to proportions vast. / Corpulency, thy name is Luddulal!" (*Indo-English Poetry in Bengal* 102). In this soliloquy, we recognize the typecast figure of the glutton from classical comedy.

Ghosh's best-known works include "Willow Drops" (1873–1874), "The Last Day" (1886), and "Shiva Ratri," "Bhagobati Gita," and *Miscellaneous Poems* (1903). Ghosh appears to have been a devout Hindu, as observed in his hymn of salutation to the goddess Durga in "Bhagobati Gita" (Song of Bhagobati). The speaker sits alone meditating on the goddess in a dimly lighted room on the night of Diwali (festival of lights) when he has a vision of the goddess speaking to him and reminding him of the Hindu work ethic or *karmayoga*, where one must perform one's duties at work without hope of material gain: "Cease, therefore, thy vain, profitless pursuit, / And work thy work in life and work it well" (*Indian Poetry in English* 55).

Rabindranath Tagore

The best-known poet of colonial India is Rabindranath Tagore (1861–1941), who founded Visva-Bharati University in Santiniketan. According to Paul Brians, Rabindranath Tagore was probably the most well-known Indian literary figure from the early twentieth century:

> He also traveled widely, speaking on public affairs, on the arts, and on religion, all over Europe, in the Americas, in China and Japan. During the second and third decades of the twentieth century, he was one of the most famous people in the world, his bearded, long-robed image vivid in the mind of a wide public that might not have read any of his works but knew him to be a great Indian [12].

Tagore's *Gitanjali* ("Song Offerings") is a collection of lyrics first composed in Bangla/Bengali and then published in an English translation by the poet himself. For Bangla/Bengali readers, Tagore transformed all genres of Bangla/-Bengali literature, especially poetry. Paul Brians writes, "Traditional poetry had been dominated by Sanskrit, a dead language that functioned like Latin in European culture; and he transformed Bengali into a vehicle for lyric poetry, experimenting influentially with styles and forms throughout his life" (11). The *Gitanjali* is a very significant example of hybridization of both theme and poetic techniques because not only was it first composed in English but it also drew heavily on the ideas of the nineteenth-century reformist and monotheistic Hindu sect known as the Brahmo Samaj[5] (co-founded by Ram Mohan Roy) as well as the mystical religious imagery in earlier Bangla/Bengali poetry inspired by the medieval Bhakti movement. In terms of European influences, there is a type of neo-Romanticism that can be traced to English Romantic poetry. Not only was Tagore's English-language poetry hybridized but his Bangla/Bengali poetry was as well. Paul Brians has observed that "he drew both on the traditional culture of South Asia and that of Europe in creating his works" (11).

A.N. Dwivedi's *Indian Poetry in English* briefly summarizes Tagore's immense contributions:

> His multipronged genius produced lyrics, poetic plays, plays of ideas, social plays, novels, short stories, essays in criticism.... He was an actor, a producer, a musician, a painter, and an orator of extraordinary power ... his important works are: *The Gardener* (1913), *The Crescent Moon* (1913), *Fruit-Gathering* (1916), *Stray Birds* (1917), *Lover's Gift and Crossing* (1918), *Fireflies* (1928), and *The Child* (1931). Tagore may properly be called the "innovator" of prose poems in Indo-Anglian literature. He sought beauty and happiness everywhere, and considered Man in relation to Nature, the Universe, and God, Love, Devotion, Friendship, Natural piety, and Childhood find room in many of his poems [75].

While it is almost impossible to do justice to Tagore's contributions in just one section of one chapter, the purpose of this study is to examine his themes and poetic techniques from the perspective of almost two hundred years of South Asian poetry in English from different continents. In this context, as Dwivedi points out, Tagore originated the prose poem in English in South Asia, and he combined the mysticism of earlier Bangla/Bengali religious poetry with an easy-to-read lyrical style that was a significant cultural hybrid. Only a few representative lyrics have been discussed in this chapter to provide examples of his poetics.

Nationalism is prominent in the often-anthologized "Where the Mind Is Without Fear," an eight-line prose poem that presents images of a nation with liberty of spirit, intellectual freedom, and tolerance for all. It may be assumed that this is the poet/speaker's prayer for a sovereign state free from colonial rule: "Where the mind is led forward by thee into ever-widening thought and action — / Into that heaven of freedom, my Father, let my country awake" (*Indo-English Poetry in Bengal* 159). In the longer lyric titled "The Child," a mother and child are described in the early rays of the sun at dawn: "The mother is seated on a straw bed with the babe on her lap, / like the dawn with the morning star" (*Indo-English Poetry in Bengal* 155). The image of the child at dawn suggests hope for the future. One is also reminded of the emphasis on children and hope in the poems of the English Romantic poets Wordsworth and Coleridge.

Tagore's mystical and religious lyrics in the *Gitanjali* present some of the tenets of the Brahmo Samaj that de-emphasized the ritualistic aspects of orthodox Hinduism, as seen in "Come out of thy meditations and leave aside thy flowers and incense" (*Indo-English Poetry in Bengal* 159). The mysticism that is characteristic of the Bhakti movement in Hinduism is also evident in several lyrics of the *Gitanjali* where the soul of the believer seeks God as a woman in love seeks her lover: "In sorrow after sorrow it is his steps that press upon my heart; and it is the golden touch of his feet that makes my joy to shine" (*Indo-English Poetry in Bengal* 157).

There are unique spiritual and visionary elements in the lyrics of the *Gitanjali* that leave a lasting impression upon readers. The voice of the *Gitanjali* set the tone for several decades of Indian poetry in English but none of the later colonial poetry displays the emotional intensity and fine lyricism of Tagore's poetry.

Sarojini Naidu

The only other early twentieth-century poets discussed in this chapter are Sarojini Naidu (1879–1949), who moved from poetry to an active political career, and her brother Harindranath Chattopadhyay, who was a prolific writer. Sarojini Naidu joined the freedom movement under the leadership of Mohandas Gandhi and Pandit Jawaharlal Nehru, becoming president of the Indian National Congress in 1925 ("Biography of Sarojini Naidu"). After 1947, she became governor of the state of Uttar Pradesh ("Biography of Sarojini Naidu"). Sarojini Naidu was referred to as the "Nightingale of India" in her lifetime. She was born in a middle-class Bengali Brahmin family in Hyderabad in southern India. After finishing high school at a very young age, Naidu

> studied in London and Cambridge. She began writing poetry while she was in England. The exotic lyric quality of her early poems attracted the attention of two English critics, Edmund Gosse and Arthur Symons. They encouraged the young girl to write more but advised her to confine herself to Indian themes instead of trying to be "falsely English" [Nair 32].

Naidu was skilled in a number of languages. Her collections of poetry include *The Golden Threshold* (1905), *The Bird of Time* (1912), and *The Broken Wing* (1917). *The Feather of Dawn* (1961) was published posthumously at a time when her early twentieth-century themes and techniques were no longer fashionable.

Sarojini Naidu's poems were mostly composed before modernism gained influence over the English-language poetry of the Indian subcontinent. One observes late nineteenth- and early twentieth-century British influences in her poems. According to K. R. Ramachandran Nair in *Gathered Grace*:

> Sarojini's poetry presents a kaleidoscope of Indian scenes, sights, sounds and experiences transmuted into a fantastic and sensitive vision of colour and rhythm. She is a poet of volatile imagination and lyrical tenderness endowed with an enormous sensitivity to sound, colour, rhythm and rhyme. A few of her poems border on the mysterious [32].

Only a few representative examples of Sarojini Naidu's poems are discussed in this chapter because to some extent her emphasis on the exotic (perhaps her "orientalism") has distanced her poetry from contemporary readers. An example is the song of the "Palanquin-bearers," who sing of the beauty of the woman hidden from the public eye in the palanquin[6] they carry: "Lightly, O lightly we glide and we sing, / We bear her along like a pearl on a string" (*Gathered Grace* 33). The poem "Indian Dancers" celebrates the costumes and seductive movements of dancers: "The scents of red roses and sandalwood flutter and die in the maze of their gem-tangled hair, / And smiles are entwining like magical serpents the poppies of lips that are opiate-sweet" (*Gathered Grace* 33).

In the poem addressed "To a Buddha Seated on a Lotus," the speaker seeks peace in a world where "Dream yields to dream, strife follows strife / And Death unweaves the webs of Life" (*Gathered Grace* 34). In another poem, a sonnet titled "The Lotus" (addressed to Mohandas Gandhi), the lotus becomes a lasting symbol of peace and grace: "Supreme o'er transient storms of tragic Fate, / Deep-rooted in the waters of all Time" (*Gathered Grace* 36). The lotus is an aquatic flowering plant that thrives in muddy and shallow water, such as swamps and ponds. In this poem, the waters around the roots of the lotus become symbolic of time. Elements of hybridity are evident in the use of the lotus symbol that recurs in Buddhist writings and in Hindu treatises on yoga and meditation, where the cerebral cortex is described as a lotus.[7]

Harindranath Chattopadhyay (1898–1990), the younger brother of Sarojini Naidu, is almost as well known as his sister. He was a prolific writer, producing poems and plays. He also acted in several films. His volumes of poetry include *The Feast of Youth* (1918), *The Magic Tree* (1922), *Blood of Stones* (1944), *Spring in Winter* (1955), and *Virgin and Vineyards* (1967).

According to Dwivedi, many of Chattopadhyay's poems are inspired by the Vaishnava poetry tradition (*Indian Poetry in English* 25). This tradition of vernacular Indian poetry is descended from the Bhakti movement. Recurring themes concern the beauty of nature and the transitory nature of human existence. An occasional lyric provides a startling point of view, as in the eight-line poem "Fire," in which the infant inquires about the identity of the flames consuming his dead mother on her funeral pyre and receives the answer "I am the terrible desire / That shaped you in mother's womb" (*Indo-English Poetry in Bengal* 10). In "The Clod of Clay," the speaker again juxtaposes fire and desire: "Creation with its shadow and its fire / Is but a ceaseless cycle of desire" (*Indo-English Poetry in Bengal* 14). In the quatrain titled "Mystery," Chattopadhyay's speaker offers clever paradoxes: "Life is a question to which there is no answer. Death is an answer to which there is no question" (*Indo-English Poetry in Bengal* 15).

While these early poets used hybridization and cultural translation to produce uniquely South Asian poems, they retained formal English as their choice of poetic language. To some extent, the choice of formal English muffles the voices of the Indian speakers in these poems, although contemporary Indian poetry mostly uses formal or standard English as well. To some extent, the preference for formal English over regional languages/dialects may be connected to the fact that in the nineteenth, twentieth, and twenty-first centuries, English-language poetry in South Asia is composed by college-educated, liberal, middle-class writers for whom formal English is also their familiar English because their other familiar language is an Indian vernacular language. Ferdinand de Saussure distinguishes between formal/abstract language (*la langue*) and the ever-changeable phenomenon of actual speech (*la parole*).[8] For bilingual South Asian writers, the vernacular Indian language is their *parole*, or familiar language, while English is their *langue*. One observes that in South Asia, a number of poets are bilingual or have published translations of poetry from Indian languages in English. This characteristic separates the English-language poets living and writing in the Indian subcontinent from many of the diasporic South Asian poets, especially those from the Caribbean and Fiji, who incorporate regional dialects of English with formal English in their poetry.

NOTES

1. At the risk of seeming redundant, it is important to include the basics of India's "colonial" past. The British influence began in India with the East India Company. According to Percival Spear in *A History of India*, Volume Two:

> The English company, for its part, had a considerable stake in Bengal by this time. The Mughal *farman* of 1717 had given the company virtual free trade for its goods; the network of Bengal waterways gave easy access to the interior and the resources of the area provided rich opportunities. To a flourishing trade in cotton and silk goods and yarn and sugar was added a growing trade in saltpetre for gunpowder in the European wars. The obverse side of this prospect was continual disputes with the Bengal government on what constituted free trade. The disputes were often bitter, but never led to an open breach because both sides reaped enough advantage from the trade to make compromise worth while. A more delicate point was fortification for this "touched the sceptre." The company had its fortified factory Fort William in 1696; but it did not complete it until 1716 and then soon cluttered it with warehouses and houses close to its walls [82].

Spear goes on to explain how the British East India Company laid the foundation of empire:

> If Clive founded the British Indian state (though in rather the way of a robber baron) and Warren Hastings gave it coherence (though solely hindered by his enemies in Bengal and in London) and made it politically viable, it was Cornwallis who gave it definite form and stamped on it characteristics of its own. The Company's dominion in India became a distinct state both Indian and English, for which it is convenient to use the label "Company Bahadur." This state was of the type which any other conqueror might have established, though of course it had char-

acteristic English features. In itself it presaged no revolution or transformation of India, but only the first stages of a new cycle of conquest, consolidation, prosperity, and decline. But since the administrative measures then taken radically affected the form of later Indian public life, it is worth looking at as a whole [93].

Factually speaking, India became a crown colony of Britain under the reign of Queen Victoria after the Great Revolt of 1857, which colonial British historians termed the "Sepoy Mutiny." Although the British cultural influence can be traced back for almost two hundred years, India was officially a British crown colony for ninety years, achieving independence from British rule on August 15, 1947.

2. In *A History of India*, Volume One, Indian historian Romila Thapar comments on the Bhakti movement in Bengal and parts of northern India:

> A Bengal school-teacher, Chaitanya (1486–1533), became a devotee of Krishna after experiencing a strange hysterical trance. He held devotional meetings where hymns were sung and the meaning of *Vaishnava* belief was expounded. He travelled through the country inspiring people with *Vaishnava* teaching through the cult of Radha and Krishna. Chaitanya was concerned almost solely with bringing *Vaishnava* teaching to as many people as possible, and he was motivated by purely religious feelings.
>
> Another group sought a retreat in their devotion, and to them all that mattered was self-abnegation in an attempt to discover God. Everything was to be subordinated to this single aim. Such was the message of the songs of Mirabai, the sixteenth century Rajput princess who became a wandering mendicant composing verses on her love for Krishna; or of Surdas, the blind poet of Agra; and in the mystical verses of Lalla, who lived in Kashmir and dedicated her songs to the god Shiva [305].

3. The passage on the concept of "double consciousness" by W. E. B. DuBois is excerpted from the chapter titled "Of Our Spiritual Strivings" in his book *The Souls of Black Folk*:

> After the Egyptian and Indian, the Greek and Roman, the Teuton and Mongolian, the Negro is a sort of seventh son, born with a veil, and gifted with second-sight in this American world, — a world which yields him no true self-consciousness, but only lets him see himself through the revelation of the other world. It is a peculiar sensation, this double-consciousness, this sense of always looking at one's self through the eyes of others, of measuring one's soul by the tape of a world that looks on in amused contempt and pity. One ever feels his twoness, — an American, a Negro; two warring souls, two thoughts, two unreconciled strivings; two warring ideals in one dark body, whose dogged strength alone keeps it from being torn asunder.
>
> The history of the American Negro is the history of this strife, — this longing to attain self-conscious manhood, to merge his double self into a better and truer self.

4. The "f" has been modernized to "s," and the "u" to "v," in this quotation.

5. Discussing the founding of the Brahmo Samaj by Ram Mohan Roy, Percival Spear states that Roy

> considered that the recognition of human rights was consistent with basic Hindu thought. He expressed this idea in his Brahmo Samaj or Divine Society, founded in 1828. He substituted theism for classical monism and denounced suttee, infanticide, idolatry, and polygamy. From the west he borrowed the Christian ethic, expounded in his book the *Precepts of Jesus*, and a belief in modern science. The group was joined by the grandfather of Rabindranath Tagore, whose son became its second head. It spread its branches over India ... it became an important influence in the new class and indirectly all over India [164].

6. A palanquin is a covered box-like litter on top of horizontal poles, used as a conveyance for one person carried on the shoulders of four people (two in front and two at the back). The palanquin was used by women and men of wealth and high social status.

7. In the Hindu system of meditation often termed *kundalini yoga*, the "chakra," or center of evolutionary energy, at the crown of the human head is described as a lotus with one thousand petals.

8. Saussure's theories have been summarized in Wilfred L. Guerin et al., *A Handbook of Critical Approaches to Literature*, 6th edition (New York: Oxford University Press, 2011):

> Not available in English until 1959, Saussure's *Course in General Linguistics* in French (1916) attracted thinkers far beyond Switzerland, linguistics, and universities: it became the model for Russian formalism, Semiology or semiotics, French structuralism or deconstruction....

> Saussure's theory of language systems distinguishes between *la langue* (language, the system possessed and used by all members of a particular language community — English, French, Urdu, etc.) and *la parole* (word: by extension, speech-event or any specific application of *la langue* in speech or writing). The *parole* is impossible without the support — the structural validity, generation, meaning — conferred upon it by the *langue*, the source of grammar, phonetics, morphology, syntax, and semantics [170].

WORKS CITED

"Biography of Sarojini Naidu." www.poemhunter.com/sarojini-naidu. Accessed 8 April 2012.

Bradley-Birt, F.B. *Twelve Men of Bengal in the Nineteenth Century*. Calcutta: S.K. Lahiri & Co., 1910. HathiTrust Digital Library. Accessed 8 April 2012.

Brians, Paul. *Modern South Asian Literature in English*. Westport, CT: Greenwood Press, 2003. Print.

Du Bois, W.E.B. *The Souls of Black Folk*. 1903. Electronic Text Center: University of Virginia Library. Accessed 8 April 2012.

Dwivedi, A.N. *Indian Poetry in English: A Literary History and Anthology*. Atlantic Highlands, NJ: Humanities Press, 1980. Print.

Guerin, Wilfred L., et al. *A Handbook of Critical Approaches to Literature*. 6th ed. New York: Oxford University Press, 2011. Print.

Haq, Kaiser. *Contemporary Indian Poetry*. Columbus: Ohio State University Press, 1990. Print.

"Kamalar baromasi." In East Bengal Ballet-Purbabanga-Gitika. sos_arsenic.net/loving-bengal/purbo.html. Accessed 20 February 2012.

Lahiri, K.C. *Indo-English Poetry in Bengal*. Kolkata: Writers Workshop, 1974. Print.

Mehrotra, Arvind Krishna. *The Oxford India Anthology of Twelve Modern Indian Poets*. Delhi: Oxford University Press, 1992.

Nair, K.R. Ramachandran. *Gathered Grace: An Anthology of Indian Verse in English*. New Delhi: Sterling, 1991. Print.

Puttenham, Richard [George]. *The Arte of English Poesie* [Arber facsimile edition]. Kent, OH: Kent State University Press, 1970. Print.

Ramazani, Jahan. *The Hybrid Muse: Postcolonial Poetry in English*. Chicago: University of Chicago Press, 2001. Print.

Spear, Percival. *A History of India*. Vol. 2. New York: Penguin, 1978. Print.

Thapar, Romila. *A History of India*. Vol. 1. New York: Penguin, 1966. Print.

• THREE •

Strangers in Their Own Lands: English-Language Poetry in the Indian Subcontinent Since 1947

The post-independence era in the Indian subcontinent brought a gradual increase in the publication of South Asian poetry in English. However, English-language poetry continued to be suspect in terms of quality, often competing for recognition against the more well-established traditions of poetry in vernacular Indian languages. For example, the English-language poets publishing in western India faced competition from the rich traditions of Gujarati and Marathi poetry. In southern India, English-language poets competed for readers with those publishing in the languages of Tamil, Kannada, Telegu, and Malayalam. In northern India, the large body of poetry in Hindi, and in Pakistan, the large body of Urdu poetry continued to draw more readers than English-language poetry. In eastern India and Bangladesh, the rich tradition of Bengali poetry provided challenges for English-language poets seeking to expand their reading public. While the English-language poets had the advantage of having access to a global audience without requiring translation services, they were also viewed in some circles as receiving more attention because they were writing for an audience outside of the Indian subcontinent. This transnationalism is one of the greatest strengths of postcolonial English-language poetry from the Indian subcontinent. The use of the English language with the conventions of the British standard combined with imagery, scenarios, and voices from South Asia gave rise to a body of poetry in which hybridization and cultural translation were key elements. Prior to Homi Bhabha's critical nomenclature of hybridization as an important characteristic of postcolonial writing, this quality of Indian English poetry was at times seen as a minus rather than a plus, with the poets being viewed as mediocre imitators of English Romantic and Victorian poets.

This chapter seeks to locate the voices of poets writing in English from South Asian countries in the postcolonial era (since 1947). In examining the temporal and spatial dimensions of this body of poetry, one must also examine the specifics of cultural translation and hybridization in the poems that combine the forms and techniques of British and American poetry with motifs and images that are often found in vernacular Indian poetry. This body of poetry, even more than the poetry of the colonial era, is recognizably transnational in that it combines the techniques of traditional and contemporary poetry from vernacular Indian languages with the methodologies of modern and postmodern poetry published mainly from the United Kingdom and the United States. The presence of these threads is analyzed in discussions of specific poets and their representative poems.

The poets discussed in this chapter have been grouped into three clusters: selected poets from Pakistan, women poets from India, and male poets from India. In focusing upon these three groups, one can identify the specific characteristics of each group and engage with the dilemmas of critics seeking to establish a canon. This chapter refers to poems published in the following anthologies: A.N. Dwivedi's *Indian Poetry in English: A Literary History and Anthology* (1980), Eunice de Souza's *Nine Indian Women Poets: An Anthology* (1997), R. Parthasarathy's *Ten Twentieth-Century Indian Poets* (1976), K. R. Ramachandran Nair's *Gathered Grace* (1991), A.K. Mehrotra's *Oxford India Anthology of Twelve Modern Indian Poets* (1992), Kaiser Haq's *Contemporary Indian Poetry* (1990), Vilas Sarang's *Indian English Poetry Since 1950* (1990), and Yunus Said's *Pieces of Eight: Eight Poets from Pakistan* (1971).

The Question of Canon

The question of canon in post-independence/postcolonial English-language poetry from the Indian subcontinent is a complex one. Several editors have compiled anthologies of poems that have appeared in other sources. These editors have tried to create their own version of a canon of postcolonial poetry in English from South Asia. Omissions and biases are evident in that Indian editors have published Indian poets, and Pakistani poets have been anthologized separately although Bangladeshi editor Kaiser Haq crosses national boundaries in his anthology *Contemporary Indian Poetry*. Most of the anthologies contain a large representation of male poets, with between one and three women poets included in each anthology. Hence, one anthology devoted to women poets is cited in this chapter to show the emergence of women's English-language poetry in South Asia. After all, there has been a steady publication of English poetry by South Asian women from the time of Aru Dutt and Toru Dutt through the early twentieth-century years of Saro-jini Naidu.

Very significant scholastic contributions to this disputed area of post-colonial English-language poetry from India appear in Bruce King's seminal study titled *Modern Indian Poetry in English* (2001). King's study is important in that it traces the history of postcolonial Indian English poetry and discusses both the cliques in Indian publishing circles and the biases of the editors of early anthologies. King separates the voices of the women poets for richer and more focused analysis. However, he groups a number of diasporic poets in a chapter titled "Exile," although at least one poet (Shiv K. Kumar) was to return to India to continue with a long teaching and writing career (209–230). The chapter "And Return" includes R. Parthasarathy, who lived in the United Kingdom, returned to India, and then relocated to the United States, where he retired after working as a professor. King's work is most valuable as a landmark attempt to create a canon as well as to identify the poetic move-ments that these Indian English poets subscribed to (as evident from their poetic manifestos).

It is worthwhile to summarize some of Bruce King's lasting contributions to scholarship in this area of South Asian poetry. King states that there is no continuity between pre-independence Indian English poetry and post-inde-pendence English-language poetry from India: "The nationalist political needs for a usable past, with its emphasis on national classics, mythology, and rep-resentation of typical characters no longer seemed relevant" (11). King also points out that the poets belong to an educated social class: "most are part of a new, urban, English-speaking elite of the universities, communications, and professions" (50), and many have studied and traveled abroad (51). King also surveys the history of publishing companies that have released Indian poetry in English. His book includes very useful charts on biographies of poets and chronological lists of published books of poetry. This chapter is indebted to some of the biographical information in King's charts.

Bruce King states that the canon of Indian poetry in English is largely determined by the poets themselves instead of literary critics from academic circles (60). However, this situation is changing with more forthcoming schol-arly research and the inclusion of Indian literature in English in the curricula of Indian universities. But more critical attention is being paid to fiction in comparison to poetry. Hence, the purpose of this study is to establish a transnational approach to English-language poetry published from South Asian countries and English-language poetry published in other continents by poets from the South Asian diaspora. Bruce King has based his analysis of poems and the concept of a canon of Indian poetry in English on the poets and poems included in several anthologies (King 60–79). The present chapter uses some of the same anthologies as well as later collections to show that certain poets have been included in a majority of the anthologies. King has also pointed out the excellent work done by the late Purushottam Lal's Writers Workshop in publishing Indian English poetry:

> In 1950 modern Indian English poetry hardly existed and as late as 1960, when the Writers Workshop started, was still fighting to survive. In general those poems which have become established as classics have used Indian subject-matter, have been explicit in meaning and not difficult in form [72].

It is important to note that in 1959, P. Lal and K. Raghavendra Rao formulated a code for modern Indian English poetry that they termed "The Kavita Manifesto," which proclaimed that they had made a clean break with the neo–Romanticism of the era of Sarojini Naidu. This modernist manifesto had eight major clauses as recorded by A.N. Dwivedi (*Indian Poetry in English* 28–29).

Bruce King has discussed the critical views of several editors of poetry anthologies and their attempts to create a canon (73–90). King views Nissim Ezekiel's contributions as being most important:

> Of the group of poets attempting to create a modern English poetry in India, Nissim Ezekiel soon emerged as the leader who advised others, set standards and created places of publication. His main significance is not, however, as a promoter of poetry; it is in his will to be a poet, his continuing involvement in the poetry scene [91].

However, while Ezekiel's poetry has been widely praised, King shows a preference for the poets and editors from western India over poets and editors from other regions. Regarding the late Purushottam Lal's poetry, King writes that "he is now more likely in India to be viewed as insignificant except as a publisher" (73). Pritish Nandy is also dismissed as being "popular" but not of real "literary interest" (King 67).

The present study discusses the contributions of male poets from India writing in English in four regional groups: western, southern, eastern, and northern. In this chapter the poets from western India include Nissim Ezekiel, Dom Moraes, Adil Jussawalla, Gieve Patel, and Saleem Peeradina. R. Parthasarathy and Shiv K. Kumar are discussed as English-language poets from southern India, while Pritish Nandy and Jayanta Mahapatra are grouped as Indian English poets from eastern India. Poets from northern India represented in the Indian English canon include Arvind Krishna Mehrotra, Keki Daruwalla, and Vikram Seth. While exclusions are not always satisfying or acceptable to readers, every effort has been made to include well-established poets as representative of the canon of Indian English poetry. Many of the poets are bilingual and there are some linkages to vernacular Indian literatures as well as cultures from different regions of a large and very densely populated country. Indian cultures tend to differ from one region to another, and this strategy helps to locate the poets' voices in temporal and spatial terms. This study also establishes comparisons between Indian English poetry and English-language poetry from Pakistan. Due to the prolific publication by many of the poets discussed in this chapter, selectivity is based upon a few representative samples of themes and techniques for each poet.

English-Language Poets from Pakistan

Selected representative English-language poets from the Pakistani canon have been published by Oxford University Press in three anthologies: *First Voices: Six Poets from Pakistan* (1965), *Pieces of Eight: Eight Poets from Pakistan* (1971), and *Wordfall: Three Pakistani Poets* (1975). This chapter discusses some of the poems published in the second anthology because it has the largest representation of poets. This chapter also selects from poets who have well-established reputations over several decades. In the introduction to *Pieces of Eight*, Yunus Said defends the English-language poetry of South Asians:

> And then we are not an English-speaking people.... Mr. Stephen Spender went on record, during a P.E.N. meeting in Tokyo some years ago, as saying that non–English-speaking peoples should not write in English.
> A language is ... the common heritage of man, for words are only verbal expressions, not symbols of race, religion or culture [*Pieces of Eight* viii].

While Said's use of the word "man" for the human race dates his writing as preceding the women's movement, Said's objection to Stephen Spender's limited views on language and race is significant because this view has its parallels in the attitudes of South Asians who prefer for their people to write in vernacular languages instead of English. It is evident that English-language poets from South Asia have faced ethnocentrism in both the East and the West.

In a review article published in 1998, Carlo Coppola tries to establish a canon of Pakistani poetry in English based on the poets anthologized by Oxford University Press. A significant omission in Coppola's choices is Zulfikar Ghosh, who is discussed later in the present study. Coppola considers Taufiq Rafat (1927–1998), Daud Kamal (1935–1987) (who is excluded from all three Oxford University Press anthologies), Maki Kureishi (1927–1995), Salman Tarik Kureshi (born in 1942), Adrian A. Husain (born in 1942), Alamgir Hashmi (born 1951), and U.S. immigrant poet Shuja Nawaz to be significant English-language poets from Pakistan in recent decades (203–220). This chapter discusses a few representative poems by Adrian Husain, Taufiq Rafat, and Salman Tarik Kureshi to show recurring themes, motifs, and techniques in

English-language poetry from Pakistan. These poets have been chosen because they are the most frequently anthologized and discussed. Diasporic Pakistani poet Zulfikar Ghose is settled in the United States, and has been grouped among South Asian poets in America discussed in chapter seven. British-born Pakistani poet Imtiaz Dharker now writes from Mumbai, India, and she is discussed in the section on women poets in India.

In *Pieces of Eight*, Adrian Husain is described as writing from the United Kingdom and Pakistan. According to this anthology Adrian Husain was born in 1942 in Kanpur; attended schools in England, Italy, and Switzerland; and then went to New College, Oxford (Said x). Husain speaks a number of European languages. He began composing poetry at the age of sixteen, and has published poems in a number of English journals (Said x). One of these publications, *House at Sea*, received the Guinness Award at the 1968 Cheltenham Festival (Said x). The late modernist elements in Husain's poetry place him in the modern British tradition. In "The Sirens," the speaker alludes to *The Odyssey*: "But soon they vanish and the world is as before, / a stormy exile and Ithaca a drunk mariner's illusion" (*Pieces of Eight* 26).

In "House at Sea," Adrian Husain writes in the surrealist mode between reality and fantasy. The house at sea is a setting for the "unhomeliness" of the expatriate poet/speaker whose home is adrift on the sea and whose world has come apart. The speaker expresses his alienation: "My books are gagged, my nationality's dissolved. This is no / land to die in. My quaint scribe's wisdom rubbing out" (*Pieces of Eight* 30). In the allusiveness of his poetry to European classics, Adrian Husain's poetry has similarities to the poetry of the late Syed Hassan, whose work is discussed in chapter five.

Carlo Coppola considers Taufiq Rafat to be Pakistan's most prominent English-language poet:

> Rafat, whom many consider Pakistan's premier English-language poet, writes poetry that is full-bodied and rich, direct and readily accessible to the reader's sensibilities, and devoid of excessive artifice. His is a poetry that links Suhrawardy, Ali, and other older Pakistani writers to such younger voices as Adrian A. Husain, Salman Tarik Kureshi, and Alamgir Hashmi [206].

Coppola has also pointed out Rafat's frequent and rich use of nature imagery (204). In *Pieces of Eight*, there appears a brief biography of Rafat that mentions that he has been writing poetry since the young age of twelve (x). "His poems have appeared in magazines in Australia and in the United States, in English anthologies and in *First Voices*. He has also written a full-length play in English" (Said x).

Rafat's poetry is vividly descriptive and full of empathy for living creatures. In the poem "Sacrifice," he presents painful images of a goat sacrifice as a ritual in laying the foundation of a friend's house. The speaker can almost feel the point of the knife at his own throat as the she-goat is ritually slaughtered. This poem closes with a critique of ritualistic animal sacrifice: "We are not laying the foundations of a house / But another Dachau" (*Pieces of Eight* 53). In another poem that begins with the words "The squalor in which some people live / Disgusts me," the speaker uses self-irony to suggest that in an earlier generation his family lived in poor and unsanitary conditions (*Pieces of Eight* 54–55). The poem "Once Upon a Time" presents a male speaker on the verge of turning forty who gazes at his reflection in a mirror. The speaker faces middle age, bourgeoise values, family responsibility, and an inner desire to escape: "I've ever wanted to be: / A hermit in a mountain cave" (*Pieces of Eight* 59). There is an underlying pacifist message in the poem "Bunched, like an Embryo," in which the speaker is a male soldier in a trench afraid that he will die in the shelling and never see his wife and children again. He speculates on how his friends and family will behave on receiving the news of his death. Then he hears his name being called: "All is quiet; the shelling is over; / And I rose from the trench, triumphant" (*Pieces of Eight* 62).

Salman Tarik Kureshi's poetry displays recognizably modernist elements. In *Pieces of Eight*, Kureshi's brief biography states, "Salman Tarik Kureshi was born in Lahore in 1942. Educated at Lahore and Multan, he has taken an active part in amateur theatre" (x). According to Coppola, Kureshi "shares with Kureishi a penchant for themes about the divided self and postcolonial rootlessness" (210).

As a business executive based in Karachi, Pakistan, Kureshi has traveled widely. Coppola aptly points out that Kureshi's poetry attempts to reconcile opposing elements: "His language and imagery are a thoughtful blend of brawn and sinew, delicacy, and grace" (212). Kureshi's poetry displays modernist influences with a sense of self-irony as the speaker in "Villanelle: The Intellectual" states, "My views are politic; for these I steal / from published sources. Eliot was a freak" (*Pieces of Eight* 40). The critiques of modernism in postmodern circles leave the speaker with little choice but to conform to the new fashions in poetry. Kureshi writes in easy and informal language that is distinct from the greater formality of diction in many English-language poets from Pakistan. In the poem "Attitude" the speaker, who is a frequent traveler, experiences "unhomeliness" on returning to the point of origin: "Glad to be home, you open the door / and wonder where you are" (*Pieces of Eight* 38).

Women Poets from India

Just as the previous section discussed a group of representative poets from Pakistan who have been anthologized and critiqued separately from mainstream English-language poets writing in India, this section examines major themes, motifs, and poetic methods in the work of women poets from India in the postcolonial era. Although pre-independence poetry in India included significant contributions from the Dutt sisters and Sarojini Naidu, the voices of Indian women after 1947 are distinctly different in many ways.

This section discusses the poetry of five women poets: Kamala Das, Eunice de Souza, Imtiaz Dharker, Mamta Kalia, and Melanie Silgardo. Four of the selected poets (Das, de Souza, Kalia, and Silgardo) are discussed in Bruce King's *Modern Indian Poetry in English*, whereas Imtiaz Dharker is a more recent immigrant to Mumbai, India, from the United Kingdom. After reviewing seven anthologies compiled by different editors (A.N. Dwivedi, R. Parthasarathy, K.R.R. Nair, A.K. Mehrotra, Kaiser Haq, Vilas Sarang, and Eunice de Souza), five women poets have been selected. Most of the poems discussed are from Eunice de Souza's anthology. In this chapter, exclusions from de Souza's nine women poets include expatriate Sujata Bhatt (who is discussed in chapter nine), Smita Agarwal, Charmayne D'Souza, and Tara Patel, who have not been included in most of the predominantly male anthologies published in the 1990s. Contemporary women poets from India are discussed in chapter four.

In the introduction to her anthology *Nine Indian Women Poets* (1997), Eunice de Souza writes that her collection "consists of two generations of women poets in India.... Their language, style, rhythms and forms are inventive, original, and contemporary. There is, in addition, a wide range of subjects — time, history, social problems, religious search, the environment, painters, writers, language" (6). She explains her principles of selection in that she has selected those who have published books and are innovative in methodology. She also states that anthologists make enemies (6). Eunice de Souza makes a valid point that any principles of selectivity that are applied for the purpose of establishing a canon of English-language poetry are likely to encounter resistance in some circles. It is quite likely that a study such as this one will have a similar reception with regard to exclusions as well as selections of representative poets and poems. Bruce King has pointed out that in the English-language poetry from India, the assessment of lasting poetic quality has often come from the poets themselves and reviewers and editors instead of academic critics (61). Hence the evaluations of poets as editors and reviewers have been taken into consideration in examining poetry by these five women poets from India.

The late Kamala Das (1934–2009) is perhaps the best-known English-language woman poet from India in the post–1947 era. Das's poetry appears in almost all Indian anthologies. Kamala Das was born on March 31, 1934, in Malabar in Kerala (Dwivedi 297). She was raised in a literary family, home schooled, and married at the age of fifteen to K. Madhava Das. Her husband was significantly older than her and a great supporter of her writing (Bahri). In December 1999, Das converted to Islam from Hinduism. She also formed a political party. She wrote in English as well as Malayalam, the language of her ethnic community and the state language of her native Kerala. She used the pen name "Madhavikutty" when writing in Malayalam. Das was a novelist and writer of short fiction in addition to being a poet. Her collections of poetry include *Summer in Calcutta* (1965), *The Descendants* (1967), *The Old Playhouse and Other Poems* (1973), *The Anamalai Poems* (1985), and *Only the Soul Knows How to Sing* (1996), as well as a collection of poetry with Pritish Nandy (1990) (Bahri). According to Eunice de Souza:

> Women writers owe a special debt to Kamala Das. She mapped out the terrain for post-colonial women in social and linguistic terms. Whatever her vernacular oddities, she has spared us the colonial cringe ... in her best poems she speaks for women, certainly, but also for anyone who has known pain, inadequacy, despair [*Nine Women Poets* 8].

Kamala Das's eroticism expressed from the woman's point of view was new to Indian English poetry, although not a new approach in the tradition of love poetry in vernacular Indian languages. Eunice de Souza correctly points out that women poets writing in ancient India in Sanskrit and Prakrit often expressed their sexuality openly: "Prakrit poems written by women or in the voices of women are often sexually explicit in a way that few modern women can match" (2). Later generations of diasporic South Asian women poets discussed in chapters nine and ten also use erotic imagery.

From the commentary of Bruce King and from a close reading of Das's poems, one can infer that Das's evident affiliations with the confessional mode of writing, as well as her use of Indian English expressions, created a unique body of poetry. King finds that Das's poems express aspects of the selves of their speakers and a varying range of emotions related to love and sex (151). In "An Introduction" from *Summer in Calcutta*, Kamala Das has addressed the topic of poetic language and choice of idiom for the Indian English poet as one of establishing ownership of one's own poetic language: "All mine, mine alone. It is half-English, half/Indian, funny perhaps, but it is honest" (*Nine Women Poets* 10). Another example of the type of explicitly erotic imagery that shocked the Indian reading public in Das's early career appears in "The Looking Glass": "Gift him what makes you woman, the scent of / Long hair, the musk of sweat between the breasts" (*Nine Women Poets* 15).

In "The Old Playhouse," the speaker describes the process of becoming a traditional wife: "Beneath your monstrous ego I ate the magic loaf and / Became a dwarf. I lost my will and reason" (*Nine Women Poets* 16). In the short poem titled "The Stone Age," the speaker is a married woman who is having an extramarital affair. As she watches her lover asleep, she reflects, "And sleeps. Ask me why life is short and love is / Shorter still, ask me what is bliss and what its price" (*Nine Women Poets* 17). While Kamala Das's erotic poems appear most often in anthologies, there are also poems with vivid memories of people and places. In "My Grandmother's House," the speaker remembers, "I received love.... That woman died, / The house withdrew into its silence, snakes moved" (*Ten Twentieth-Century Indian Poets* 23). Memories of early life, people, and places also recur in the poems of the diasporic poets Ramanujan, Sharat Chandra, Alexander, and Ondaatje. King compares Das to other poets from southern India such as Ramanujan, Parthasarathy, Sharat Chandra, and Alexander (148). Das is very successful in creating immediacy of feeling, a sense of the transient quality of life as well as its sensory experiences, and a dramatic speaking voice in her different female personae, who are often strong, earthy, and candid.

Like Kamala Das, Mamta Kalia has had a long career as a bilingual writer. Kalia writes in her native Hindi as well as in English. According to Eunice de Souza, Kalia was born in 1940 and received an M.A. in English literature in 1963 from Delhi University (18). She has been the principal or chief academic officer of a women's college in Allahabad, India. Kalia has won several awards for her publications in Hindi, and her books in English include *Tribute to Papa* (1970) and *Poems '78* (1978) (de Souza 18).

According to Bruce King, Mamta Kalia, Kamala Das, Eunice de Souza, and Melanie Silgardo have made a more significant impact on the immediacy of expression in Indian English poetry than earlier women poets and male poets (155). Mamta Kalia's women speakers expose the hollowness and subordination of women's lives in the patriarchal structure of Indian society in the era immediately before the Indian women's movement of the 1980s. Kalia is quite recognizably a confessional poet who creates feminist voices, such as that in "Tribute to Papa," a poem that expresses a significant degree of anger and is in some ways a reminder of the late Sylvia Plath's poem "Daddy." The female speaker in this poem views her father, who seeks control over his family in the home, as an overly religious man and a loser in his career: "These days I am seriously thinking of disowning you, Papa, / You and your sacredness" (*Nine Women Poets* 20). In the brief lyric "Compulsion," the speaker confesses her forbidden desires, such as "I want to pick my nose / in a public place" (*Nine Women Poets* 21). The woman speaking in "Brat" discovers her fleshly connection to her own mother as she describes images of prenatal existence: "By that cordial cord inside you. / I must have been a rattish thing" (*Nine Women Poets* 24).

There is social commentary on marriage and family life in South Asia in the poem "After Eight Years of Marriage," in which the speaker visits her parents for the first time after her marriage. In a large country such as India, brides often travel far from their parents after marriage. Also, in Indian extended families, women living as housewives traditionally had to adjust to a number of relatives living under the same roof in addition to the new husband selected in an arranged marriage: "that it wasn't easy to be happy in a family of twelve" (*Nine Women Poets* 25). The impossibility of answering the parents, who appear not to have inquired about their daughter's feelings in eight years, is clearly expressed in the words "They asked me, 'Are you happy, tell us.' / It was an absurd question" (*Nine Women Poets* 25).

In the angry confessional lyric "Anonymous," the speaker is an unnamed middle-class Indian housewife in the late twentieth century who has become like other housewives of her generation caught up in repetitive housework and "worthless movies at reduced rates," a woman who has lost both her sense of self and her self-esteem: "I put on weight every month / like Kamla or Vimla" (*Nine Women Poets* 26). Despite the fact that Mamta Kalia turned more toward writing in Hindi as a resident of Allahabad in northern India, her confessional poems clearly defined the Indian feminist viewpoint of the late twentieth century through her anonymous women speakers.

Eunice de Souza (born in 1940) and her former student Melanie Silgardo (born 1956) have emerged as two prominent Indian women poets writing in the confessional mode. Both de Souza and Silgardo are of Goan ancestry and their poems depict family history, memories of early life, and Goan scenarios. Eunice de Souza's poems are more satiric while Silgardo's poems are somewhat more compassionate.

Bruce King has pointed out similarities between Eunice de Souza and Sylvia Plath in which the confessional mode is combined with "self-ironic wit" (156). Based on King's biographical chart, Eunice de Souza was born in Pune in a Roman Catholic family of Goan ancestry (392). Her parents were educators. She received her B.A. in English from Sophia College in Mumbai, her M.A. in English from Marquette University in the United States, and her Ph.D. from the University of Mumbai. She lives in Mumbai and is a retired professor. She has published several poetry collections such as *Fix* (1979), *Women in Dutch Painting* (1988), *Ways of Belonging* (1990), and *Selected and New Poems* (1994). Her poems are widely anthologized, and she has edited several works.

Eunice de Souza's first collection of poems (*Fix*) was not received well by the Goan Roman Catholic community (*Nine Women Poets* 38). In "Catholic Mother," the speaker satirizes a couple who have had seven children in seven years and are being held up as pillars of society by the Roman Catholic clergy. The "father of the year," Francis X. D'Souza, is an Indian citizen who expresses a negative attitude toward India's majority religion: "(these Hindu buggers got no ethics)" (*Nine Women Poets* 39). The poem "For A Child, Not Clever" addresses a slow learner who has learned not to speak of poor academic performance: "sometimes, you say, as if / explaining things: I'm not clever" (*Nine Women Poets* 40).

In the poem titled "Autobiographical," the confessional mode is reminiscent of Sylvia Plath as the speaker/persona recalls a suicide attempt, the death of her father, an out-of-body experience and the painful criticism of her enemies directed against her single status: "Really I'm writhing with envy / and anyway need to get married" (*Nine Women Poets* 41). In "The Road," the female speaker remembers her strict, almost puritanical upbringing in a traditional Goan Catholic community through memories of her first communion and of Sister Flora in primary school. As an adult she encounters criticism, for "now she wears lipstick / now she is a Bombay girl" (*Nine Women Poets* 45). In "Bequest," the speaker opens with the image of Christ holding his bleeding heart that she found to be disturbing in her childhood and she connects it at the end of this brief poem with images of organ donation (*Nine Women Poets* 44–45). The poem "Landscape" subverts the traditional idea of the beautiful natural landscape in depicting the seashore of a large Indian city (probably the overcrowded megalopolis of Mumbai where de Souza lives): "The crows will never learn / there is garbage enough for everyone" (*Nine Women Poets* 45). A similar surrealistic strategy is used in "Jaisalmer," a city in Rajasthan rich in the history of medieval Hindu Rajput warriors, where the speaker viewing Rajput paintings reflects, "The life of the hero on the scabbard of a sword. / Faces in profile, erect penis in profile" (*Nine Women Poets* 46).

Both Eunice de Souza's anthology *Nine Indian Women Poets* and Bruce King's critical study *Modern Indian Poetry in English* classify Melanie Silgardo as a significant woman poet from India writing in English. Silgardo belongs to the same Goan Roman Catholic community as de Souza, with whom she once studied. She earned a B.A. and M.A. in English at the University of Mumbai, and has had a long career as an editor living in London. Many of her poems have been published outside of the Indian subcontinent, and her work has not received as much attention as it deserves in Indian English poetry circles. Her collection *Skies of Design* (1985) was published in London and was awarded the Best First Book Commonwealth Poetry Prize, Asian Section (de Souza, *Nine Women Poets* 27).

Melanie Silgardo's poems combine both confessional and surrealistic techniques. "The Earthworm's Story" reads almost like a parody of the confessional mode in which the speaker is a suffering earthworm: "It does not matter / if that's your foot over me" (*Nine Women Poets* 33). The masochism of these lines, as well as the gentle irony pointed at the voice of the postmodern poet in a decentered world, makes this brief poem quite striking in method and tone. In the poem "1956–1976 A Poem," the speaker is a twenty year old with "The insane need / To roll up the sky" (*Nine Women Poets* 29).

As in the poems of Mamta Kalia and Eunice de Souza, Silgardo's women speakers contend with patriarchal authority while growing up with fathers who were strong authority figures. The speaker in "For Father on the Shelf" remembers the days when her father was drunk: "You never knew I wet my pillow / oftener than I had ever wet my bed" (*Nine Women Poets* 32). In "Skies of Design," the speaker is a woman recovering from a relationship that is over: "All power, now, I take away from you. / As from my father, my brothers" (*Nine Women Poets* 34).

In Silgardo's poems, there is compassion for nature's creatures such as, the bird flying on a broken wing who is still singing even though it is destined to fall to an inevitable death: "Bird flying on a broken wing / soon your voice will break" (*Nine Women Poets* 36).

Like de Souza and Silgardo, Imtiaz Dharker presents voices of a minority community in India — the Muslim community. Dharker, like a number of diasporic South Asian poets, has migrated twice to two different countries. She was born in Lahore, Pakistan, in 1954 (de Souza, *Nine Women Poets* 48). She relocated to the United Kingdom with her family and was educated there. She later moved to India, and lives and writes in Mumbai. Dharker is also a documentary filmmaker and a visual artist. She served from 1975 to 1985 as consulting poetry editor of the magazine *Debonair*, a general commercial Indian magazine that prints poetry (*Nine Women Poets* 48). Imtiaz Dharker's poetry is not discussed in Bruce King's study. Her first collection of poems (*Purdah*) was published in 1989, followed by *Postcards from God* (1994), *I Speak for the Devil* (2001), *The Terrorist at My Table* (2006), and *Leaving Fingerprints* (2009) ("Imtiaz Dharker").

Dharker's poems present a persona or speaker who expresses empathy for the lives of marginalized South Asians, such as veiled Muslim immigrant women in Britain, the people of Mumbai's slums, and those viewed as "terrorists." In *Nine Women Poets*, Eunice de Souza finds Dharker's interest in oppressed groups to be a poetic flaw (49). Sometimes, there is considerable emotion encapsulated into a single poem, such as "The Right Word," in which the speaker presents the terms "terrorist," "freedom fighter," "hostile militant," "guerilla warrior," and "martyr" as words that have been used to describe the same individual ("Imtiaz Dharker").

Eunice de Souza praises a poem by Dharker titled "Living Space," about a shack in a very poor area somewhere in India. This poem is very rich in visual imagery, a reminder that Dharker is also a visual artist: "The whole structure leans dangerously / towards the miraculous" (*Nine Women Poets* 54).

According to de Souza, the poem "Living Space" captures the rickety and shabby quality of life in India as well as a spirit of survival (49).

In the early poem "Purdah 1," the speaker is a Muslim woman speaking of other veiled Muslim women: "We sit still, letting the cloth grow / a little closer to our skin" (*Nine Women Poets* 50). It is almost as if within the confines of the traditional South Asian "burkha," the women become more and more introverted. In "Battle-line" the speaker describes scenes after border skirmishes between adjacent countries who are compared to "distrustful lovers / who have fought bitterly" (*Nine Women Poets* 51). In "Namesake" the speaker describes the life of a ten-year-old boy in a slum, where the speaker of the poem describes the scene instead of letting the scene speak for itself. It is this tendency to "tell" instead of "show" that sometimes places the experiences of Dharker's poems at a distance from readers. However, in a poem such as "Minority," the speaker has a strong voice that describes the status of being a minority, a foreigner and an immigrant in different countries: "I don't fit / like a clumsily-translated poem" (*Nine Women Poets* 55). In poems such as these, autobiographical elements are recognizable.

English-Language Poets in Western India

It can be observed that in the post–1947 era, Mumbai has been the most significant cultural center for Indian English poetry, where a group of poets flourished under the mentorship of Nissim Ezekiel. Anthologies of Indian English poetry have an overrepresentation of male poets and an abundance of poets from western India. This chapter builds upon Bruce King's attempts to establish a canon of modern and postmodern Indian English poetry. English-language poetry from India in the post–1947 era is recognizably modern, postmodern, confessional, and surrealist in the poets' uses of late twentieth- and twenty-first-century methodologies.

Bruce King has appropriately emphasized the contributions of the late Nissim Ezekiel, Gieve Patel, Keki Daruwalla, Saleem Peeradina, Santan Rodrigues, Manohar Shetty, Arun Kolatkar, Dilip Chitre, and Adil Jussawalla from western India. This chapter is more selective in discussing the contributions of Nissim Ezekiel and his group by highlighting Dom Moraes, Adil Jussawalla, Gieve Patel, and Saleem Peeradina as male poets from western India.

Nissim Ezekiel (1924–2004) was born and educated in Mumbai, India. He also studied in London. Ezekiel worked as a professor of American literature at the University of Mumbai. He grew up speaking Marathi in Mumbai's Jewish community, and it is possible that the themes of self-identity and marginalization explored in his poems may be related to his background. On this topic, R. Parthasarathy's *Ten Twentieth-Century Indian Poets* quotes Ezekiel himself: "I am not a Hindu, and my background makes me a natural outsider: circumstances and decisions relate me to India" (28). According to Parthasarathy's anthology, "In 1964, he was a Visiting Professor at Leeds University; in 1974, an invitee of the U.S. government under its International Visitors program; and in 1975, a Cultural Award Visitor to Australia. For some time, he was Director of Theatre Unit, Bombay" (*Ten Twentieth-Century Indian Poets* 28). Ezekiel published *A Time to Change* (1952), *Sixty Poems* (1953), *The Third* (1959), *The Unfinished Man* (1961), *The Exact Name* (1965), *Three Plays* (1969), *Snakeskin and Other Poems* (1974), *Hymns in Darkness* (1976), *Latter-Day Psalms* (1982), and *Collected Poems 1952–88* (1989). Ezekiel's obituary reads, "Ezekiel received the Sahitya Akademi cultural award in 1983 and the Padma Shri, India's highest civilian honour in 1988" (Joffe).

By the mid–1950s, Nissim Ezekiel, as editor of the magazine *Quest*, became a mentor to several English-language Indian poets writing in the late modernist style. Ezekiel's own earlier poems reveal the influences of post–World War II British poetry; some of these poems, such as "The Night of the Scorpion" and "The Patriot," are included in high school textbooks (Joffe). Lawrence Joffe's obituary also states that Ezekiel served as a mentor to Dom Moraes, Adil Jussawalla, and Gieve Patel.

The speakers in Ezekiel's poems are rational and analytical, as in the well-known poem "Night of the Scorpion," which presents a critique of Indian superstitions and folk remedies. The speaker's mother is stung by a scorpion and suffers for twenty hours, being subjected to various remedies (some probably more painful than the sting itself). The poem closes with the mother's comment on her willingness to sacrifice herself for her children: "Thank God the scorpion picked on me / And spared my children" (*Ten Twentieth-Century Indian Poets* 32).

In the often-anthologized poem "Background, Casually," the speaker seems to be Ezekiel himself presenting his own experiences and views. The speaker begins with his marginalization as a Jew in a Roman Catholic school and describes his voyage on a cargo ship, his life in London, and his return to India, where he discovers that he belongs: "The Indian landscape sears my eyes. / I have become a part of it" (*Ten Twentieth-Century Indian Poets* 36).

Ezekiel's speaker in "Goodbye Party for Miss Pushpa T.S." breaks free from the formal English that characterizes the first century of South Asian poetry in English to speak in the Indian English vernacular (Saussure's *la parole*) used in western India. Miss Pushpa is going abroad, and the speaker (presumably male) wishing her farewell describes her incredibly submissive qualities: "Whatever I or anybody is asking / she is always saying yes" (*Ten*

Twentieth-Century Indian Poets 38). This poem demonstrates that Ezekiel had a fine ear for folk speech and created dramatic voices in his poems. Ezekiel was also keenly aware of other South Asian English-language poets, as seen in "Poem of the Separation," where two lovers are separated by ten thousand miles and the woman breaks off the relationship, sending in her latest letter "Ramanujan's translation of a Kannada religious poem" (*Ten Twentieth-Century Indian Poets* 31).

Among poets from western India influenced by Ezekiel is Gieve Patel (born in 1940), a Mumbai-based physician whose poetry receives negative commentary in Parthasarathy's anthology: "Patel's poems are unspectacular take-offs on the Indian scene on which he comments with clinical fastidiousness" (*Ten Twentieth-Century Indian Poets* 85). The setting of many of Patel's poems is his native city of Mumbai, with some references to his Parsi (Zoroastrian) upbringing, as in "Naryal Purnima," wherein the Parsi speaker reflects upon his early life on the day of a Hindu festival: "Quite English. The local gods hidden in / Cupboards from rational Parsi eyes" (*Ten Twentieth-Century Indian Poets* 91). An occasional poem is strikingly surrealistic; in "O My Very Own Cadaver," the speaker describes a terrifying fantasy of an out-of-body experience: "I see my body float on waters / That rush down the street" (*Ten Twentieth-Century Indian Poets* 98).

Dom Moraes (born in 1938) is another Mumbai-based poet influenced by Ezekiel. Some editors of Indian anthologies have not been comfortable with the inclusion of Moraes, who returned to India from England in 1974. Dom Moraes's first book of poems, *A Beginning* (1957), won the Hawthornden Prize at Oxford in 1958. Moraes has been a prolific writer with several volumes of poetry, biography, travelogues, collections of his articles, and an autobiography. The voices of Moraes's speakers are expatriate voices, and as Arvind Krishna Mehrotra aptly comments, "For nearly three decades Moraes's readers, too, saw him as an 'English poet,' and even though this has now changed, the foreignness of his verse has not gone away" (91).

An example of the British themes, imagery and language in much of Moraes's poetry appears in the soliloquy of the wizard Merlin of Arthurian legends, who now plays the role of a scarecrow and reflects on his glorious past: "What is Merlin but a mad mendicant / Working as hodman and scarecrow" (*Indian English Poetry Sicne 1950* 98).

Adil Jussawalla (born in 1940) also came under Ezekiel's influence. He was born in Mumbai, raised in a Parsi (Zoroastrian) community, and educated in Mumbai and Oxford. He worked in London for some time and returned to India permanently in 1970. He has published collections of poetry and has also edited an anthology (Sarang 112). Jussawalla's poetry displays late modern and postmodern formal English but there is energy and sympathy for the poor and oppressed, as seen in "The Waiters," where servers at a restaurant are described as follows: "Blacker than mud their Tamil minds recall, / Dark skins serving dishes to the sallow" (*Indian English Poetry Since 1950* 112).

Bruce King finds the influences of British poetry on Jussawalla to be significant (244). Themes of alienation and disillusionment recur in Jussawalla's work (King 246–47). In that sense, Jussawalla fits the paradigm of the stranger in his own land. King has discussed Jussawalla's poetry at length because he has focused on Ezekiel and his followers in much detail. Other than Ezekiel and his followers in western India, the literary reputations of Saleem Peeradina and Arun Kolatkar are well established.

Arun Kolatkar (born 1932) in Kolhapur, Maharashtra, India, is a bilingual writer who uses both the English and Marathi languages. His reputation as an English-language poet is based upon his award-winning collection *Jejuri* (1976), which received the Commonwealth Poetry Prize (Mehrotra 33). According to Mehrotra, Kolatkar is clearly modernist in his technique: "The passionate masters of this new faith — Kolatkar's precursors — were Ezra Pound, William Carlos Williams, Louis Zukofsky, to mention only poets, and only Americans" (54).

The poem "Irani Restaurant Bombay" is filled with visual images that suggest not only modernism but also surrealism: "as when to identify a corpse one visits a morgue and politely the corpse rises from a block of rice" (Mehrotra 58). The placement of visual objects is significant in Kolatkar's poems and reminds readers of Kolatkar's formal training in the visual arts. The poems in *Jejuri* create unforgettable images of a small town in Maharashtra, India: "You pass by the ruin of the temple / but the resident bitch is nowhere around" (Mehrotra 71).

Saleem Peeradina was born in Mumbai, India, in 1944. He was educated at Mumbai and Wake Forest University. His first collection (*First Offence*) appeared in 1980 and brought him critical acclaim as an Indian poet writing in English. After working in Mumbai, Peeradina emigrated to the United States in 1989 and is now an associate professor of English at Siena Heights University in Adrian, Michigan ("Saleem Peeradina"). He published the collection *Group Portrait* in 1992, and also *Meditations on Desire* in 2003. Peeradina became recognized as an editor and critic for his anthology *Contemporary Indian Poetry in English: An Assessment and Selection* (1972). Peeradina has not been included in chapter seven because of his greater recognition in Indian poetry circles (also confirmed by Bruce King's comments on Peeradina's work). Interestingly, Peeradina is excluded from the anthology *Indivisible* (2010), as are several other South Asian immigrant poets in the United States, such as Waqas Khwaja, Darius Cooper, and the late Syed Hassan.

Peeradina's poetry creates unique images of contemporary urban life in

India. Many of his poems specifically refer to scenes of city life in Mumbai. Poems such as "Group Portrait" and "Transition" contain an almost bewildering collection of images — visual, auditory, olfactory, and kinetic. Bruce King finds Peeradina's fragmented imagery to be successful in bringing together many aspects of modern life in a way that could not be accomplished in more formalized poems (135). Some of the images remain with the reader, as in the poem "Group Portrait"—"Four heads on a two-wheeler is a tight-rope dance" (*Indian Poetry in English* 132)—and also "In the bloodstream of this insomniac city / A plane lifts off, receding in the direction" in the poem "Transition" (*Indian Poetry in English* 134).

Poets from Southern India

Rajagopal Parthasarathy was born at Tirupparaiturai near Tiruchirapalli, Tamil Nadu, in 1934 and educated in Mumbai and Leeds University, United Kingdom. He returned to Mumbai, where he taught English in the same department as Nissim Ezekiel, then moved to Chennai (formerly Madras) in 1971, where he joined Oxford University Press as regional editor. He moved to New Delhi in 1978 and worked as an associate professor of English and Asian studies at Skidmore College in Saratoga Springs, New York. Again, because he received considerable recognition in India before moving to the United States in the second half of his career, R. Parthasarathy is discussed as an Indian poet instead of an immigrant South Asian poet in the United States. He is included in *Indivisible* (2010) and has appeared in readings with one of the editors of this anthology. Parthasarathy has been successful with his English translations of Tamil poetry in the later stages of his career.

Parthasarathy's collections of poetry include *Rough Passage* (1977) and *Poetry from Leeds* (1968). Parthasarathy's poetry combines late modernist and postmodern methodologies. He shows interest in appropriating a language that is suitable for English poetry by Indians and also addresses themes of exile, alienation, and self-identity that are common to the diasporic South Asian poets' experiences. In "Homecoming," the speaker (who is of Dravidian descent, like the poet himself) returns with a perception of "My tongue in English chains" (Parthasarathy, *Ten Twentieth-Century Indian Poets* 74). In "Exile" the speaker observes of another man that "He has spent his youth whoring / after English gods" (*Ten Twentieth-Century Indian Poets* 75).

Parthasarathy moved to editing, criticism, and translating Tamil poetry in the second half of his career upon emigrating to the United States, whereas Shiv K. Kumar worked in the United States and returned to a permanent academic position in India as a professor of English at the University of Hydrabad in Andhra Pradesh in southern India. Kumar's poetry on the expatriate's perspective is discussed in chapter seven.

Shiv Kumar (born in 1921 in Lahore), was educated in India and Cambridge. He has been a visiting professor at several British and American universities. Kumar was awarded the Padma Bhushan Award in India. He has translated the Urdu-language poetry of Faiz Ahmed Faiz in a collection titled *Selected Poems of Faiz Ahmed Faiz* (1995). He also received the Sahitya Akademi Award in 1987 for *Trapfalls in the Sky* (1986). Other collections of his poetry include *Articulate Silences* (1970), *Cobwebs in the Sun* (1974), *Subterfuges* (1976), *Woodpeckers* (1976), *Woodgathering* (1998), and *Thus Spoke the Buddha* (2002).

Shiv K. Kumar has had a long career as a poet, fiction writer, playwright, translator, and critic. He has been anthologized as an Indian postcolonial poet. Kumar's poems use the confessional style, and contain both humor and irony, as well as a kind of self-irony not common in Indian English poetry (*Ten Twentieth-Century Indian Poets* 33). Parthasarathy comments that the hallmark of Kumar's technique is that "often he takes a simple fact or incident and develops it to a point where it acquires a new meaning" (*Ten Twentieth-Century Indian Poets* 33). In the poem "Indian Women," the speaker describes village women who wait patiently for the return of their men, who have left presumably in search of work: "In this triple-baked continent women don't etch angry eyebrows" (*Ten Twentieth-Century Indian Poets* 54). The poem "Pilgrimage" ends with the speaker's ironic view "that the gods had trapped us / into belief" (*Ten Twentieth-Century Indian Poets* 55).

The Poets from Eastern India

While a number of English-language poets continue to publish from the states of West Bengal and Orissa in eastern India, the Writers Workshop prints both neglected poets of the past and those publishing collections for the first time, and Jayanta Mahapatra's journal *Chandrabhaga* also created opportunities for new regional English-language poets. This section briefly discusses the contributions of two well-established poets, Pritish Nandy and Jayanta Mahapatra, both of whom appear in several anthologies and have also been discussed in Bruce King's book. King views Nandy's work as prolific but of unequal quality (27–28), and is more favorable to Mahapatra (30).

Pritish Nandy, born in 1951 and educated in Kolkata, is an ethnic Bengali with beginnings in Kolkata, West Bengal, where he became associated with publisher, poet, and scholar P. Lal of the Writers Workshop from the early days of his writing career. Nandy and Lal also mentored Jayanta Mahapatra and other younger poets from Orissa, a state bordering West Bengal in eastern India.

Nandy began in the late modernist mode and swiftly acquired the idioms of the counter-culture of the late 1960s and early 1970s. His poetry began to represent popular culture rather than serious art. By 1981 he had published seventeen volumes of poetry. After *The Rainbow Last Night* (1981), Nandy stopped writing poetry and relocated to Mumbai. Since then, he has been a successful journalist, translator, filmmaker, and right-wing politician. He returned to poetry in 2010 with a collection of poems titled *Again* (Johari).

Nandy's poems are in free verse and he uses the rhythms of common speech. However, images appear to be loosely clustered without the fragments always creating a temporal and spatial arrangement that makes the reader reflect deeply. It is almost as if the images and emotions are expressed too quickly, as in the poem "Calcutta If You Must Exile Me," which closes with the words "And I will show you the hawker who died with Calcutta in his eyes / Calcutta if you must exile me destroy my sanity before I go" (*Gathered Grace* 101).

The poem "Love" presents a male speaker in a third unsuccessful relationship where the breakup is either a violent fantasy or a memory of domestic violence: "So, when life took over, one dusklit autumn night, I caught her by her / hair and dragged her to the edge of the forest, where I left her" (*Gathered Grace* 102). Most of the academic anthologies of Indian English poetry have excluded Nandy but positive reviews in India of *Again* (2010) suggest that he still has a following from his popularity in the 1960s and 1970s as an icon of popular culture.

Unlike Nandy, Jayanta Mahapatra (born in 1928) has been recognized for the artistic quality of his poetry. Mahapatra is the most prominent Indian English poet from eastern India. Mahapatra has lived all his life in Cuttack, Orissa. He also writes in the Oriya language. He taught physics at Ravenshaw College in Cuttack until his retirement in 1986. Mahapatra has received the Indian Sahitya Akademi Award as well as the highest Indian honor of Padma Shri. He is also the recipient of many international poetry awards. His literary journal *Chandrabhaga* (published from 1979 to 1985) opened up opportunities for several talented new writers from eastern India. As a poet, he has his own methodology developed independently from the Mumbai circles of poetry. Mahapatra has published about eighteen collections of poetry. His first volumes were *Swayamvara and Other Poems* (1971) and *Close the Sky Ten by Ten* (1971).

Bruce King is uncertain which poems by Mahapatra should be considered a part of the canon (71). Mehrotra views Mahapatra's magazine *Chandrabhaga* as an "example of the limiting view of poetry" (5). R. Parthasarathy offers a valuable insight on Mahapatra's style: "The economy of phrasing and startling images recall the subhasitas (literally, that which is well said) of classical San-skrit" (*Ten Twentieth-Century Indian Poets* 59).

In Mahapatra's poetry, the control of language and imagery incorporate both modernism and postmodernism as well as the sensitivity of Oriya ver-nacular poetry in describing human relationships. For example, "The Whore-house in a Calcutta Street" closes with a moment frozen in time encapsulating the prostitute's disinterestedness and loneliness: "'Hurry, will you? Let me go,' and her lonely breath thrashed against your kind" (*Ten Twentieth-Century Indian Poets* 62). Mahapatra's poems often capture moments of reflection and tranquility, as in "Grass," where the speaker states, "Now I watch something out of the mind scythe the grass, know that the trees end" (*Ten Twentieth-Century Indian Poets* 63).

In the poem "The Abandoned British Cemetery of Balasore," the speaker reflects upon India's history, reads the names of the dead, and walks away from the weight of the past to reflect upon the future where the young can also die: "Of what concern to me is a vanished Empire? Or the conquest of my ancestors' timeless ennui?" (Mehrotra 26). Only a few lines of Mahapatra's prolific poems have been cited here as examples of his method.

At this time books and dissertations on Mahapatra continue to be written and these works analyze and categorize his poems in both depth and detail. Arvind Krishna Mehrotra is a harsh critic of Jayanta Mahapatra. However, Mehrotra includes Mahapatra in his anthology with the comment that "with some few exceptions, Mahapatra's work is a meditation on a single theme: the daily tragedy of having to wake up in a sun-filled room" (20).

Poets from Northern India

Arvind Krishna Mehrotra has compiled an influential anthology and has maintained a stable reputation as an Indian English poet from northern India. Like Mamta Kalia, he has had a long career in Allahabad, Uttar Pradesh. Bruce King places Mehrotra and Mahapatra in the same chapter as experimentalists (183–208). While Mehrotra's body of work is smaller and finely polished, Mahapatra's body of poetry is much larger. Mehrotra's poetic style has evolved through the influences of late modernism, postmodernism, and surrealism to a degree of temporal and spatial consciousness (King 184). In the 1960s, Mehrotra started some short-lived avant-garde magazines. It is important to recognize Mehrotra's ideological dedication to English-language poetry in a setting where using Hindi gives the poet a much larger reading public and swifter recognition. Mamta Kalia changed the language of her poems but Mehrotra maintained his standing as an established Indian English poet.

Mehrotra was born in Lahore in 1947, and was educated in Allahabad and Mumbai. He is a professor of English at the University of Allahabad. He has been a visiting writer in the United States and other countries. Parthasarathy states that Mehrotra cites *Manifesto of Surrealism* (1924) as an important influence (*Ten Twentieth-Century Indian Poets* 64). In 2009, Mehrotra became one of the nominees for the prestigious chair of Professor of Poetry 2009 at Oxford, competing for votes against Nobel laureate Derek Walcott and Ruth Padel (Flood). Mehrotra's art is internationally known for its quality. His reputation is based on four collections of poetry: *Nine Enclosures* (1976), *Distance in Statute Miles* (1982), *Middle Earth* (1984), and *The Transfiguring Places: Poems* (1998).

Images of recollections, of special moments frozen in time, frequently occur in Mehrohtra's poetry. The male speaker in "Continuities" remembers his early life: "My first watch is a fat and silver Omega / Grandfather won in a race fifty-nine years ago" (*Ten Twentieth-Century Indian Poets* 68). In "Letter to a Friend," a newlywed husband speaks of the unromantic early days of setting up a home with his wife, who spent all day in chores until "The postman came up the steps and she spent, Hours reading letters from her family" (*Ten Twentieth-Century Indian Poets* 71). In this poem, the style of life of the India of Mehrotra's youth is frozen in time. This was an era when there were few household appliances that housewives could purchase and when people actually wrote letters. "Remarks of an Early Biographer" is about a writer. In this poem, Mehrotra's talent for unusual phrasing is evident in the lines "As a child he divided words / With a blade, or turned them" (*Ten Twentieth-Century Indian Poets* 72).

Internationally recognized as a prolific fiction writer, Vikram Seth was born in 1952 in Kolkata, India, and educated in India and the United Kingdom. Like the poet Sudeep Sen, Seth lives in New Delhi, India, and also has a home in the United Kingdom. He studied at Oxford University, Stanford University, and Nanjing University (China). His published collections of poetry include *Mappings* (1980), *The Humble Administrator's Garden* (1985), *All You Who Sleep Tonight* (1990), *Beastly Tales* (1991), *Three Chinese Poets* (1992), and *The Frog and the Nightingale* (1994). Seth's *Golden Gate* (1986), a novel in verse and a hybrid genre, was selected for the Sahitya Akademi Award of 1988 (Mehrotra 148). *The Humble Administrator's Garden* received the Commonwealth Poetry Prize for Asia (Mehrotra 48).

Vikram Seth's poetry has received mixed critical responses. Adil Jussawalla once compared some of his poems to pop songs (Mehrotra 149). And Arvind Krishna Mehrotra comments, "In ten years, Seth's craft has flourished; the poetry has stayed where it was. Whereas he's added polish, refinement, and civility to his work, and given his language the sweetness of plain water, he has been unwilling to risk anything more than the simplest imaginative structures" (149–151).

Seth's poetry is socially aware but does not suggest any solutions to social problems. In the poem "The Humble Administrator's Garden," misappropriation of funds underlies the beauty of Mr. Wang's lovely garden: "The means by somewhat dubious means, but now / This is the loveliest of all gardens (*Twelve Modern Indian Poets* 157). In "Guest" the speaker is a homosexual: "There was no real hope. 'Guy loving guy? / Man — that's a weird trip — and not for me'" (Mehrotra 151). In the lyric "Soon," the speaker is terminally ill with HIV-AIDS in a hospital bed knowing there is no hope: "He whom I love, thank God, Won't speak of hope or cure" (*Twelve Modern Indian Poets* 160).

The final male poet from northern India is Delhi-based Keki N. Daruwalla, who was born in 1937 in Lahore. His family later moved to India. Daruwalla belongs to the Zoroastrian Parsi community. Daruwalla studied English at the University of Punjab and joined the Indian Police Service (IPS), where he has had a long and successful career. He received the Sahitya Akademi Award in 1984 and the Commonwealth Poetry Prize in 1987. Daruwalla first published with Writer's Workshop in Kolkata, and was praised by Nissim Ezekiel for his early poems. His published works includes *Apparition in April* (1971), *Under Orion* (1980), *Winter Poems* (1980), *The Keeper of the Dead* (1982), *Crossing of Rivers* (1985), *Landscapes* (1987), *A Summer of Tigers* (1995), *Night River: Poems* (2000), *The Map-Maker: Poems* (2002), *A House in Ranikhet* (2003), *The Scarecrow and the Ghost* (2004), and *Collected Poems (1970–2005)* (2006). Daruwalla's reputation is well established. Several critical studies of his work have been published in India.

Bruce King places Daruwalla in the same chapter with Ezekiel, Ramanujan, Patel, and Shiv Kumar as established poets in the canon of post-independence Indian poetry in English. Daruwalla's images are concrete and sharply defined. Parthasarathy writes that "Daruwalla has been praised for his bitter, satiric tones, which is rather exceptional in Indian verse in English." He also points out Daruwalla's effective use of landscapes of the Indian countryside (*Ten Twentieth-Century Indian Poets* 13). This characteristic makes Daruwalla's poetry somewhat different from the majority of post–1947 Indian English poets, whose poems generally use urban imagery.

In "The Epileptic" the speaker is a detached observer describing a woman with her husband and children who is having an epileptic seizure in a public place (*Ten Twentieth-Century Indian Poets* 13). "The Ghagra in Spate" brings to life the destruction brought to rural communities by a river that changes its course often: "And through the village / the Ghagra steers her course" (*Ten Twentieth-Century Indian Poets* 15). Most of Daruwalla's poems present the voice of a detached speaker. An exception is "Fire-Hymn," in which, like

Daruwalla himself, the male speaker is a Zoroastrian. This brief poem begins with the childhood memory of a Hindu cremation where his father showed him partially burned body parts. As a Zoroastrian and a fire worshipper, the speaker does not endorse cremation but is left with no choice after a personal tragedy: "as I consigned my first-born to the flames — the nearest Tower of Silence was a thousand miles" (*Ten Twentieth-Century Indian Poets* 18).

Daruwalla's early poetry contains scenarios of natural disasters, riots, and human suffering that may be related to his exposure to such events as a police officer. Mehrotra, an academician, is not favorably impressed: "That the news is delivered in verse should make all the difference, but seldom does" (77). In Daruwalla's later poems, landscapes and human experiences are presented with the recurrence of an emerging worldview that is almost existentialist in the sense that little meaning emerges from the pain and suffering depicted. In his decentered, postmodernist presentation of physical reality, Daruwalla has similarities to North American poets of his generation.

The poets discussed in this chapter are now viewed as representative of the canon of postcolonial English-language poetry from the Indian subcontinent. The regional clusters of poets that developed in the Indian republic in the post–1947 era have continued to flourish in the twenty-first century. Similar clusters of contemporary English-language poetry in India are discussed in chapter four. However, the political scene continues to keep Indian poets disconnected from their counterparts in Pakistan. And South Asian poets, as editors and reviewers, continue to influence the academic discussions of English-language poetry in the Indian subcontinent.

WORKS CITED

Bahri, Deepika. "Kamala Das." Postcolonial Studies, Emory University. www.english. emory.edu/Bahri/Das.html. Accessed 15 July 2011.

Coppola, Carlo. "Some Recent English Language Poetry from Pakistan." *Ariel: A Review of International English Literature* 29:1 (January 1998): 203–20. ariel.synergiesprairies.ca. Accessed 8 April 2012.

de Souza, Eunice. *Nine Indian Women Poets: An Anthology*. New Delhi: Oxford University Press, 1997. Print.

Dwivedi, A.N. *Indian Poetry in English: A Literary History and Anthology*. Atlantic Highlands, NJ: Humanities Press, 1980. Print.

Flood, Alison. "Little-Known Indian Writer Joins Race for Oxford Poetry Professor." *The Guardian*. 23 April 2009. www.guardian.co.uk/books/2009/afor/23/mehrotra-oxford-poetry. Accessed 14 April 2012.

Haq, Kaiser. *Contemporary Indian Poetry*. Columbus: Ohio State University Press, 1990. Print.

"Imtiaz Dharker." www.imtiazdharker.com. Accessed 14 April 2012.

Joffe, Lawrence. "Nissim Ezekiel." *The Guardian*. 9 March 2004. www.guardian.co.uk. Accessed 15 July 2011.

Johari, Aarefa. "After Literary Hiatus, Pritish Nandy Takes to Poetry 'Again.'" *Hindustan Times*. 28 May 2010. www.hindustantimes.com. Accessed 14 April 2012.

King, Bruce. *Modern Indian Poetry in English*. New Delhi: Oxford University Press, 2001. Print.

Mehrotra, Arvind Krishna. *The Oxford India Anthology of Twelve Modern Indian Poets*. Delhi: Oxford University Press, 1992. Print.

Nair, K.R. Ramachandran. *Gathered Grace: An Anthology of Indian Verse in English*. New Delhi: Sterling, 1991. Print.

Parthasarathy, R., ed. *Ten Twentieth-Century Indian Poets*. Delhi: Oxford University Press, 1976. Print.

Said, Yunus, ed. *Pieces of Eight: Eight Poets from Pakistan*. Dhaka: Oxford University Press, 1971. Print.

"Saleem Peeradina." www.sienaheights.edu. Accessed 14 April 2012.

Sarang, Vilas. *Indian English Poetry Since 1950: An Anthology*. New Delhi: Orient Longman, 1990. Print.

FOUR

Transnationalism and Hybridity in Contemporary Indian Poetry

In the twenty-first century, anthologies are being compiled with groups of Indian poets who have lived in India as well as overseas. The works of these contemporary poets represent the growing elements of transnationalism and hybridity in contemporary Indian poetry in English. The poets discussed in the previous chapter are well established in the canon of South Asian poetry in English in the postcolonial era. The late modernism that appears in post–1947 Indian English poetry is evident in the poems analyzed in this chapter. Most of the contemporary poetry analyzed in chapter four is recognizably postmodern, hybridized, and often transnational in theme and methodology.

Many of the poems discussed in this chapter were first published in periodicals, chapbooks, and collections from India as well as other countries. Some of the publications are now out of print, as poetry journals are sometimes short-lived. For greater accessibility of primary sources for readers, the poems anthologized and reprinted in Jeet Thayil's *The Bloodaxe Book of Contemporary Indian Poets* (2008) have been discussed. These poems are fairly representative of the poetic methodologies of the poets whose work is reviewed in this chapter. These poets include K. V. K. Murthy, Mukta Sambrani, Mamang Dai, Srinivas Rayaprol, Tabish Khair, Vijay Nambisan, Vivek Narayanan, Manohar Shetty, H. Masud Taj, Bibhu Padhi, Tishani Doshi, Arundhathi Subramaniam, Anjum Hasan, Dipankar Khiwani, Leela Gandhi, Anand Thakore, Ruth Vanita, Kersey Katrak, Rukmini Bhaya Nair, Menka Shivdasani, Gopal Honnalgere, Daljit Nagra, Shanta Acharya, Ranjit Hoskote, Karthika Nair, Sridala Swami, Amit Chaudhuri, Debjani Chatterjee, Jerry Pinto, Lawrence Bantleman, E. V. Ramakrishnan, Revathy Gopal, Sampurna Chattarji, K. Satchidanandan, and C. P. Surendran. While this list is representative, it should not be viewed as comprehensive. Some of these poets have been publishing consistently over a period of time while others have limited publications but significant innovations in poetic methods. Some of the poets discussed in this chapter have also been included in Bruce King's revised edition of *Modern Indian Poetry in English.*

Jeet Thayil's anthology brings together poets who live and publish in India as well as diasporic poets of Indian origin whose poetry is read in Indian circles. Some of the poets discussed in this chapter are deceased but are best grouped with contemporary Indian English poets because of their postmodern poetics. Using the classifications of this study, the present chapter discusses contemporary (and postmodern) Indian English-language poets according to the following groups:

(1) Contemporary women poets in India
(2) Contemporary male poets in India
(3) Contemporary women poets from India living overseas
(4) Contemporary male poets from India living overseas

One exception to these four clusters is British Indian poet Daljit Nagra, who has been included because of his depiction of the voices of Indian expatriates in his poems.

Contemporary Women Poets in India

Contemporary women poets publishing in India may be grouped and studied by region. Indian English writing is largely produced in the large metropolitan cities where there is a stable readership and where English-language culture continues to flourish. These centers of English- language culture appear to be in and around the large cities of Mumbai, Bangalore, Chennai (Madras), Kolkata (Calcutta), and New Delhi. These regional concentrations of postcolonial Indian English poets have also been discussed in chapter three. Contemporary Indian English women poets include groups from western and southern India, with limited representation from eastern and northern India.

From the mid-twentieth century onward, Indian English poetry has flourished in Mumbai, as noted in chapter three. The poetics of four contemporary women poets from Mumbai are noteworthy — namely, the works of Menka Shivdasani, Revathy Gopal, Sampurna Chattarji, and Arundhathi Subramaniam. The hybrid poems of Menka Shivdasani (born in 1961) contain surrealistic imagery and depict conflicts within the self. For instance, in "Spring Cleaning" the woman speaker is cleaning her own psyche only to find a skeleton in her closet, the remains of a man from a past relationship: "What the hell / does one do with human remains?" (Thayil, *Bloodaxe Book* 260). In the poem "At Po Lin, Lantau," the woman speaker, who is visiting an area with a Buddhist monastery, admits to thinking idly, "And I wonder what it's like to make love to a monk" (*Bloodaxe Book* 261). Shivdasani's poetry is full of innuendo, of suggestions of the untold tales of the lives of her women speakers, as in the poem "Epitaph," where the poet-speaker withholds her pain only to conclude, "That's when the poem writes itself / like an epitaph" (*Bloodaxe Book* 262).

Unlike Menka Shivdasani's poetry, the poems of Arundhathi Subramaniam, Sampurna Chattarji, and the late Revathy Gopal present diverse points of view of the concept of "place." In these poems, the speakers comment on the temporal and spatial locations of the self. Arundhathi Subramaniam (born in 1967) presents speakers who are recognizably women in the process of reinventing themselves, as seen in the poem "Home," where the speaker expresses her alienation and *angst* both within her "home" and in her woman's body: "A home, like this body, / So alien when I try to belong" (*Bloodaxe Book* 178). In the space of a Mumbai commuter train, the speaker of Subramaniam's "5.46, Andheri Local" finds within herself the energy and power of the Hindu goddess Kali: "million-tongued, multi-spoused / Kali on wheels" (*Bloodaxe Book* 178).

Subramaniam brings up the question of the Indian English poet's Indian identity in her poem "To the Welsh Critic Who Doesn't Find Me Identifiably Indian." The poet-speaker seeks a unique poetic language and metaphors that can hybridize the English language and vernacular Indian languages: "Smear my consonants / with cow-dung and turmeric and godhuli" (*Bloodaxe Book* 177). The inclusion of the word "godhuli" (Hindi for "dusk," associated with the pastoral image of the cattle returning home at sunset) hybridizes this poem by connecting the speaker's literary work to ancient and medieval Indian poetry.

For Mumbai-based poet Sampurna Chattarji (born in 1970), locations appear in her poems with a hint of the ominous. It is almost as if the poems are describing scenes in which women and girls appear where nothing actually happens but where something disastrous could happen. Chattarji's poems contain time capsules, as in "Still Life in Motion," where a young girl is wandering in the streets of a city before daybreak: "The bristly boy at the shop / eyes her too-short skirt" (*Bloodaxe Book* 356). In the poem "Boxes," Chattarji captures scenes of the overcrowding and congestion in which working-class families live in Mumbai and other large Indian cities: "In one side of her one-room home, a stove, where she / cooks dal in an iron pan. The smell of food is good" (*Bloodaxe Book* 359).

For the late Revathy Gopal (1947–2007), time and place are related to major historical events, such as the events in the Indian subcontinent in 1947, the year of her birth and also the year that marked India's release from colonial rule. In the poem "Freedom!" the speaker reminds readers that freedom came with turmoil and suffering: "Was it the dust of departing armies, / or the blood-fog of partition" (*Bloodaxe Book* 350). In the poem "Just a Turn in the Road," the speaker reminds readers that the British colonized India by defeating other European colonizers, that the major decisions of the colonial powers were made in Europe: "ships sunk, local rajahs bought and sold, / small accruals in a war that happens elsewhere" (*Bloodaxe Book* 351). Gopal's poems of loss and disintegrating relationships demonstrate remarkable phrasing that encapsulates very intense emotions, as in "Time Past, Time Present," where the speaker closes with this statement: "See me as I was, one last time. / Watch as I fall to earth" (*Bloodaxe Book* 355). In "Carved in Stone" the woman speaker concludes, "I shall not say your name again, not even by chance. / One day, perhaps, love may die of disuse, left to rust in wind" (*Bloodaxe Book* 355). The speaker's pain and anger resonate in these bitterly ironic lines.

In southern India, three contemporary women poets (Sridala Swami, Tishani Doshi, and Anjum Hasan) are well established in Indian poetry circles. Tishani Doshi (born in 1975) is of Welsh-Gujarati parentage. Educated in the United States, she lives in Chennai (formerly Madras), and is a writer, dancer, and journalist. Doshi's poems present speakers who express a sense of their dislocation in terms of place and time. The external dislocations turn the speakers to their own private spaces, which allow fragments of sensory experiences to surface. These sensory experiences are often dislocated in place and time, even disturbingly fragmented, apparently surfacing from deep within the speaker's psyche, seemingly without logical connections to the speaker's present condition. In "Countries of the Body," from Doshi's award-winning collection of the same name, the poem presents scenarios of clandestine and forbidden encounters whenever individuals seek to express their sexuality via adulterous relationships, one-night stands, and possibly same-sex encounters, as in the last stanza: "How two woman will lead each other out of a country / To sort out wombs, scars, faces. Exchange the others for her own" (*Bloodaxe Book* 133).

In the poem" Homecoming," the speaker captures the sounds and sights of Doshi's native Chennai, where the traditional customs and attire of Tamil Nadu blend with the modern, as in the following image: "And Tamil women on their morning walks / In saris and jasmine and trainers" (*Bloodaxe Book* 156). In "The Day We Went to the Sea," the visual imagery captures the crowding of family beaches: "Mothers in Madras were mining / The Marina for missing children" (*Bloodaxe Book* 156). The dislocation and panic conveyed by these lines provides a startling contrast to conventional images of mothers and children on family beaches.

Dislocations of place and time similar to those in Doshi's poems surface in the postmodern poetry of Sridala Swami (born in 1971), who lives in Hyderabad in southern India. The speakers in Swami's poems have conversations with a listener who represents an aspect of the speaker's own self, as in the images of the human brain in a jar after an autopsy in the unusual poem titled "Post Mortem": "without you without you without you / I am only a dissonance, an object adrift, a wretched" (*Bloodaxe Book* 321). The incomplete line that ends in "wretched" leaves the identity of the speaker unclear. The problems of human relationships also surface in fragmentary references in Swami's poetry, as in "Cryogenic," in which a female Odysseus goes on her journeys while leaving behind a frozen male partner. The freezing negates the possibility of an interesting reconciliation: "Perfectly preserved, he knows nothing" (*Bloodaxe Book* 320). The scenario in this poem suggests the need for both growth and change in maintaining strong relationships. In Swami's "Slip Dreams," the other self is compared to a male vulture: "He is a vulture awake. / He devours me with his words" (*Bloodaxe Book* 322

The poetry of Anjum Hasan (born in 1972) covers different aspects of time and place through the memories of the speakers in her poems. Originally from eastern India, Hasan is from the city of Shillong in the state of Meghalaya, where she was educated. Hasan now lives and works in southern India in the large metropolis of Bangalore. Memories of a young girl's early life surface in the brief poem titled "Shy," in which the speaker remembers her days in a Roman Catholic school: "or running into a nun round a corner / and made idiot by that prim mouth" (*Bloodaxe Book* 179). A sense of place that is both meaningless and stagnant appears in the imagery of Hasan's "To the Chinese Restaurant," where young people are eating out and counting their money with the realization that "Life's not moving / We sit at a red table among the dragons" (*Bloodaxe Book* 180).

In "Jealousy Park," the speaker views the green of the park, with its swings and seesaws, as the color of jealousy, which overwhelms her so that she concedes, "My baby hunger melts into those other / faces of unfinished childhood: the longing" (*Bloodaxe Book* 182). Ultimately, in Anjum Hasan's poetry, the concept of place is in the imagination, as in her poem "Rain," in which the speaker states, "Always the 'where' of where you are is a place in the head / established through skin, and you recognise the address" (*Bloodaxe Book* 183).

Also from northeastern India is the poet and journalist Mamang Dai (born in 1959), who works in Itanagar, Arunachal Pradesh. Mamang Dai's nature poetry is recognizably animistic in its messages. The incantatory rhythms of Dai's poetry suggest hybridization with the vernacular chants of the peoples of the eastern Himalayas. Her poems present recurring images of light, mountains, rivers, and water. The speaker of the poem "The Missing

Link" refers to a myth of the region: "and the cloud woman always calling from the sanctuary of the gorge" (*Bloodaxe Book* 66). In "Remembrance," the speaker refers to memories of guerrilla separatists in the northeastern hills of India: "In the hidden exchange of news we hear / that weapons are multiplying in the forest" (*Bloodaxe Book* 67).

In Dai's lyric "No Dreams," the landscape in the mountains is strangely beautiful: "The hills are washed with light. / The river sings" (*Bloodaxe Book* 68). In the lyric "Small Towns and the River," the speaker celebrates the river that his/her hometown is located on as a river of both life and death, as generations live their lives in the small town. The final lines of the poem are ironic in their comment on the lives of ordinary people: "In small towns by the river / we all want to walk with the gods" (*Bloodaxe Book* 70).

Distinctly different from the work of most of the other women poets publishing in India is the poetry of New Delhi–based academician Rukmini Bhaya Nair, whose poems reflect the influences of cognitive linguistics and critical theory that are her areas of scholarly expertise. Nair's poetry is both hybridized and innovative in its use of words. Nair uses two-line stanzas to great effect, as seen in "Renoir's Umbrellas": "Holds out her hands to you / Through bars of rain" (*Bloodaxe Book* 252). In "Convent," the speaker captures a moment when young girls in a convent school are giggling at prayer time: "And she wonders about prayer / The pity of it, the point" (*Bloodaxe Book* 254). Innovative and provocative in language and theme, Nair's poem "Genderole" challenges the reader to decode the single lines, each of which has words running together as a single word in an imitation of the lengthy word combinations of classical Sanskrit. The poem "Genderole" offers a critique of traditional Hindu treatises on the roles of women as good wives, concluding with the ironic twist that if women had been men, their contributions would not have been the same: "MyworstfearisankarathathadI —, indeedbeenyouImightnotafterallhaveconceivedanythingnewtl" The woman speaker in Nair's poem addresses the Hindu philosopher Sankaracharya as an authority from whom traditional roles of Hindu women have been derived. Nair even uses the Sanskrit punctuation of a straight-line "l" for a period in this cleverly composed hybrid poem.

Contemporary Male Poets in India

Contemporary Indian English male poets are also located in regional groups, with the largest number in western India, followed by southern India and limited representation in eastern and northern India. These concentrations are similar to the groups noted in chapter three as representative of the canon of postcolonial Indian English poetry. Male poets living in western India include Manohar Shetty, Vijay Nambisan, Dipankar Khiwani, Kersey Katrak, Ranjit Hoskote, Jerry Pinto, Anand Thakore, and E.V. Ramakrishnan.

Manohar Shetty was born and educated in Mumbai, later relocating to Goa. The poems of Manohar Shetty (born in 1953) capture the chaos, and to some extent the corruption, of life in urban locations in western India. In the poem "Stills from Baga Beach," the speaker captures scenes in imagery that cannot be coerced into a unified meaning as the poem juxtaposes women tourists from England on the beach with a German studying Vedanta philosophy while the temple elephant, "Swastika on its domed / Forehead, lumbers" across the sand (*Bloodaxe Book* 121). In "The Hyenas," the speaker holds a sleeping asthmatic child whose slumber is disturbed by the sounds from the governor's banquet grounds: "They laugh with the Governor's gang / of kingmakers, fatcats, gold-toting ogres" (*Bloodaxe Book* 120). The hyenas symbolize the corruption of the political arena in India. Shetty's poetry is characterized by unusual imagery, such as "I come from the labyrinths: / Traffic lights park in my eyes" in the poem "Gifts," where the speaker bears gifts for a silent listener (*Bloodaxe Book* 123).

The poet Vijay Nambisan (born in 1963) was educated in the Indian state of Tamil Nadu, has lived in the state of Bihar, and has been located in the hill resort town of Lonavala in the state of Maharashtra. Nambisan has been grouped with the poets from western India in this chapter. Nambisan's postmodern poems are intensely subjective. His poetic personae are often conflicted and the poems allow the trials and tribulations of life in contemporary India to surface, as seen in the images of a train station in "Madras Central": "That is axiomatic. Come we will go and drink / A filthy cup of tea in a filthy restaurant" (*Bloodaxe Book* 102). In the poem "Dirge" Nambisan's speaker is a poet who remembers the poets of western India (well established in the canon of Indian English poetry) who have died: "So Arun and Dom and Nissim — I will shun their hard-earned grief / And much though I will always miss 'em, in softer shadows find relief" *Bloodaxe Book* 104). These lines refer to the deaths of the three poets Arun Kolatkar, Dom Moraes, and Nissim Ezekiel in the same year — 2004. Nambisan's poet-speaker would like to live to the age of ninety.

The poetry of Mumbai-based Dipankar Khiwani (born in 1971) presents themes of loss and nostalgia that appear in South Asians' English-language poetry across continents. In "Delhi Airport" the speaker presents recollections of a stopover in New Delhi (Khiwani's birthplace): "And yet this city somehow clings to me / in smells, exhaustion, dust yet in my hair" (*Bloodaxe Book* 191). In "Night Train to Haridwar" the poem's speaker is traveling on a long-distance train with the following self-reflection: "I smile at myself: Journey, halts indeed! / I should have been a poet, adrift at sea" (*Bloodaxe Book* 191). The image of the poet sailing on the ocean suggests the poet's ability to voyage into unknown reaches of the mind. And the imagery of trains and train stations connects Khiwani's poem to images of trains and train stations in Indian literature as symbols of ongoing journeys in human life. Factually, trains continue to provide long-distance transportation to very large numbers of Indians.

The transience of human life emerges as a theme in the poetry of Kersey Katrak (1936–2007), who also lived in Mumbai. Katrak's imagery of the aging human body is recognizably surrealistic as well as startling. In Katrak's poem "From Malabar Hill," the title locates the speaker in an upscale neighborhood of Mumbai. The speaker notes that the human body "Creates its bright arterial jungle and undergrowth of nerve, / Pap, genital and thigh" (*Bloodaxe Book* 244). In the poem "Ancestors," the speaker imagines that he sees his father who has recently died: "He was once my father. He comes, simply familiar / As one who has the right" (*Bloodaxe Book* 246). The image of the speaker's father is a reminder of the lasting influence of one's male parent in the strongly patriarchal cultures of South Asia.

Poet and art critic Ranjit Hoskote (born in 1969) lives in Mumbai. Hoskote's poetry is almost deliberately difficult and full of incongruous imagery that suggests the difficulties of finding meanings in life's experiences. Hoskote's poem "Passing a Ruined Mill" is dedicated to the late Nissim Ezekiel, and displays Hoskote's late modernist and even postmodern poetics. His poems present startling metaphors such as "And there he sat, while the paper rustled away, / shedding the weave of his words like a blotted skin" (*Bloodaxe Book* 291). In the unusual piece titled "Footage for a Trance," the speaker describes the fragmented recollections of being in a trance as if the trance is being filmed. This poem's closing is surrealistic in that the gardener finds the speaker's skin abandoned in the garden before the speaker's flight: "drooping, ravelled at the seams: / My skin, abandoned in flight" (*Bloodaxe Book* 294). In the poem "Colours for a Landscape Held Captive," the speaker celebrates the imagery and themes in the poems of the late Agha Shahid Ali, who had migrated to the United States. The speaker is moved by the landscapes in Ali's poetry: "those surfaces that melted as you spoke, / laying bare depths in which we'd drown" (*Bloodaxe Book* 296).

Images of shapes take on life in the poetry of Mumbai-based writer and journalist Jerry Pinto (born in 1966). In a poem titled "House Repairs," the speaker describes the demolition of a bathroom wall and the overnight building of a new wall. However, the speaker and his family find that the new wall is really the old wall "With a suicide note still scrawled on it / With blood still fresh splashed on it" (*Bloodaxe Book* 324). There is clearly the indication of an untold story within this poem, suggesting that Pinto's method is hetero-glossic.

Between different versions of stories and different angles of drawings there are similarities in vision, as outlined in Pinto's poem "Drawing Home," where images are viewed as appearing in the eyes of different cameras: "You could play one camera, I could be the other. / We could ask for a neutral third" (*Bloodaxe Book* 325). In contrast, the brief poem "Window" states that a window offers only a limited vision: "What can you do with a window? / It will always remain four-cornered" (*Bloodaxe Book* 325).

Unlike some of the other contemporary poetry in Mumbai, the work of Anand Thakore (born in 1971) is clearly late modern in style with the influence of British speech, as in "What I Can Get Away With," in which the speaker's bourgeois tone mimics the speech of postcolonial India's urban elite: "This whiskey's pretty good, though the waiters aren't too bright, / And what they will get away with I will never get" (*Bloodaxe Book* 240).

The poet E. V. Ramakrishnan (born in 1951) is located in western India, where he teaches English at the University of South Gujarat. Ramakrishnan's postmodern poetry presents surrealistic imagery of a world where menace lurks behind ordinary scenes, such as the situations presented by the speaker of "Terms of Seeing" (*Bloodaxe Book* 347–48). In this poem, the speaker recalls times of his/her schooldays when the children raided the hiding places of the bootleggers: "Mud pots. The crematorium in the corner / Revealed an occa-sional roasted vertebra" (*Bloodaxe Book* 347). The speaker of "Stray Cats" cre-ates an eerie atmosphere by referring to negative myths about a common domestic animal, suggesting that stray cats jump on rooftops "and hold their weekly meetings / in the graveyard like wandering mendicants" (*Bloodaxe Book* 348). Like Kersey Katrak, Ramakrishnan's poem "Things You Don't Know" is concerned with the life of the human body: "The porous skin filters a humid world, / stays in a state of high alert." (*Bloodaxe Book* 350).

Postmodern contemporary Indian poets based in southern India include K. V. K. Murthy, Srinivas Rayaprol, and Gopal Honnalgere. K. V. K. Murthy (born in 1950) is originally from the state of Andhra Pradesh and works in the city of Bangalore in Karnataka. Murthy's poetry is influenced by the work of Dom Moraes and presents surrealistic imagery, as in the poem on exhibits set in a museum where the woman visitor sees, just before closing time, "not love-light in a statue's eyes, / but history's finely sculpted lies" (*Bloodaxe Book* 38). Thoughts of death and dying surface in "Hospital Journal," in which the speaker states that the hospital may be viewed as either hell or purgatory in the poem's allusions that hybridize the poem between European and Indian artistic traditions: "Not Dante but Bosch, this: the stylised fright / of ether, smells and swabs, and groans" (*Bloodaxe Book* 37). And in Murthy's poem

"Just Dead," the speaker presents the imaginary point of view of one who has recently died and entered a domain where human language and meaning have no relevance. The poem itself is intense and frightening in its expression of a state of nonbeing: "makes no sense, without a name — / For ghost after all is earthspeak" (*Bloodaxe Book* 36).

The late Srinivas Rayaprol (1925–1998) was born in Andhra Pradesh, studied at Stanford University in the United States, and then returned to Andhra Pradesh. His views on poetry tended to favor late modernism over the experimentation of postmodern poetry after the 1960s. Rayaprol's views found favor with American poet William Carlos Williams (*Bloodaxe Book* 70). In his poetics, Rayaprol has similarities with some of the poets discussed in chapter three. In Rayaprol's poems, images capture multiple layers of meaning, as in the piece titled "Poem," where the speaker describes the way women in India grow old working in their kitchens day after day: "a hundred years / stirring soup" (*Bloodaxe Book* 71).

Rayaprol's poems are both transnational and hybridized, as in "A Taste for Death," in which the speaker remembers a roommate, Christoph, who is probably deceased. The poem's speaker is a poet and the roommate Christoph was a fiction writer: "and I cannot turn a sudden tear / For the memory of your love" (*Bloodaxe Book* 72). The poem "Travel Poster" presents scenes from different countries and continents as in a poster, only to close with the observation, "And all round this world / eternal dissatisfaction" (*Bloodaxe Book* 73). The poet-speakers of "Married Love" and "Middle Age" present the confessions of middle-aged men. In "Middle Age," the speaker describes his aging face and body, concluding with "Husband and father / friend and inadequate lover I" (*Bloodaxe Book* 74). In "Married Love," the speaker is greeted by his wife and daughters when he returns home after work only to eat the dinner his wife has cooked and leave again "for my evening is planned / for a meaningless excursion to the bars" (*Bloodaxe Book* 74). The irony behind "I Like the American Face" lies in the speaker pointing out the expressions on the faces of Americans photographed for magazines as images of success: "and always ready / to break into a false-toothed smile" (*Bloodaxe Book* 75). In contrast, the speaker in "A Poem for a Birthday" provides an image of sincerity and friendship: "I have never needed a new face / to meet the faces of my friends" (*Bloodaxe Book* 76).

According to Jeet Thayil, the late Gopal Honnalgere (1942–2003) corresponded with Robert Lowell and W. H. Auden (263). Honnalgere was from the state of Karnataka, and he taught art and writing in school. In the poem "The City," the male speaker presents scenarios from a crumbling marriage amid the consumerism that characterizes urban middle-class lives in post-colonial India. The speaker concludes, "Marriage a refrigerator, / It freezes eggs, apples, and bananas" (*Bloodaxe Book* 266). In the poem "Theme," the speaker is a visual artist in search of a theme that includes his wife and home: "mangalore tiled roof / and two coconut trees" (*Bloodaxe Book* 269). In the humorous piece "How to Tame a New Pair of Chappals" ("chappal" is a Hindi word for sandals of the flip-flop type), the speaker describes the process of breaking in a pair of sandals as if they were indentured workers: "then gradually increase the distance / they should never know the amount of work they have to do" (*Bloodaxe Book* 270). The speaker's sympathies clearly suggest the exploitation of workers in postcolonial India.

Contemporary male poets in northern India include Vivek Narayanan and C.P. Surendran, both located in New Delhi. Vivek Narayanan (born in 1972) was educated in Africa and the United States. He composes story poems that are prose poems with elements of exaggeration and fantasy. Narayanan's hybridized poetics combine rap and fiction with postmodernism to create unique images of contemporary life in India. In "Three Elegies for Silk Smitha," the speaker presents three scenarios with women that are evocative of Indian films and television with their recurring episodes of melodrama. In the closing scene of this poem, a woman dressed in white has committed suicide: "My last of her is borrowed too: / She hangs from the fan of a bright North Madras apartment" (*Bloodaxe Book* 116). In "Learning to Drown," the speaker appears to be fantasizing about images of suicide by drowning with echoes from nineteenth-century American poet Emily Dickinson's poem "Because I could not stop for death." Narayanan creates hybridized and allusive lines: "doubled as witness and mistress. I kindly stopped for time / because by then he could not stop for me" (*Bloodaxe Book* 113).

The poems of C.P. Surendran (born in 1959) capture the ironies of life in contemporary India. Journalist and poet Surendran's short poems reproduce moments of recollection in the memories of speakers, as well as memories of lost love, as in "Milk Still Boils": "He no longer thinks about her, / Or him. Just them" (*Bloodaxe Book* 363). In "Curios," after three years of separation, a man lets a woman into his home and, in a typically Indian gesture of hospitality, makes tea: "He lets her in, / Puts on some tea" (*Bloodaxe Book* 364). "Family Court" presents the setting where marriages are dissolved daily: "People come together to be separated" (*Bloodaxe Book* 363). The paradox in these lines emphasizes the ephemeral nature of human relationships. In the episodes from "Catafalque," the speaker describes his father as ill and dying: "My father on the cot in white, straight as a corpse in a coffin, the hours hushed about him in ambush, their scissor hands" (*Bloodaxe Book* 366). This poem emphasizes the significant role of fathers in India's ancient patriarchal culture, just as images of dying fathers appear in the poems of several other contemporary Indian English poets.

Contemporary male poets in eastern India include Bibhu Padhi and Amit Chaudhuri. Bibhu Padhi (born in 1951) is from the state of Orissa, where he lives and teaches. Padhi's poetry shows a strong influence of modern and post-modern American literature. Padhi also writes on philosophy. His poems contain memories, nostalgia, and sometimes a pervasive sadness. Padhi's poem "Something Else" carries the subtitle "Remembering Raymond Carver" (*Bloodaxe Book* 149). The poem's theme is philosophical in suggesting that there is in the world that the speaker inhabits, a larger meaning or meanings that words alone cannot capture. The speaker realizes that "something is always missing in the things / we use, the persons we care for" (*Bloodaxe Book* 130). Like a number of other contemporary Indian male poets, Padhi's speaker in "Stranger in the House" discovers the continuity of generations, connecting himself to his father and his son: "I see the dust of my father's year rise / from the corner where my son plays" (*Bloodaxe Book* 148). In "Grandmother's Soliloquy," the speaker is frail and she thinks her family does not expect her to live much longer. But her will to live is strong: "that I might live on to name your / unborn son, hold his small voice in mine" (*Bloodaxe Book* 152).

The poet Amit Chaudhuri was born in Kolkata, raised in Mumbai, and currently lives in Kolkata. Chaudhuri (born in 1962) is the editor of a literary anthology. His poems show neo–Romantic influences and hybridization in the influence of the sounds of the Bangla/Bengali language, as well as the use of alliteration and assonance. The poems focus on details and create frozen time capsules, as in the sections from "St. Cyril Road Sequence" that may be referring to the poet's childhood in a Mumbai suburb. The speaker remembers "the tangent outline of a dragonfly / against a leaf, its wings whirring so fast" (*Bloodaxe Book* 184). Then there is the poet-speaker's memory of being rejected at age seventeen by influential editor and poet Nissim Ezekiel: "told me, for fifteen minutes, / that my poems were 'derived'" (*Bloodaxe Book* 186). This poem confirms the regionalized groups that hold their sway in postcolonial Indian literary circles.

Women Poets from India Located Abroad

Several contemporary Indian women work overseas but continue to write for poetry circles in India. This group includes Mukta Sambrani, Leela Gandhi, and Ruth Vanita in the United States; Shanta Acharya and Debjani Chatterjee in the United Kingdom; and Karthika Nair, who works in France.

Mukta Sambrani (born in 1975) is from Pune in western India. Sambrani moved to the United States in 1999. Sambrani's writing is postmodern with surrealistic imagery. Her prose poems contain hybrid themes and motifs, transnational experiences and imagery, as seen in the writings of her fictional speaker Anna Albuquar. In the poem "Names Anna Forgets. Narayan Vishwanath, Padmapani," Anna forgets the names of Hindu deities: "From his navel emerges the creator, Anna shifts now familiar discomfort of the atheist, / Anna sees him reclining, his name committed to amnesia like ocean, now empty" (*Bloodaxe Book* 58–59). The hybrid imagery suggests a world empty of meaning.

Hidden meanings underlie the brief poems of Ruth Vanita (born in 1955), who teaches at the University of Montana. Vanita's poems contain references to clandestine encounters, perhaps of same-sex lovers, as in "Sita" (the model wife of Hindu culture): "From being the perfect wife, there's only one way out — / Not one you planned. Or imagined even" (*Bloodaxe Book* 242). In the brief poem "Fire," the speaker contemplates the answer to the objects to be grabbed as he / she runs for safety in the event of a fire, only to concede: "Knowing that everything can only turn / To ash, except what lives" (presumably in the speaker's mind and spirit (*Bloodaxe Book* 243).

For well-known postcolonial studies scholar and literary critic Leela Gandhi (born in 1966), poetic composition is inspired by the Western literary canon. Born in Mumbai, Leela Gandhi was educated in Delhi and the United Kingdom, and is a professor at the University of Chicago. Gandhi's poetry contains themes of love and loss, and is full of literary allusions. For example, the response of a perceptive reader appears in "Homage to Emily Dickinson, after Pain," where the speaker states, "Our formal feeling when it comes, comes belatedly. / Like a chill on a good night, a season's afterthought" (*Bloodaxe Book* 193).

Gandhi effectively uses the form of the sonnet, even including Elizabethan diction in the sonnet titled "Noun," in which the speaker almost pleads, "Let me call you lover once / And I'll agree that this love's a tenancy" (*Bloodaxe Book* 194). The transience of love is emphasized in these lines. In yet another sonnet, Gandhi compares the literary critic to the poet in "On Reading You Reading Elizabeth Bishop," where the speaker reading American poet Elizabeth Bishop humbly concedes that "I, consigned to where her margins end, / Must annotate your litany, with apologies" (*Bloodaxe Book* 195).

The contemporary expatriate Indian women poets in the United Kingdom include Shanta Acharya and Debjani Chatterjee. Shanta Acharya (born in 1953) is from Orissa, and lives in London with a career in investment management. Acharya's poetry presents philosophical themes as well as themes of love. In "Shunya," the speaker ponders about the nature of the zero (Sanskrit adjective meaning "nothing") as a concept and its myriad applications: "reflecting the sum of the universe, / reducing all to Itself, always transforming"

(*Bloodaxe Book* 288). Acharya's poem "Bori Notesz" (Camp Notebook) is a tribute to the Hungarian poet Miklos Radnoti, who died in the Holocaust. The poem's speaker attempts to capture Radnoti's intensity of emotions: "judge me only by my thoughts of you in a world rebuilt / where my song will live and be heard" (*Bloodaxe Book* 289).

The poet Debjani Chatterjee (born in 1952) was born in India, and educated in Japan, Bangladesh, India, and Hong Kong (*Bloodaxe Book* 308). She lives in Sheffield, Yorkshire, United Kingdom, and has published books of poetry and prose. In Chatterjee's postmodern poetry, the inadequacy of words to explore thoughts and feelings is presented in "Words Between Us," where the breakdown of a relationship corresponds with a breakdown in communication: "Language breaks down and sounds have no meaning. / You and I cross and there is no meeting" (*Bloodaxe Book* 309). Debjani Chatterjee's poetic technique has similarities to songs in her use of refrains that are repeated at the end of every stanza to emphasize the theme of the poem, as in the lament "All Whom I Welcome Leave without My Leave," where the opening line which is the same as the title) becomes a refrain that reiterates the loss of loved ones: "While graying hair and shades of old age cleave / To me, those I love abandon station" (*Bloodaxe Book* 308).

The recent poetry of Karthika Nair (born in1972), originally from the state of Kerala in southern India and now working in Paris, France, is currently receiving positive reviews from critics. Her poems capture moments in time that are replete with sensory details and emotions, as seen in "Interregnum," where the speaker copes with separation from a partner who is traveling in other countries: "Do your hands still stray unbidden at night / Angling to fold my beat within your heart?" (*Bloodaxe Book* 316). In Nair's "Snapshot on the Parisian Metro, or Landscape on Line 3," the speaker captures details of the images of the diverse passengers on the subway as if in a photograph from which a visual artist can create a painting. Even the expressions on the faces of the subway passengers come to life, such as the woman in white silk holding a bouquet who "closes her eyes, and smiles / from Republique to Parmentier" (*Bloodaxe Book* 318).

Male Poets from India Located Abroad

Like several women poets from India who work abroad but keep their ties to Indian literary circles, the contemporary male poets Tabish Khair and H. Masud Taj also work overseas — Khair in Denmark, and Taj in Canada. The late Lawrence Bantleman had emigrated to Canada but is remembered chiefly in Indian poetry circles, and U.K.-born and -raised Daljit Nagra is a poet of the South Asian diaspora whose themes and use of Indian English expressions link his writings to the poetry of the Indian subcontinent.

Tabish Khair (born in 1966) is from Ranchi in the state of Bihar and teaches in Aarhus University in Denmark. Khair's postmodern poetry is transnational in themes and imagery, using both diasporic as well as Indian subjects. The expatriate Indian speaker of "Nurse's Tales, Retold" discovers in the east wind "A warm smell like that of shawls worn by young women / Over a long journey of sea, plain and mountains" (*Bloodaxe Book* 84). In "The Birds of North Europe," the expatriate speaker observes that, unlike birds in India that sometimes fly into people's homes and nest in the corner beams of balconies, in northern Europe, birds display different behavior: "Twenty-four years in different European cities and he had not lost / His surprise at how birds stopped at the threshold" (*Bloodaxe Book* 85). In the poem "Lorca in New York," the speaker presents, among other disconnected images, the unpleasant reality of anti–South Asian racism: "Watch the voice outside that ethnic shop —*Fucking Paki / Place is always open*— put a stainless steel lock" (*Bloodaxe Book* 86).

H. Masud Taj (born in 1956) is from Moradabad in northern India, and is an architect and calligrapher working in Ottawa, Canada. Taj went to the same school in Mumbai as Manohar Shetty, and his poetry displays realism similar to that seen in Shetty's imagery, as in the imaginary and disturbing speech of a dying cockroach killed by a blow from a rolled-up newspaper: "My sides burst symmetrically — / Is there life after death?" (*Bloodaxe Book* 126). A critique of contemporary society is offered in "The Travelling Non-vegetarian," which questions traditions and customs: "The man who spoke with suitcases / Said neckties were nooses, wristwatches handcuffs" (*Bloodaxe Book* 125).

The late Lawrence Bantleman (1942–1995) was from Pune in western India and had also emigrated to Canada. Bantleman worked as a writer and editor and was very much a part of the Indian poetry scene. Bantleman's postmodern poems present speakers who are in love with words as well as unusual and striking imagery. In the poem "Words," with very creative use of diction, the speaker creates the sights and sounds of an Indian bazaar: "Vegetable sellers, transmigratory / Hindu tomato yellers, men of spinach" (*Bloodaxe Book* 343). In "One A.M.," the speaker imagines Time personified and moving with feline grace: "How artfully he moves, / Catpawing through a clock" (*Bloodaxe Book* 346). The speaker of "Septuagesima" ponders the significance of pre-Lent rituals by clergy in a world where "God must go down while Man goes on / To Easter and Christmas Isles!" (*Bloodaxe Book* 345)

The last poet discussed in this chapter provides a transition to the poets analyzed in chapter five in that Daljit Nagra (born in 1966) is from London, and continues to live there, but writes of the language and experiences of British South Asians. For his readers, Nagra's ethnic speakers bridge the gap between India and the South Asian diaspora. In Nagra's poems, the voices of South Asian Punjabi immigrants speak in Punjabi-accented, ungrammatical English quite similar to the voices of the Caribbean immigrant speakers in some of the poems of David Dabydeen. This innovative use of the spoken word makes Nagra's contemporary poetry significant because the majority of modern and postmodern South Asian poets tend to favor the use of the formal *langue* over any regional or ethnic *parole*. Thus in "Singh Song!" (with the play on "sing song" suggesting the cadences of the Punjabi immigrants' English), the speaker is expected to work twelve hours daily in one of his father's shops: "and he vunt me not to have a break / but ven nobody in, I do di lock" (*Bloodaxe Book* 274). Nagra's poems also satirize the culture shock registered by Punjabi immigrants coming from northern India to London and their inability to view women as their equals, as in the monologue "The Speaking of Bagwinder Singh Sagoo," which opens by saying, "Why now not be naked, you naughty western woman? / Not four month since I Delhi-Heathrow to you" (*Bloodaxe Book* 272).

In closing this chapter, it is necessary to recognize the landmark contributions of poet and editor Jeet Thayil, whose anthologies *The Bloodaxe Book of Contemporary Indian Poets* (2008) and *60 Indian Poets* (2008) have made accessible the works of many contemporary Indian English poets as well as some neglected and even forgotten poets from India. The perspective of Thayil's anthologies is transnational in recognizing that it is important to transcend national boundaries in the systematic study of the English-language poetry of South Asians in the late twentieth and twenty-first centuries.

WORKS CITED

King, Bruce. *Modern Indian Poetry in English.* New Delhi: Oxford University Press, 2001. Print.

Thayil, Jeet, ed. *The Bloodaxe Book of Contemporary Indian Poets.* Highgreen, Northumberland, UK: Bloodaxe Books, 2008. Print.

_____, ed. *60 Indian Poets.* New Delhi: Penguin India, 2008. Print.

• FIVE •

Hybridity and Dislocation: Poets of the South Asian Diaspora in the United Kingdom and Australia

Hybridity and dislocation are common elements in the poetry of the five poets of South Asian origin discussed in this chapter. Four of the poets — the late Tambimuttu, David Dabydeen, Sudeep Sen, and Moniza Alvi — have been published from the United Kingdom, while Fiji-born Australian poet Sudesh Mishra writes and publishes in Australia. The examination of this body of poetry under the umbrella of transnational poetics allows one to discover connections in the experiences of the South Asian diaspora over time and space. One cannot examine the English-language poetry of the South Asian diaspora without discussing Sri Lanka–born Tambimuttu's global perception of twentieth-century poetry in English. Following Tambimuttu's death in 1983, there has been a steadily growing body of South Asian poetry in English published by diasporic South Asians. David Dabydeen is a British poet, fiction writer, and essayist born in Guyana, while Sudeep Sen was born in India, and Moniza Alvi was born in Pakistan. Australian poet Sudesh Mishra is discussed with this group because of certain common elements between his poems and those of David Dabydeen. In the speakers' perceptions of alienation, anxiety, and the need for self-reflexivity, these five poets are similar to many of the South Asian poets discussed in chapters three, five, six, seven, and nine.

Vijay Mishra's *Literature of the Indian Diaspora: Theorizing the Diasporic Imaginary* (2007) makes a clear distinction between the writers of the old South Asian diaspora, who came following indenture (both voluntary and forced), and the post–1960s immigrants who are publishing contemporary literature. Mariam Pirbhai adapts Vijay Mishra's theory in her work on the novels of indenture titled *Mythologies of Migration, Vocabularies of Indenture: Novels of the South Asian Diaspora in Africa, the Caribbean, and Asia-Pacific*

(2009). This chapter applies the Mishra-Pirbhai distinction to the hybridized and transnational poetry published by poets of the South Asian diaspora.

Life Vijay Mishra, Mariam Pirbhai distinguishes between the "old" South Asian diaspora, in which indentured workers were taken to the Caribbean, Africa, and Fiji, and the "new" diaspora of educated immigrants from the 1960s onward (3–6). Mishra also first coined the term "old Indian diaspora" (Pirbhai 8). Of the poets discussed in this chapter, David Dabydeen and Sudesh Mishra are descendants of the old diaspora, while Tambimuttu, Sudeep Sen, and Moniza Alvi may be viewed as members of the new diaspora. All five poets have relocated from their lands of birth and present transnational perspectives in their poetics. Foreignizing and domesticating images become a complex phenomenon in the light of these transnational relocations.

Tambimuttu

While the name of the late Tambimuttu is quite familiar in some circles, his poetry may be unfamiliar to many readers because his work has not yet become fashionable in anthologies or easily accessible books. The materials for this chapter were accessed in the Rare Book Collection of the University of South Carolina in Columbia, South Carolina. The largest collection in the United States of Tambimuttu's work as editor, critic, and poet is probably archived by the Northwestern University library in Evanston, Illinois, where 106 boxes of materials await scholarly attention. There is another large body of material in the British Library in the United Kingdom. Tambimuttu was somewhat controversial in his own lifetime because of his unorthodox methodology as both editor and critic. Contemporary scholars are unsure as to whether he was ahead of his time in his global (transnational) perception of English-language poetry or else simply a marginal literary personality. This ambivalence is evidenced by the relative neglect of Tambimuttu's work by editors of anthologies and the absence of a volume of his "Collected Works."

This chapter takes the position that Tambimuttu's global perception of poetry was an early precursor of the theory of transnational poetics. His work as an editor and critic in the postcolonial era was identifiably postnational in that he promoted literary works and artists for their quality rather than for the cultural contexts that generated the works. The confusing terminology that now surrounds South Asian poetry in English was not a problem for Tambimuttu when he accepted poetry for publication.

In a paper presented in Amsterdam at the Third Sri Lanka Conference in April 1991, T. Wignesan considers Tambimuttu to be a very important poet from Sri Lanka (2). His full name was Meary James Thurairajah Tambimuttu. The family was Tamil, and they claimed descent from the kings of Jaffna, a city in northern Sri Lanka also known as Jaffnapatam. He was known to his circle as Tambi. He was born in 1915 and died in 1983. His family had prominent connections in India and Sri Lanka. He was married three times with one child, his daughter Shakuntala. Raised as a Roman Catholic, he turned to the beliefs of Hinduism and Buddhism in his adult life. Educated in Jesuit schools in Sri Lanka (then Ceylon), Tambimuttu gave up a university program of study on botany, and arrived in London in 1938. In the 1940s, he rose to prominence among literary circles in London as a man of letters — handsome, artistic, well dressed, and often lionized. By 1949, he was well known not only in England but also in Sri Lanka. From 1952 to 1968, he worked out of New York. Ben Sonnenberg's article "Tambimuttu in New York" (September 21, 1997), published in the *New York Times*, describes the memory of "a Ceylonese poet, brown-skinned, longhaired. A bohemian, verbose, and skinny. Very British sounding, too" (Sonnenberg 1).

Tambimuttu was either admired immensely or disliked exceedingly. T. Wignesan states, "for he was and is a controversial figure, controversial mainly because of his role in publishing English poets in England" (2). He was eulogized by the poets he published, and condemned by those whom he rejected. He was the founder-editor of *Poetry London*, and editor of the publishing houses Editions Poetry London and the Lyrebird Press (in the late 1960s). In the 1950s, he started a brand-new magazine, *Poetry London–New York*, with the financial backing of a very wealthy woman named Mrs. Carleton Palmer (who wrote and published poetry under the name of Winthrop Palmer). Tambimuttu's *Poetry London–New York* published Jack Kerouac, James Merrill, Herbert Morris, Richard Farina, Karl Shapiro, Gavin Ewart, Roy Campbell, Robin Skelton, Allen Ginsberg, and W.H. Auden. *Poetry London–New York* eventually collapsed financially amid the politics of publishing in New York. Tambimuttu then returned to London, where he continued to work as an editor.

On the British literary scene in the 1940s and 1950s, *Poetry London* included the work of artists such as T.S. Eliot, Dylan Thomas, Lawrence Durrell, and George Orwell. Among poets from India that Tambimuttu published were modern writers such as Amrita Pritam, Jibanananda Das, and Buddhadeva Bose (March-April 1956 edition of *Poetry London–New York*, Vol. 1, No. 1). Tambimuttu showed a distinct preference in his poetry magazine for poetry criticism written by poets. And in later decades, poets have often served as reviewers and editors of collections of South Asian poetry in English. In one of Tambimuttu's last editions for the Lyrebird Press in 1972 there appeared Pritish Nandy's English translation titled *Poems from Bangla Desh: The Voice of a New Nation*. At the height of his recognition in London in 1948, Tambimuttu also published with Richard March a volume of essays collected in celebration of T.S. Eliot's sixtieth birthday. These essays came from all over the world, for in the heyday of high modernism, in Tambimuttu's publishing house, poetry represented a global culture of its own kind. In this volume, Tambimuttu wrote the poem "Natarajah" (Dancing Shiva) for T.S. Eliot: "May you prosper, sir, between dawning and adorning, / Sweeney give you the things I lack" (*T.S. Eliot: A Symposium*). In the same volume, Tambimuttu published an essay by Indian Bengali poet Bishnu Dey on the lasting influence of T.S. Eliot on "modern" poetry in the Indian subcontinent. The publication of this essay ushered in the modernist post-independence era in postcolonial Indian poetry. In recent decades, the perspective of "subaltern studies" has been a recognized element in postcolonial theory, but it is a challenge to find a subaltern aspect to Tambimuttu's poetry journal and its published essays and poems. It appears that to Tambimuttu's editor's eye for the quality and integrity of fine poetry, there were poets, fine poetry, and (possibly) no subalterns.

Tambimuttu himself wrote only a limited number of poems, among which is the long World War II poem *Out of This War: A Poem* (1941). In this work, Tambimuttu captures the moments of living in London under the constant threat of World War II air raids: "Where shall the innocent, curly head shelter from the blast, / The bombs and tombs are falling on Leicester Square" (*Out of This War* 11). Out of the war, the speaker/persona envisions the rise of a mythical hero who will "ride the sky." The imagery and techniques of high modernism are clearly discernible in Tambimuttu's poetry.

Among Tambimuttu's final contribution to the world of letters was the *Poetry London/Apple Magazine*, published with support from the Beatles — one volume in 1979, another in 1982. He helped in founding the Government Arts Councils in Sri Lanka and India, and was appointed consultant to an Indian Government Arts Council project shortly before he died in 1983. In 1989, Jane Williams edited a collection of memories of friends and relatives titled *Tambimuttu: Bridge Between Two Worlds*, published in London by Peter Owen. T. Wignesan states that it is difficult to find Tambimuttu's primary works. Indeed, twenty-seven years after his death, this South Asian literary figure and poet who brought to public notice so many poets in the United Kingdom, the United States, and the Indian subcontinent remains relatively obscure. Once again, as shown in chapter three, the relative difficulty of keeping journals that publish poetry and other forms of creative writing alive and adequately funded in an age of technology needs to be noted.

Sudeep Sen

Contemporary poet Sudeep Sen may be viewed as transnational poet who publishes in the United Kingdom, India, and the United States. Sudeep Sen was born in New Delhi, India in 1964. His family is of Bengali ancestry, and his Hindu Bengali heritage is discernible in his poetry. Sen was educated in India and the United States. According to Kwame Dawes, Sudeep Sen was born in 1964 in New Delhi, India. He received a B.A. in English at the University of Delhi, and then studied at Davidson College in North Carolina (Dawes 1). Sen received his master's degree in literature and writing at Hollins College, Virginia. He then completed an M.S. in journalism at Columbia University, New York. Sen worked as a journalist in New York and returned to New Delhi to work as a documentary filmmaker and a journalist. In 1992–1993, Sen served as an international poet-in-residence at the Scottish Poetry Library in Edinburgh (Dawes 1). Sen is recognizably a transnational poet who divides his time between New Delhi and London, with occasional visits to the United States to read and to lecture.

Sen's works of poetry include *Leaning Against the Lamp Post* (1983, 1996), *Lunar Visitations* (1990), *Kali in Ottava Rima* (1992), *New York Times* (1993), *Parallel* (1993), *Dali's Twisted Hands* (1994), *South African Woodcut* (1994), and *Postmarked India: New and Selected Poems* (1997). Chapbooks published by Sen include *Retracing American Contours: 1987–90* (1999), *Almanac* (2000), and *Lines of Desire* (2000). Other works include *A Blank Letter* (2000), *Perpetual Diary* (2001), and *Monsoon* (2002). Sen continues to publish poetry collections. Sen has also written verse drama and translated poems written by poets from Bangladesh.

In this chapter, Sudeep Sen's volume *Dali's Twisted Hands* (1994), one of his longest collections, has been selected as representative of Sen's poetics and methodology. According to Kwame Dawes, "This volume is the perfect introduction to the poetry of Sudeep Sen because it contains poems that explore the range and complexity of Sen's work. It reflects his significant capacity as a formalist, his thematic range and his maturing vision. There are poems in this volume that chart his various journeys throughout the world and his many encounters with poets and artists" (11).

The opening section of *Dali's Twisted Hands* suggests Sen's transnational perception of poetry. "April's Air" has an epigraph from Japanese poet Matsuo Basho and links to forms of Japanese poetry / writing such as "tanka" and "haiku": "In the emperor's court, the scribe / recorded time in *tanka* and *haiku* on paper made of mashed rice" (*Dali's Twisted Hands* 15). Sen's transnational perception of poetry also emerges in "Rhyme Royal for an Unknown Chinese Wine" (*Dali's Twisted Hands* 16) and "Musee Dorsay Paris" (*Dali's*

Twisted Hands 17). In the lyric "August 9, 1964," Sen uses a series of couplets to create the imaginary scene of his own birth: "her live chamber cloistering his helplessness, / sharing her blood, breed, and breath" (*Dali's Twisted Hands* 23). One can compare this description to the birthing imagery in the poems of Meena Alexander and Sujata Bhatt.

In the second section of *Dali's Twisted Hands*, the poem "Line Breaks" presents a series of images that have no clear connections and suggest the disconnectedness of memories. Often, everyday scenes and activities are presented in Sen's poems as frozen time capsules, as in the third section, "Ink Spills from My Indian Blood," where in the poem "The Box-office Hit," the poet speaker describes waiting to buy a ticket for a Bollywood Hindi film: "I spend, waiting in the unending queue / for hours under the scorching sun" (*Dali's Twisted Hands* 44). This scenario belongs to the poet's youth, when there used to be long lines in front of Indian movie theaters. Images of Hindu deities and beliefs surface in "Govind Dev Temple, Vrindavan": "Govind Dev stands steadfastly, propped with monumental / blocks of red and other sandstone" (*Dali's Twisted Hands* 43).

Time and again, Sen's poetry captures images of the life of the urban Bengali communities in Kolkata and New Delhi, as seen in "Calcutta": "and from somewhere, an old dhoti-clad man / carrying the night's wisdom, walks swiftly" (*Dali's Twisted Hands* 48). In "During the Street Play," the speaker alludes to the 1989 killing of Safdar Hashmi: "He is, perhaps, just a local / student, armed with pamphlets" (*Dali's Twisted Hands* 50). This poem is dedicated to the Marxist playwright Safdar Hashmi, killed during the performance of his play "Hulla Bol" (*Dali's Twisted Hands* 50). Meena Alexander also refers to the untimely death of Safdar Hashmi, suggesting that his death had a significant impact on South Asian literary circles.

Sudeep Sen captures the rhythm of mundane daily activities in Bengali households in a time now past when women were mainly homemakers in the poem "Between the Flight of Two Sparrows": "while the woman's pupils fume at the / cumin and onions frying furtively" (*Dali's Twisted Hands* 47). In "The Garland of Stars," the speaker refers to Hindu marriage practices, such as the use of vermilion powder ("sindoor") and its significance: "I love your love for her, and hers for you, I / know that the *sindoor* in (her) hair affirms an enchantment" (*Dali's Twisted Hands* 62). The poem referring to the American poet Donald Hall is significant because the two poets meet in Delhi. Hall flies from the United States and Sen from England, "traveling together unknowingly / to meet once again in Delhi" (*Dali's Twisted Hands* 53). In his allusions to the Berlin Wall, Sen's speakers are referring to the walls that exist between people in contemporary society: "of forced division, an autocrat's craze. / East had met West again, but was it the same?" (*Dali's Twisted Hands* 68).

Moniza Alvi

Unlike Sudeep Sen, who works between India and the United Kingdom, Moniza Alvi is a Pakistani-born South Asian immigrant poet resident in the United Kingdom. Alvi was born in 1954 to a Pakistani father and an English mother. The family moved to England in Alvi's infancy. Moniza Alvi worked as a high school teacher for some time, and now works as a freelance writer and a tutor for the Poetry School ("Moniza Alvi"). In 2002, Alvi received the Cholmondeley Award for her poetry. Her collections include *Carrying My Wife* (2000), *Souls* (2002), *How the Stone Found Its Voice* (2005), *Europa* (2008), *Split World: Poems 1990–2005* (2008), and *Homesick for the Earth, Versions of Poems by Jules Supervielle* (2011).

The poems discussed in this chapter come from Alvi's collection *Carrying My Wife* (2000), published in a volume that also includes *The Country at My Shoulder* (1993), *A Bowl of Warm Air* (1996) and *Presents from Pakistan*. There are 158 poems in this collection that are representative of Alvi's poetic method, which combines narrative elements, dramatic voices, and surrealistic imagery.

The title sequence of *Carrying My Wife* is unusual in the choice of a male speaker or persona by a woman poet. The speaker is a husband with an imaginary wife who has disappeared, as described in "Missing" (*Carrying My Wife* 13). The speaker remembers intimate details in "Toothbrush" (*Carrying My Wife* 15), and fantasizes about his wife's infidelity in "My Wife and the Composer" (*Carrying My Wife* 16). Like Sudeep Sen, Alvi has the ability to turn everyday scenes and activities into surrealistic scenarios.

In the title poem "Carrying My Wife," the speaker states, "I carried my wife inside me — / Like a cable car I pulled her" (*Carrying My Wife* 19). He reiterates that they were an indoor couple who had a quiet life. Now that she is missing, he looks at her clothes: "In cheerful moods I'd see all the garments / my wife had ever worn — they'd be dancing (*Carrying My Wife* 21). He also notes the mix of Western and ethnic South Asian ensembles. In "Man Impregnated," the speaker envies his imaginary wife's pregnancy and wakes up with a "glass abdomen" (*Carrying My Wife* 23). More surrealistic imagery surfaces in "The Unremembered Dream": "We sat there on the edge of the bed / hoping the dream night emerge" (*Carrying My Wife* 27). Even as the speaker recounts patchy memories of his lost wife, other South Asian stories emerge, as in the poem on the Sikh immigrant in the United Kingdom named Ranjit Singh who has achieved a degree of financial success: "He had the air of a Bombay lord, / not a garage mechanic from Wembley" (*Carrying My Wife* 45). The speaker also remembers the homes of his parents' South Asian immigrant friends in "I Thought My Parents Were Married": "But each couples' Indian food / was always subtly different" (*Carrying My Wife* 46).

The voice of the man with the missing imaginary wife gives way to a speaker who is a young South Asian immigrant girl, asking, "Was I more Indian or more English? / I blurred, as I would forever" (*Carrying My Wife* 47). In "Thoughts of a Pakistani Woman in an English Jail," the speaker expresses an emerging sense of self: "Here, for the first time I knew I'm me, / not this man's daughter, that wife's" (*Carrying My Wife* 51). Surrealistic imagery appears again in "Incident at the Zoo," set in Lahore, Pakistan, where a she-bear tears a human child in half because the parents place the child too close to the bear's cage (*Carrying My Wife* 52–53). The poem "Storyteller" appears to be a thinly disguised autobiography in which the speaker listens to an imaginary storyteller "turning the page / or briefly clearing her throat" (*Carrying My Wife* 58). These images capture Alvi's own interest in narrative plots.

In the last poem of *Carrying My Wife*, a woman throws herself to her death from a church tower, and the speaker/poet wonders, "But was it wise to end the novel in this way, / the narrative jumping off the ledge" (*Carrying My Wife* 63). The heteroglossic elements in the poems are referenced in the above lines. The reader is left wondering as to who is the woman who jumps to her death — the missing wife or the missing immigrant South Asian woman referred to in another poem? The mystery of the multiple dramatic voices and heteroglossic narratives in Alvi's "Carrying My Wife" remains unclear.

The collection titled *A Bowl of Warm Air* has a number of poems that capture vignettes of life in the United Kingdom for South Asian immigrants. In "The Double City" (London), there is the historic London that tourists visit as well as the poor ethnic South Asian neighborhood of Southall, where South Asian women in saris chant for the release "of the battered Kiranjit / who killed her husband" (*Carrying My Wife* 69). Several poems in this collection bring to life scenes and images from Pakistan and India based on experience as well as imagination. Alvi creates the voices of South Asian immigrants whose memories of lost homelands surface in surrealistic imagery. One recalls Bhabha's "unhomeliness" and Ramabai Espinet's motif of the "nowhere place" that the immigrant inhabits.

The collection titled *The Country at My Shoulder* (1993) is similar to *A Bowl of Warm Air* in its immigrant voices (both young and adult) evaluating South Asian and English settings and events. The final section of *Carrying My Wife* is titled *Presents from Pakistan*. The presents in the section's title poem are ethnic clothes and jewelry from Pakistan that the young female speaker does not really want to wear because she wants to dress like her peers in the United Kingdom. There are also memories of Pakistani immigrants whom the speaker/poet knew in England. The South Asian ethnic elements and the English setting and landscape are fused into an unreal dream world in Alvi's poems. Perhaps this characteristic is a reinforcement of the unhomeliness of exile, of alienation, of anxiety, and of the quest for self-identity that recurs in the poetry of the South Asian diaspora.

David Dabydeen

A different category of immigrant consciousness and sense of history appears in the poetry of the Guyanese-born David Dabydeen, who is now settled in the United Kingdom. He is a cousin of the Canadian poet Cyril Dabydeen. David Dabydeen (born in 1955) spent his early life in an agricultural setting: "Dabydeen's family moved several times during his early years to avoid race riots between the Indo-Guyanese and Afro-Guyanese" (Bahri). His father went to England, later sending for all of his children. In the next stages of his career,

> Dabydeen earned a Bachelor of Arts with honors from Cambridge University in 1978 and his Ph.D. in eighteenth century literature and art from the University of London in 1981. While at Cambridge, he wrote poems which were eventually published in his first book, *Slave Song*, some six years later in 1984. He continued his studies at Oxford and Yale from 1983–87, lecturing in Caribbean Studies [Bahri].

David Dabydeen is currently a professor and acting director of a center for Caribbean studies at Warwick University in the United Kingdom.

David Dabydeen's art is unique among the Guyanese-born Indo-Caribbean poets discussed in this study because Dabydeen's poetry explores a multicultural Guyanese identity that encapsulates both the tragic history of African slavery and the oppressive history of South Asian indenture. Mark McWatt's comments regarding Dabydeen's collection are relevant: "In this work we are presented with fourteen poems, each of which is a carefully constructed mask by means of which the poetic persona inhabits the men and women — slaves and indentured laborers — who worked the sugar lands of Guyana; but these poems, in raw Guyanese Creole, are only part of the text of *Slave Song*" (15–16).

While Dabydeen's poetic personae are masked, he also juxtaposes reproductions of paintings with some of his poems. There is a discernible emphasis on visual images together with surrealistic elements in the narratives of his speakers. The use of Guyanese Creole heightens the authenticity of the voices of Dabydeen's speakers. A significant amount of research underlies Dabydeen's poems, which are steeped in both Guyanese history and Guyanese folklore. The characters in *Slave Song* are vividly realized. The poet's own translations pale in comparison to the immediacy and energy of Dabydeen's Creole. In *Turner: New and Selected Poems*, the visual imagery is very striking in the graphic details that bring history to life. In both volumes, Creole is preserved as if by an anthropologist. The emerging image of Guyanese culture in Dabydeen's poetry is a blending of African and South Asian elements. This is an unusual perspective in an Indo-Caribbean poet because Indo-Caribbean writers have tended to depict the two communities separately, as in the fiction of the late Samuel Selvon that is set in rural Trinidad.

Slave Song (1984, revised 2005) is a collection of fourteen poems in Guyanese Creole accompanied by fourteen translations into formal English. This volume also includes a number of illustrations of colonial themes that are oppressive and even violent images of the slavery era. The speakers represent characters who have experienced considerable oppression because of race, class, and gender. In the introduction to Slave Song, Dabydeen explains:

> I have retained the full vulgarity of the language for it is a profound element in Guyanese life: for instance, in The Canecutter's Song, I wanted to show the Creole mind straining and struggling after concepts of beauty and purity (imaged in the White Woman), but held back by its crude, physical vocabulary. The canecutter aspires to lyrical experience and expression but cannot escape his condition of squalor nor the crude diction that such a condition generates. So to describe her beauty he struggles to transform vulgar words and concepts into lyrical ones, the result being both poignant and funny [Slave Song 14].

The poor canecutter to whom Dabydeen refers becomes infatuated with a blonde woman in a lace dress: "O Shanti! Shanti! Shanti!— / So me spirit call, so e halla foh you" (Slave Song 24). He goes on to express his lust for her in profane language because he has no other means of verbal expression.

In the poem "Men and Women," an abusive husband who left his wife and children returns to find that she is old and does not recognize him. He apologizes to her: "Bu me still saary / Kase me drink rum an beat yu" (Slave Song 32). "For Ma" begins with an image of a meal cooked in the kitchen of a rural, possibly Indo-Guyanese family: "Roll roti! roll roti! roll roti! / Curry cookin in de karahee" (Slave Song 33). This poem celebrates the hard work done by women daily on farms in the Guyanese countryside year after year and generation after generation.

The poem "Slavewoman's Song" presents a woman speaker who asks another crying and wailing slave woman the reason for her grief: "Tell me wha ya howl foh / Tell me noh?" (Slave Song 34). The speaker asks if the causes of grief are one of the following: the taking away of her child, being struck on the head or bitten in the hand, her husband being taken away and fed to the alligators in the Demerara River, missing her lost parents in Africa, becoming pregnant by her master — all these scenarios bring to life the violence and abuse suffered by African women in slavery times in the Caribbean. In the poem "Two Cultures," the speaker is a rural Guyanese person who criticizes a young man who returns from England with European-style city clothes and speaking formal English: "Yu dadee na Dabydeen, plant garden near Black-brush Pass? / He na cut wid sickle an dig wid faak?" (*Slave Song* 36). This speaker forbids the youth from the city to approach his/her daughter because poor country people have their pride. The dramatic voices of the speakers in *Slave Song* present a variety of characters and scenes from Guyanese history and rural Guyanese life, combining the cultural heritages of Afro-Caribbeans and Indo-Caribbeans into one rich whole.

In *Turner: New and Selected Poems* (1995, revised 2002), eight poems are reprinted from the earlier volume *Slave Song* with the title poem "Turner" and twelve other poems. This title poem was inspired by J.M.W. Turner's well-known painting of a slave ship. David Dabydeen describes the purpose of his poem in the preface to this collection: "My poem focuses on the sub-merged head of the African in the foreground of Turner's painting. It has been drowned in Turner's (and other artists') sea for centuries. When it awak-ens it can only partially recall the sources of its life, so it invents a body, a biography, and peoples an imagined landscape" (7). The poetic method is recognizably surrealistic as the drowned African struggles to reinvent a land-scape, flora, and fauna under the sea. Ultimately, he is left with nothing: "No stars, no land, no words, no community, / No mother" (*Turner: New and Selected Poems* 42).

If the title poem "Turner" closes with nihilism, "Old Map" also alludes to the tragic histories that the map unfolds: "Green of seamen's hopes and gangrene, / Yellow of the palm of the dead Amerindian" (*Turner: New and Selected Poems* 43). The poem "El Dorado"— the title is ironic — contains yet another New World tragedy of an oppressed group as a character named "Jun-cha" dies of jaundice, or yellow fever, without proper medical treatment: "They bury him like treasure, / The coolie who worked two shillings all day" (*Turner: New and Selected Poems* 44).

Leaving behind the hopelessness of rural Guyana, and seeking work in England, allows the son of a coolie to make a transition into the lower social classes of the United Kingdom, where in "Coolie Son (The Toilet Attendant Writes Home)," the speaker states, "I is a Deputy Sanitary Inspecta, / Big-big office, boy! Tie round me neck!" (*Turner: New and Selected Poems* 65). The condition of the Guyanese immigrant in the United Kingdom is one of social disadvantage. It is as if the journey of the Africans and South Asians from their original homelands to the Caribbean, and thence, after generations, to Europe, continues to perpetuate the conditions of socioeconomic exploita-tion originated by colonialism. Perhaps this phenomenon is currently associ-ated with globalization, which includes the migration of Africans and Asians to European countries in search of higher wages and "better" conditions of employment. However, it is a known fact that new immigrants often take jobs that natural-born citizens will not accept. David Dabydeen's Guyanese immigrant voices in his poetry are reminiscent of the late Samuel Selvon's earlier fictional portrayals in *The Lonely Londoners* of the problems faced by immigrants from the Caribbean in the United Kingdom.

Sudesh Mishra

There are recognizable similarities between the condition of Guyanese immigrants in the United Kingdom and the problems of dislocation and relocation faced by Fijian Indian immigrants in Australia and New Zealand. The voices of this community are heard very clearly in the poetry of Fiji-born poet Sudesh Mishra. Mishra write very powerfully of the history of South Asians' indenture and of the lives of South Asian "coolies" brought to Fiji under British colonialism.

Sudesh Mishra (born in 1962) is a fourth-generation Fijian of Indian origin and a descendant of indentured workers ("Sudesh Mishra"). Coming to Australia as a student, he completed his Ph.D. in English literature at Flinders University. His first volume of poetry, *Rahu* (1987), received the Harris Jones Memorial Prize in 1988. Mishra takes an ironic view of the ongoing political strife in Fiji. He has also published *Tandava* (1992), *Memoirs of a Reluctant Traveller* (1994), and *Diaspora and the Difficult Art of Dying* (2002). Mishra held the Asialink Literature Residency at Jawaharlal Nehru University in New Delhi when he composed the title poem of the fourth volume, *Diaspora and the Difficult Art of Dying*. This long prose poem first appeared in *Subaltern Studies* in India. Currently, Mishra teaches professional writing at Deakin University in Melbourne, Australia. He has taught literature courses at Stirling University in Scotland and the University of the South Pacific, Suva campus. Mishra's career is typical of the intercontinental journeys of the writers of the South Asian diaspora. His works of literary criticism include *Diaspora Criticism* (2006) and *Preparing Faces: Modernism and Indian Poetry in English* (1995).

In his first four volumes of poetry, Sudesh Mishra depicts the contemporary South Asian experience as one of fragmentation and dislocation. Yet this transnational and diasporic experience expressed in poetry from different countries has, according to Mishra, "an underground logic of colours, tropes, sounds, textures, moods, secrets." This chapter explores the motifs of fragmentation and dislocation as well as the "underground logic" of the diasporic (and postnational) South Asian experiences as depicted in Mishra's *Diaspora and the Difficult Art of Dying*.

Sudesh Mishra's poetry is filled with motifs of the experience of being a South Asian from Fiji. The history of the settling of South Asians in Fiji is perhaps only familiar to those well versed in the history of British colonialism. To understand the historical allusions in Mishra's poetry, it is important to recognize that people of Indian ancestry account for over one-third of Fiji's population. The majority of Indo-Fijians are Hindu and a minority is Muslim. The majority of Fijians are Christian, mostly Methodist. Fiji consists of 332 islands in the Southwest Pacific Ocean. In 1874, Fijian chiefs ceded their islands to Britain. Fiji was proclaimed a possession and then a colony of the British Crown, In the 1880s, large-scale cultivation of sugarcane began. Over the next forty years, more than 60,000 indentured laborers from India were brought to the islands to work on the plantations. Indentured servitude ended by 1920. Racial conflict between Fijians and Indians has been central to the history of modern Fiji. The political history of Fiji has been extremely unstable in recent decades. As a result, many Indo-Fijian professionals, businessmen, and intellectuals have emigrated to Australia and New Zealand. The Indo-Fijians have a strong sense of their heritage and history. For example, in 1979, the Fiji Indians celebrated the hundredth anniversary of their arrival on the islands with many public events. The history of the indentured laborers, who came under an agreement called "girmit" in their folk parlance, was discussed and celebrated at their centenary celebrations (Munro 94). And Sudesh Mishra's poetry is highly evocative of the history of the Fijian Indians.

The cover of the slim volume titled *Diaspora and the Difficult Art of Dying* looks like a drop of oil spreading on the rough surface of a tarred road. The picture is evocative of the central concern of this volume, described in the preface by the poet as the mixture of "colors, tropes, sounds, textures, moods, secrets" (*Diaspora and the Difficult Art of Dying* 3). The title piece of this volume appears to be a memory poem of generations, beginning with the recollections of an elderly "girmitiya" (as the indentured laborers were called). The speaker recalls his beginnings in India in a poor rural community. He remembers being the eldest of three sons and leaving his village on foot, in search of a better life, then being deceived into entering the world of indenture like "three thousand seven hundred and forty eight girmitiyas": "but my destiny was an arkathi with a tongue sweeter than sucrose" (*Diaspora and the Difficult Art of Dying* 73). The speaker sets sail from the port of Calcutta (now Kolkata), hoping to make money. He goes on to describe the diverse ethnic groups and religions from the Indian subcontinent that formed a new brotherhood on the voyages to the islands of Fiji.

Mishra's speaker cross-references the affinity of Fijian Indians to the Indians who accepted indenture and traveled to Mauritius, Trinidad, Surinam, and Guyana. He confesses his alienation and permanent dislocation: "and between the hell of girmit [indenture] and the hell of basti [slum] was an ocean of alchemy" (*Diaspora and the Difficult Art of Dying* 74). This speaker ultimately realizes that over time Fiji has become his homeland, and memories of India have been replaced by familiarity with the Fijian landscape and Fiji's flora and fauna. The voice of the speaker changes to that of his son, Mahadeo, who becomes a carpenter, a tradesman. Then the voice of the speaker becomes that of Mahadeo's daughter, Subadra, who works as a bank clerk and marries a civil servant. They send their son to study abroad. Then the spirit of the speaker melts into the body of her son, Rajesh, who is a writer composing stories of the Fijian islands. In this long prose poem, Mishra creates four generations of a Fijian Indian family.

The poems in *Diaspora and the Difficult Art of Dying* seem to have been arranged to suggest the fragmentation and dislocation of the diasporic experience. The emotions and experiences of the speakers are wide ranging and set in different countries. In this chapter, the poems of *Diaspora and the Difficult Art of Dying* are grouped into the following categories: (1) poems about Fiji, (2) poems about India and Indian culture, (3) poems set in Italy, and (4) poems with dramatic voices.

In the first cluster of poems about Fiji, images of life from the sea are predominant. Yet other images are unusual in conception, as in "Suva; Skye," in which the speaker compares a half-spent mosquito coil to the swan "arching / its ancient neck" (*Diaspora and the Difficult Art of Dying* 47). Social realism emerges in "Unemployment Blues," where the unemployed male speaker in the act of shaving and viewing his last can of shaving cream before yet another interview seems to be a Fijian Indian who has received political asylum in Australia: "Yes, these are the dole-days, Australatus" (*Diaspora and the Difficult Art of Dying* 45). In the poem "Fiji," Cinderella's ball turns into a postmodern nightmare, with the prince characterized as a "leery, syphilitic brat": "And so she gave to the vomiting wretch / Her exquisite, slippered, severed foot" (*Diaspora and the Difficult Art of Dying* 72). In "Flood," the mud left by flood waters is compared to memory: "Which is the tract of memory / Composed of silt and sileage" (*Diaspora and the Difficult Art of Dying* 51). In "Fisher-King," Mishra combines the imagery of pulling in fishing nets and fishing lines with the imagery of playing musical instruments: "Then riff, jazz, and the harp swarming like hives. / On the strand the fish turned like kitchen knives" (*Diaspora and the Difficult Art of Dying* 28). In the poem "A Wishing Well in Suva," the speaker wishes for a flood to destroy the town: "Let the tsunami come, / Let it come as an ogre in grey armature" (*Diaspora and the Difficult Art of Dying* 48). In "Cane," sugarcane farming becomes symbolic of imprisonment: "'Prison bars,' says the resident farmer / When pressed, his tone uncrimped by irony" (*Diaspora and the Difficult Art of Dying* 58). In "Khara" (which means "drought" in Hindi), the imagery evokes the parched land waiting for rain: "The sky / Bloody as a she-goat's viscera" (*Diaspora and the Difficult Art of Dying* 59).

In terms of thematic connections, the second group of poems is about India and Indian culture. These poems are "Sanskriti," "Sufi," "Dowry," "About Aji," and "Mrs. Mukherjee." "Sanskriti" means "tradition" in Hindi. Here tradition seems to become synonymous with Hindu superstitions: "The Brahmin of the temple of Shiu / Forgetting himself" (*Diaspora and the Difficult Art of Dying* 55–56). In "Sufi," the speaker describes the fruitless efforts and death of a dung beetle in a remote memory from days in Jaisalmer, a city in a desert region of western India (*Diaspora and the Difficult Art of Dying* 55). "Dowry" brings forth images of the speaker's mother searching in her old dowry chest, whereas the poem "About Aji" describes the hard labor done by the grandmother of the speaker in processing nuts: "Scooped and gritty and black as grief, to oar / The louring sand like a galley slave, stroke" (*Diaspora and the Difficult Art of Dying* 30). In "Mrs. Mukherjee," the speaker visits the home of a cultured older South Asian woman, an ethnic Bengali (*Diaspora and the Difficult Art of Dying* 32–33). Imagery of events from colonial India surfaces in this visit, presumably evoked by Mrs. Mukherjee's conversation and from items in her home.

A third group of poems in *Diaspora and the Difficult Art of Dying* is about Italy. These poems are "Piazza San Marco," "Capri," and "Venice." In "Venice," among all the memories of its artistic heritage, the speaker discovers a diasporic South Asian: "a runaway from an agra slum, / hawker of red florentine roses" (*Diaspora and the Difficult Art of Dying* 6). The phrase "vats of vivaldi" (containing the name of the famous composer) adds an ironic twist and a tone of disbelief to the imagery in this poem because this story is told by "a wag." "Piazza San Marco" juxtaposes images of a grotesque nature to suggest the unreal world of the speaker's travels: "A girl shrieks under a spray of corngold teeth. / Someone, not a stranger, bought this treasure" (*Diaspora and the Difficult Art of Dying* 49). The poem "Capri" describes the cliffs and waters of the bay in clear light: "but the light just before / and the light just after" (*Diaspora and the Difficult Art of Dying* 21).

The fourth category of poems in *Diaspora and the Difficult Art of Dying* are several poems for dramatic voices scattered through the volume. These poems include "Envoi," "Ambulance Driver," "Still Life in Gaza," "A Bilimbili for Madeleine" and other pieces. Mishra's interest in dramatic voices is further developed in his plays titled *Ferringhi* and *The International Dateline*.

"Envoi" is the opening piece of *Diaspora and the Difficult Art of Dying*. The persona of the "envoi" is clearly that of the poet, and the processes of inspiration leading to reflection and composition are described with startling and surrealistic imagery: "Every day straggler word-bees fly up / His nostrils to swarm in the cold bone-urn" (*Diaspora and the Difficult Art of Dying* 5). Then the word-bees die and are absorbed. In the spring, there comes composition, naming "all that namelessness" (*Diaspora and the Difficult Art of Dying* 5)."Ambulance Driver" is written for the nameless drivers of ambulances (*Diaspora and the Difficult Art of Dying* 13). "Still Life in Gaza" presents a speaker who is Palestinian addressing a listener who is Israeli. In its conclusion, this dramatic lyric uses Hindi words to suggest a dream of peace and harmony: "A Gaza of Ghazals / Where rocks turn to raisins" (*Diaspora and the Difficult Art of Dying* 16).

This discussion of the major movements or groups of poems in Sudesh Mishra's *Diaspora and the Difficult Art of Dying* seeks to establish that amid the reality of fragmentation and dislocation, the poet establishes underlying connections in meaning relevant to the diasporic experience. As in the title piece, the spirit of the diasporic Indian of the old and new diasporas endures in every generation through dislocations that are also temporal and spatial, and also through intercontinental journeys.

WORKS CITED

Alvi, Moniza. *Carrying My Wife*. Newcastle upon Tyne, UK: Bloodaxe Books, 2000. Print.

Bahri, Deepika. "David Dabydeen." Postcolonial Studies, Emory University. www.english. emory.edu/Bahri/Dabydeen.html. Accessed 15 July 2011.

Dabydeen, David. *Slave Song*. Leeds, UK: Peepal Tree, 2005. Print.

_____. *Turner: New and Selected Poems*. Leeds, UK: Peepal Tree, 2002. Print.

Dawes, Kwame. "Sudeep Sen: Biography, Major Works & Themes, Critical Reception." In Kwame Dawes, *Sudeep Sen: A Bio-Bibliographical Critical Sourcebook*, 1–19. Columbia: University of South Carolina, 1996.

March, Richard, and Tambimuttu. *T.S. Eliot: A Symposium from Conrad Aiken*. London: Editions Poetry London, 1948. Print.

McWatt, Mark. "His True-True Face: Masking and Revelation in David Dabydeen's *Slave Song*." *The Art of David Dabydeen*. Ed. Kevin Grant. Leeds, UK: Peepal Tree, 1997: 15– 25. Print.

Mishra, Sudesh. *Diaspora and the Difficult Art of Dying*. Dunedin, New Zealand: University of Otago Press, 2002. Print.

Mishra, Vijay. *The Literature of the Indian Diaspora: Theorizing the Diasporic Imaginary*. London: Routledge, 2007. Print.

"Moniza Alvi." www.moniza.co.uk. Accessed 9 April 2012.

Munro, Doug. "In the Wake of the Leonidas: Reflections on Indo-Fijian Indenture Historiography." *The Journal of Pacific Studies* 24.1 (2005): 93–117. www.usp.ac.fj/jps/Doug-Munro.pdf. Accessed 8 April 2012.

Pirbhai, Mariam. *Mythologies of Migration, Vocabularies of Indenture: Novels of the South Asian Diaspora in Africa, the Caribbean, and Asia-Pacific*. Toronto: University of Toronto Press, 2009. Print.

Sen, Sudeep. *Dali's Twisted Hands*. New York: Peepal Tree, 1994. Print.

Sonnenberg, Ben. "Tambimuttu in New York." Bookend. *New York Times* 21 Sept. 1997:

1–4. www.nytimes.com/books/97/09/21/bookend/bookend.html. Accessed 24 February 2003.

"Sudesh Mishra." www.deakin.edu.au. Accessed 9 April 2012.

Tambimuttu. *Out of This War: a Poem*. London: The Fortune Press, 1941. Print.

Wignesan, T. "Tambimuttu: Poet, Critic, Editor/Publisher." http://members.aol.com/_ht_a/wignesh/TAMBIMUTTU. Accessed 24 February 2003.

• SIX •

Diaspora, Dislocation and South Asian Poetry in Canada

English-language poetry published by writers of South Asian ancestry from Canada includes works by poets as diverse as Michael Ondaatje, Rienzi Crusz, Cyril Dabydeen, Arnold Itwaru, and Sasenarine Persaud. All of these poets are immigrants to Canada, and are very versatile in that they write both poetry and fiction. All five South Asian Canadian poets in this group are male as the Indo-Canadian woman poet Ramabai Espinet is discussed in chapter nine due to her similarities to Meena Alexander, Sujata Bhatt, Chitra Divakaruni, and Mahadai Das. While Michael Ondaatje and Rienzi Crusz spent their early years in Sri Lanka, Cyril Dabydeen, Arnold Itwaru, and Sasenarine Persaud relocated from Guyana to Canada. In this chapter, the poets from Sri Lanka and the poets from Guyana are discussed separately to focus on specific themes and images in their works.

Canadian Poets from Sri Lanka

There are striking similarities between the nostalgic memories of Sri Lanka in the poems of Ondaatje and Crusz and the memories of life in South Asia that surface time and again in the poems of Agha Shahid Ali and Zulfikar Ghose. The most well-known literary figure of the five poets analyzed in this chapter is Michael Ondaatje. Ondaatje is best known for his Booker Prize–winning novel *The English Patient*, which was adapted for film in 1996. Ondaatje was born in Colombo, Sri Lanka, in 1943, and moved to England with his mother in 1954, eventually moving to Canada. He received his B.A. at the University of Toronto and his M.A. at Queen's University, and since 1971 has taught in the English department at York University, Toronto, Ontario (Bahri). Ondaatje has received numerous awards and honors, including the

Canadian Governor-General's Award for Literature in 1971 and 1980 (Bahri). Michael Ondaatje has published poetry collections, novels, and plays, and has also produced edited works. Some of his poetry collections include *The Dainty Monsters* (1967), *The Man with Seven Toes* (1969), *The Collected Works of Billy the Kid: Left-handed Poems* (1970), *Rat Jelly* (1973), *There's a Trick with a Knife I'm Learning to Do: Poems, 1963–1978* (1979), *Secular Love* (1984), *The Cinnamon Peeler: Selected Poems* (1989), *Handwriting* (1998), and *The Story* (2006). Ondaatje's novels include *Coming Through Slaughter* (1976), *In the Skin of a Lion* (1987), *The English Patient* (1992), *Anil's Ghost* (2000), *Divisadero* (2007), and *The Cat's Table* (2011).

While Michael Ondaatje has become well known for his contributions to fiction and film, his contributions to Canadian poetry are significant. In his fiction and film scripts, Ondaatje uses mainstream subjects but in his poetry memories and images of his early life in Sri Lanka and of his Eurasian ancestry surface repeatedly. In this chapter, a few selected poems from Ondaatje's three-part collection of poems titled *Handwriting* (1998) have been analyzed to demonstrate his ties to South Asian poetry in North America.

The opening poem of *Handwriting* is titled "A Gentleman Compares His Virtue to a Piece of Jade," and the speaker repeatedly uses images from life in Sri Lanka almost as a way of "foreignizing" the speaker's voice and experiences, as in the image of "That tightrope-walker from Kurunegala / the generator shut down by insurgents" (*Handwriting* 5). The central image of handwriting recurs in such poems as "The Distance of a Shout": "Handwriting occurred on waves, / on leaves the scripts of smoke" (*Handwriting* 6).

The poems of *Handwriting* are filled with references to the sights and sounds of Sri Lanka, where Ondaatje spent his early life. In "Buried," the speaker refers to a past event: "750 AD the statue of a Samadhi Buddha / was carefully hidden escaping war" (*Handwriting* 8). In "The Brother Thief," four men "steal the bronze / Buddha at Veheragala" (*Handwriting* 14) and one of them, in the middle of the night, steals the gemstones that are in the statue's eyesockets. "Buried 2" alludes to the tooth of the Buddha buried and secretly moved "from temple to temple for five hundred years" (*Handwriting* 21).

We are reminded of Sinhalese superstitions in "The First Rule of Sinhalese Architecture": "Never build three doors / In a straight line" (*Handwriting* 19). In "The Medieval Coast" the speaker describes "A village of stone-cutters. A village of soothsayers. / Men who burrow into the earth in search of gems" (*Handwriting* 20). Ondaatje places romanized poetic phrases in Sinhalese in juxtaposition with their English translations, such as "All those poets as famous as kings" (*Handwriting* 29). Ondaatje uses phrases translated from love poetry in Sanskrit and vernacular South Asian languages (for instance, "Kadamba branches" and "The Bhramarah bee is drunk," to evoke the ancient and medieval civilization of Sri Lanka.

The second part of *Handwriting* is titled "The Nine Sentiments (Historical Illustrations in Rock and Book and Leaf)" and each poem has a low-ercase roman numeral for its title. For instance, the speaker in the poem titled "vii" describes the women by the river at Boralesgamuwa in terms of ancient and medieval temple carvings: "The three folds on their stomachs / considered a sign of beauty" (*Handwriting* 39).

The third section of *Handwriting* consists of memories after leaving Sri Lanka, as seen in "Flight," in which the speaker watches an elderly Sri Lankan woman in an adjacent seat comb her hair: "Pins in her mouth. She rolls her hair, / curls it into a bun like my mother's" (*Handwriting* 47). The expatriate Sri Lankan speaker in "Wells" remembers the nanny as "my ayah Rosalin" (*Handwriting* 50). A tenth-century legend is associated with "The Siyabasla-kara" (*Handwriting* 52–53). In "The Story" (*Handwriting* 62–63), the speaker describes Sri Lankan folk customs and beliefs, such as the belief that for the first forty days a newborn baby dreams of his previous life (both Hindus and Buddhists believe in reincarnation).

Ondaatje himself comments at the end of this book that these poems "were written between 1993 & 1998 in Sri Lanka & Canada" (*Handwriting* 77). Ondaatje also states:

> Some of the traditions and marginalia of classical Sanskrit poetry and Tamil love poetry exist in the poem sequence "The Nine Sentiments." In Indian love poetry, the nine sentiments are romantic/erotic, humorous, pathetic, angry, heroic, fear-ful, disgustful, amazed, and peaceful. Corresponding to these are the aesthetic emotional experiences which are called rasas or flavours [*Handwriting* 78].

While Ondaatje's writings are on diverse subjects, of which Sri Lankan memories are only one, Rienzi Crusz focuses in greater depth and detail on his early years in Sri Lanka and his immigrant experiences in Canada in *Insurgent Rain, Lord of the Mountain,* and *Beatitudes of Ice.* Crusz (born in 1925) is a retired librarian living in Waterloo, Ontario, Canada. He received his B.A. in Sri Lanka, emigrated to Canada in 1965, and earned a B.L.S. at the University of Toronto and an M.A. at the University of Waterloo ("Rienzi Crusz"), where he worked as a reference librarian until his retirement in 1993. Some of his poetry collections include *Flesh and Thorn* (1974), *Elephant and Ice* (1980), *Singing Against the Wind* (1985), *A Time for Loving* (1986), *Still Close to the Raven* (1989), *The Rain Doesn't Know Me Anymore* (1992), *Beatitudes of Ice* (1995), and *Lord of the Mountain: The Sardiel Poems* (1999).

Rienzi Crusz is often viewed as one of the best English-language poets from Sri Lanka. Crusz's poetry is unique in its self-reflexivity, a modernist characteristic that makes connections in his poetry from one volume to another and from poem to poem in each volume. This chapter focuses on the method by which Crusz uses self-reflexivity in the volumes *Insurgent Rain: Selected Poems 1994–1996* and *Lord of the Mountain* to develop his own poetic method.

While it is common in literary criticism to separate the poet from the speaker or persona of a poem, in Rienzi Crusz's lyrics, the reader is repeatedly made aware that the poem's persona and poet are often recognizable as the same individual. According to the South Asian Canadian critic Chelva Kanaganayakam:

> The self-reflexivity and the introspection are at least in part a consequence of a genuine concern with his own predicament of living on the cusp, of negotiating two worlds, of being anxious about his own directions. They also draw attention to all the areas of experience — the cosmic scheme — that occupy him [*Insurgent Rain* xviii].

Kanaganayakam also compares Rienzi Crusz to Derek Walcott: "It is hardly an accident that Derek Walcott appears time and again as an intertextual reference in Crusz's poetry. At its most obvious both share an awareness of racial mixture that flaunts hybridity; more significantly, they reveal a skepticism about nationalist narratives" (xvi).

The volume *Insurgent Rain* contains selected poems by Crusz spanning a time period from 1974 to 1996. The first group of poems is in a section titled "The Raging Chaos of Love." The opening poem, "Taste of Old Wine," suggests a relationship that ended in pain for the male speaker: "she slowly turned her polished head / caught me / in pale blue gun sights / and gently squeezed / the trigger" (*Insurgent Rain* 3). In "How Does One Reach the Sweet Kernel?," the speaker uses the Sri Lankan farmer's husking of a coconut with a machete as an image of love that "burst into the kernel / of the heart" (*Insurgent Rain* 3). These images are probably autobiographical. "Autograph Album" contains an autograph composed by Rienzi — the poet himself.

In "The Night Before My Birthday," the speaker (and poet) remembers "the raging chaos of love" as his ex-wife appears in a nightmare: "all rags, her face caked like a ghost, / she asks: where are the children?" (*Insurgent Rain* 8–9). In "Kamala" the speaker is a fisherman speaking to his beloved, inviting her to sit on the seashore "and read the horoscopes / of our fishing lives" (*Insurgent Rain* 17). Over a period of time, Crusz, while writing from his country of adoption (Canada), is still able to capture the sights, smells, and emotions of his early life in Sri Lanka in the themes and imagery of his poems. Hence, in "Love Poem," the poet-speaker characterized as a "brown lover" views his contribution as one perpetual summer: "only summer, / and summer and summer" (*Insurgent Rain* 9).

In the section titled "The Marshmallow Land," poem after poem contains imagery of heavy snowfall in Canada as well as the dilemmas of the immigrant arriving from a tropical island into a land of ice and snow. In many ways, Crusz's poet-speakers retreat into "a nowhere place," an interstitial space of their own making. In "The Interview," the speaker looks at his Canadian passport, views the snow-clad landscape, and escapes into memories of the elephant in his ancestral land: "the Immigrant's Song, / how I hear the elephant in my sleep" (*Insurgent Rain* 28). The speaker's Canadian identity is new and superficial because in his sleep he still hears the elephant. The elephant becomes a symbol of the poet's self in "You Cannot Tell Me That I'm Not an Elephant" in the section of *Insurgent Rain* titled "Dark Antonyms and Paradise." The poet-elephant trumpets the last call "for a dying bull," claiming "You Cannot Tell Me That I'm Not an Elephant / because I stood apart from the herd" (*Insurgent Rain* 47). Other significant elephant poems in earlier volumes include "Elephant and Ice" and "The Elephant Who Would Be a Poet." Chelva Kanaganayakam comments that the elephant in these poems symbolizes the role of the poet (*Insurgent Rain* xvii).

Over and over again, Rienzi Crusz's lyrics return to the poet's racial and ethnic identity, to his Sri Lankan roots, as poem after poem presents speakers who express a keen sense of their Sri Lankan identity and origins. Most clearly autobiographical is the poem "Roots," which describes his Eurasian origins, imagining that in 1575 "A Portuguese captain holds / the soft brown hand of my Sinhala mother" (*Insurgent Rain* 43). From this union is born Crusz's "burgher," or Eurasian, ancestor. In the section titled "The Igloo of Heaven" the lyrics express a profound sense of irony in that the immigrant from Sri Lanka views himself / herself as privileged by having become an immigrant in Canada consuming Canadian-style meals. There is a strong sense of irony in this self-chosen exile: "the Molson cool / I wear the turban of urban pride" (*Insurgent Rain* 76). In this satiric poem, supposedly a conversation with God about his/her present whereabouts, the speaker's closing imagery is startling and recognizably existentialist, juxtaposing a brown laughing face in the white setting of snow with a white skull "for the flies / in Ceylon's deadly sun" (*Insurgent Rain* 77). The poem's ending emphasizes the transience of human life.

The closing section of *Insurgent Rain* is titled "Soul of a Faltering Saint" and contains a collection of poems that are suggestive of Rienzi Crusz's strongly Catholic background. The diasporic South Asian poet Zulfikar Ghose, who is based in the United States, has described Rienzi Crusz as "a true poet of the displaced self, with sorrow beneath its bemused surface" (*Insurgent Rain*— back cover).

In the volume of poetry titled *Lord of the Mountain: The Sardiel Poems* (1999), Crusz combines poetry and prose into a unique work of art that is an autobiography of the outlaw Sardiel, a nineteenth-century Sri Lankan Robin Hood. Interesting comparisons in subject matter and poetics are found in

Michael Ondaatje's *The Collected Works of Billy the Kid* (1970) and *Coming Through Slaughter* (1976), both based upon research into the loves of the American outlaw Billy the Kid and the legendary creator of jazz, musician Buddy Bolden from Lousiana. Crusz himself comments, "Revising a figure of legend, a cultural icon, and searching for the man behind the myth is always a challenge" (*Lord of the Mountain*, Acknowledgments, no pagination). It is the recasting of Sardiel as a passionate champion of poor and repressed people in colonial times that invites the reader into Crusz's stance on the history of Sri Lanka.

In *Lord of the Mountain*, Rienzi Crusz moves from his usual lyrical mode into the composition of dramatic narratives. In his earlier volumes and in the representative mythology *Insurgent Rain*, Crusz's speakers are often dramatic voices that express the poet's own worldview and elements of autobiography. The transition into creating dramatic monologues in poetry and prose for different characters in *Lord of the Mountain* helps to tell the story of Sardiel's childhood, in which he tortured and killed lizards in the garden because they had eaten many flies. Sardiel's sister is a spokesperson for his childhood and adolescence. The reader learns of Sardiel's humiliation in school by the children of the wealthy as well as by teachers. Crusz is successful in creating Sardiel as a figure obsessed with social justice in the corrupt colonial society of Sri Lanka, where the machinery of government does not work for the poor peasant. Crusz shows the psychology of the Robin Hood–like Sardiel without romanticizing his protagonist. Sardiel's propensity for cruelty and murderous violence is shown as being apparent from childhood in the monologues of his sister. Ultimately, Sardiel's career of murders and robberies ends when he is captured by the colonial authorities. Following his capture, Sardiel converts to Christianity before going to meet the hangman's rope. From monologues, letters, and interviews, Crusz depicts a passionate man who lives, loves, and embraces a philosophy of violence, finally converting to Christianity in prison: "'Formerly' replied Sardiel, 'I surrounded myself with firearms and guns and swords to defend myself. Now with my feet and hands chained I have to defend myself against — that is the devil'" (*Lord of the Mountain* 91). Thus *Lord of the Mountain* emerges as a critique of nineteenth-century Sri Lanka with the oppressive British colonial forces, as well as the greed and corruption of the Buddhist priests, landlords, and moneylenders.

Canadian Poets from Guyana

Another significant group of diasporic South Asian poets in Canada is made up of immigrants from Guyana — Cyril Dabydeen, Arnold Itwaru, and

Sasenarine Persaud. This group of poets is interesting because their poetry covers the history of the old South Asian diaspora as well as the new late twentieth-century diaspora represented by the three poets who are educated immigrants publishing from Canada.

Guyanese-born Indo-Canadian poet Cyril Dabydeen began his writing career in Guyana before relocating to Canada for higher education. Deep-seated awareness of his South Asian roots emerges in his writings as an immigrant poet in Canada. As mentioned earlier, he is a cousin of the U.K.-based writer David Dabydeen. Cyril Dabydeen was born in 1945 in Guyana and raised in an agricultural setting. He received the Sandbach Parker Gold Medal for poetry in 1964. Dabydeen's first poetry collection, *Poems in Recession*, was published in 1972 ("Cyril Dabydeen"). In the early 1970s he migrated to Canada to pursue higher education, earning a B.A. from Lakehead University and an M.A. and M.P.A. (Master of Public Administration) from Queen's University. "He has worked for many years in human rights and race relations in Canada, and currently teaches in the Dept. of English, University of Ottawa" ("Cyril Dabydeen"). Dabydeen is a prolific writer who has published novels, short stories, and essays on culture in addition to several volumes of poetry. Dabydeen's poetry collections include *Coastland: New and Selected Poems* (1989), *Stoning the Wind* (1994), *Born in Amazonia* (1995), *Discussing Columbus* (1997), *Imaginary Origins: New and Selected Poems* (2004), *Uncharted Heart* (2008), and *Unanimous Night* (2009).

Dabydeen's ethnic poetry examines complex aspects of dislocation, the understanding of heterogenous peoples, and the diasporic South Asian experience. Dabydeen also addresses some of the social and cultural issues that affect the Guyanese diaspora as well as Indo-Caribbean immigrants in Canada. This chapter examines the dominant motifs and influences in some of Dabydeen's recent poems as well as in two earlier collections titled *Stoning the Wind* and *Born in Amazonia*. This chapter seeks to examine a selection of poems that are representative of Dabydeen's poetics as well as his perspectives on the experiences of the Indo-Caribbean diaspora.

In "A Visit to India" from Dabydeen's collection *Coastland: New and Selected Poems*, the speaker (who is a thinly disguised stand-in for Dabydeen himself) addresses the sense of dislocation of the Caribbean-born South Asian who lives with the stories of the South American forest not connecting with the ancestral land: "Where my ancestors have come from, / I pretend to acknowledge or not understand" ("Caribbean Voices" 1). For an Indo-Caribbean member of the South Asian diaspora, the images of India come from reading about India and Indian literature in classical Sanskrit with references to tigers, elephants, and Shakuntala, the heroine of Kalidasa's epic ("Caribbean Voices" 1). These reflections come in an Indian restaurant in Ottawa where the speaker — an academician — is having dinner with a visiting professor from India to discuss ways of publicizing Canadian literature in India. The idea of an India — past and present — that is an imaginary construct based upon the speaker's reading, as well as scholarly interest in postcolonial literature, is referenced with a gentle irony that makes one reconsider the extent to which readers create imaginary worlds based upon their reading to carry on the business of literary criticism in the academy.

The sense of dislocation of an Indo-Caribbean person to whom the India of his/her ancestors is basically an idea or imaginary construct is clearly expressed in "Elephants Make Good Stepladders," where growing up in the tropics of Guyana is not the same as growing up in the tropics of India and hearing stories about "India's tigers — / Not elephants" ("Caribbean Voices" 2). In the poem "Reconciliation" in the collection *Coastland,* the speaker emphasizes the similarities of peoples across continents with allusions to Mohandas Gandhi; Martin Luther King Jr.; Nelson Mandela; the philosophers Ruskin, Thoreau, and Tolstoy; and the scriptures of Hindus and Muslims. The speaker concludes, "Or the living self's errant ways, determined as we are in Africa, Asia, Canada, or continents elsewhere, to move ahead" ("Caribbean Voices" 3). The poem "Flight" celebrates the heterogeneity of peoples in the newly formed nation states in the Americas — especially in the Caribbean: "As the races combine or simply mix. / All new states we now call a country" ("Caribbean Voices" 4). This hopeful celebration contrasts with the reality of the power struggles in Guyana between Afro-Guyanese and Indo-Guyanese in the latter part of the twentieth century.

In the poem "Multiculturalism," the speaker alludes to episodes of intolerance in Canada, past and present, to suggest that multiculturalism is at best a flawed policy: "The ethnics at our door / Malingering with heritage" ("Four Poems by Cyril Dabydeen"). In "The Beauty of Toes" the speaker creates fantasy images of footprints or "toeprints" across continents, across place, and across time, suggesting the oneness of the human race ("Four Poems by Cyril Dabydeen").

The images of the similarity of human experience over time and place are more evident in Dabydeen's recent poetry. In an earlier volume such as *Stoning the Wind* (1994), the poems deal with the ironies of human life, the condition of the poor, and the dislocation of the poet/speaker. In the poem "Looking for Ghosts," the speaker alludes to his own status as a non-white immigrant in Canada: "One blonde youth says he's from Alberta, marvels that I too am from Canada" (*Stoning the Wind* 23). In poem after poem of *Stoning the Wind,* the poet-speaker juxtaposes memories of his beginnings in Guyana with his daily life in a Canadian city (probably Ottawa, as Cyril Dabydeen lives in the Ottawa area and teaches part-time at the University of

Ottawa). In "Grandma's Grammar," the poet-speaker has nostalgic memories of the *patois*, or dialect, spoken by his grandmother in Guyana: "or twisting a refrain with the selfsame Irish, Scotch, / Welsh: cockney inhabiting her breath despite Hindi" (*Stoning the Wind* 27). In the poem "Belly-Mumma," the speaker uses a Caribbean patois to describe the immigrant parent's pride in his/her Canadian-born child who is so different from the parents in his/her culture, growing up in a cold northern climate while the parents yearn for their tropical homelands in Guyana or Jamaica, "which you sometimes does dream 'bout / or suddenly rememba wid strange laughta" (*Stoning the Wind* 28).

In the poem titled "Stoning the Wind," after which this earlier collection is named, the images are from a poor village in the Caribbean where the father uses a knife (probably to cut sugarcane) seemingly cutting the wind, while the mother sews at her sewing machine (probably working as a seamstress). The influence of socialist poets Pablo Neruda and Nicholas Guillen (as pointed out by crtics) is apparent in Dabydeen's sympathy for the working classes in the Caribbean. In "Who We Are," the speaker is in Havana, paying tribute to the beauty of Cuba while recognizing her "need for pesos." Once again, we are reminded of the Afro-Cuban poet Nicholas Guillen. Cyril Dabydeen's speaker describes Cuba as "Hispanic in your smile, / African in your walk" (*Stoning the Wind* 32). In the poem titled "Officialdom," the poet-speaker ironically describes the Canadians' response to an Indo-Caribbean poet writing in English: "At our table we were amazed at how well / you read that poem" (*Stoning the Wind* 34). The poet's audience assumed that English was not his first language. The speaker realizes that his foreignness, his status as an ethnic poet, is evident in both his non-white appearance and his "foreign" accent. Yet in the beginning of this poem, the poet-speaker describes how hard he has worked at his poetry — living in a British colony, mastering poetic diction, studying Mallarme and Eliot (*Stoning the Wind* 33). Dabydeen also explores the attitudes of white Canadians toward black Canadians, and in the poem "Nuptial" he writes, "Othello is all I can think of... / Or how else will the races mix, a Moor's sigh" (*Stoning the Wind* 39). The allusion to Shakespeare's play *Othello* is evocative of social taboos and parental objections to interracial marriages in contemporary Canada.

In contrast to Canada, the land of Dabydeen's adoption, the highlight of Dabydeen's native Guyana is the mixing of heterogenous peoples. The diversity of Guyanese society is encapsulated by the poet in the closing stanzas of a poem titled "Pointe Noire," in which the speaker refers to the Indo-Guyanese leader Dr. Cheddi Jagan and describes the mixing of races in Guyana: "the waves rise and lash; black and white, / or timely brown — we always will be" (*Stoning the Wind* 46).

In yet another lyric, Dabydeen's speaker identifies himself with the

English Romantic poets Wordsworth, Coleridge, Keats, Shelley, Byron, and Cowper. In the following lines, the speaker echoes Wordsworth's poems and romantic solitude: "Declaring myself always a romantic as I wander / Lonely as a cloud in this prelude of events" (*Stoning the Wind* 47). More literary allusions are found in *Stoning the Wind*. In the poem "The Big Apple," where the setting is New York City, the speaker observes, "A few feet away, a woman / reads Marquez" (*Stoning the Wind* 48), and the lyric "Nothing Lights Up" is dedicated to Japanese Canadian writer Joy Kogawa (*Stoning the Wind* 55). In the fourth section of *Stoning the Wind*, the poem "December Is Winter" once again uses the persona of the poet-speaker who has emigrated to Canada from a Caribbean country: "If I am preoccupied with the tropics / Let it be place of birth, mud, soliloquies" (*Stoning the Wind* 65). These images of immigrant nostalgia can be compared to Rienzi Crusz's poems with images of memories of Sri Lanka.

Dabydeen weaves together imagery of confusion, fear, and pain in poems such as "Dinosaur," "The Hunt," "Days of Malaria," and "Marabunta." In poem after poem, Dabydeen presents the difficulties that immigrants and their relatives experience in adjusting to Canada's culture and climate. In the poem titled "The Immigrant Who Remained Forever an Immigrant" we learn that: "Older now, he's still a 'new Canadian' / As his plastic citizenship card fades" (*Stoning the Wind* 77).

If the setting and context were changed from Canada to any other country in the Western Hemisphere, we would still find the first-generation South Asian immigrant becoming conscious of his/her difference. And if the poems in *Stoning the Wind* closely depict the complexity of the experiences of the South Asian diaspora, *Born in Amazonia* is evocative of Dabydeen's roots in Central and South America as he celebrates creatures in the Amazon forests, such as the jaguar. There are several jaguar poems highlighting the feline's strength and striking appearance. Dabydeen's jaguar is evocative of the symbolic tiger in English Romantic poet William Blake's "The Tyger." The title poem of this volume "Born in Amazonia" describes the flora and fauna of the native lands of the Yanomami Indians (*Born in Amazonia* 33). The poem "Anaconda" brings to life this giant constrictor's method of swallowing its prey (*Born in Amazonia* 32). The poem "The Beast" depicts a nameless and frightening animal (*Born in Amazonia* 31), whereas in "Galapagos," the speaker celebrates the giant tortoises of the Galapagos Islands (*Born in Amazonia* 30). Dabydeen dedicates a poem titled "Crocodiles and Cannons" to author Gabriel Garcia Marquez (*Born in Amazonia* 46–47). And in "Jim Jones Revisited," Dabydeen re-creates the tragedy of Jonestown with graphic images: "Take count, how many bodies lie bloated / In the sun? Am I with you?" (*Born in Amazonia* 52).

Thus, Dabydeen's poetic method combines the self of the poet with the self of the speaker or persona in each poem, thereby allowing autobiographical elements of the poet's own life and his own experiences of immigration, exile, marginalization, and sense of dislocation to become key elements in his poetry. Over and over again, Cyril Dabydeen's poems contain allusions to his native Guyana as well as other Central and South American countries. The images of daily living and landscapes from tropical countries are repeatedly juxtaposed with images of everyday life in Canadian cities to suggest the major transitions that the poet-speaker has gone through as an Indo-Caribbean immigrant in contemporary Canadian society.

Arnold Harrichand Itwaru was born in Guyana in the 1940s, and received his M.A. and Ph.D. from York University ("Arnold Itwaru"). He is the director of the Caribbean studies program at New College, University of Toronto, Canada. Itwaru is both a visual artist and a writer. Itwaru writes fiction and poetry, and has won two national awards in Guyana for his poetry. His poetry collections include *Shattered Songs (A Journey from Somewhere to Somewhere)* (1982) and *Body Rites: Beyond the Darkening* (1991).

The poetry of Arnold Itwaru has recurring images of pain, suffering, and violence, sometimes combined with erotic imagery. In this chapter, Itwaru's third book of poetry, *Body Rites: Beyond the Darkening*, has been analyzed as an example of Itwaru's poetic method. Like many other contemporary North American poets, Itwaru's free verse in this volume is all in lowercase letters with no punctuation. This type of writing suggests dislocation of syntax, as in a decentered postmodern world. The self-reflexivity noted in the poems of Rienzi Crusz is also present in Itwaru's *Body Rites*, where the "I" is a thinly disguised version of the poet's own voice. Itwaru's imagery is often surrealistic. His background and training as a social scientist is also evident in repeated references to oppression and injustice; at times, the speakers in these poems represent the voices of oppressed people.

Itwaru begins *Body Rites* with two reflections that suggest the meditative and dreamlike qualities of his poetry as well as his interest in social issues. Itwaru writes, "This work returns to some of the presences of my reflection and finds in the anguished footpaths of these poems changing utterances out of which other meditations arise and join the moments of this present volume" (*Body Rites*, no pagination). This poet also points out the social relevance of his poetry: "When the actions of nation states rewrite themselves in the grue-some ecstasies of the day poetry must rethink its body in whose corporeality we fearfully dream" (*Body Rites*, no pagination).

Itwaru's interest in archetypes and mythopoiesis is also apparent in his two brief epigraphs from the *Popol Vuh*, the well-known collection of Mayan legends of creation. The opening piece of this volume closes with an image of the speaker's alter ego, "who goes there dreaming my dream" (*Body Rites* 1). The imagery associated with a carnival is usually festive but the carnival acquires a nightmarish and fiery quality in Itwaru's "and in this carnival": "serpent human demon / once more we dance within the barriers of flames" (*Body Rites* 16). In "among the lilies," there are images of the oppressed people in a tropical setting that is perhaps Itwaru's native land of Guyana: "Mother, amidst the rubble of sun / and daughters and sons in bamboo barbed wire and mud" (*Body Rites* 16). And "in this dream" depicts memories "in the blooming closures of / each rice-grown mud-grown unremembering" (*Body Rites* 17).

In "we who have survived birth" the speaker is one who has lived through bloody political turmoil and remembers "death at the ports and terminals of hope / factories of casual assassinations" (*Body Rites* 18). Imagery of the countryside devastated by war recurs in "sacred presence": "by the brick of bombed out roadways have I come / infested canals swamps streams and rivers" (*Body Rites* 19). In poem after poem, the persona is a survivor who revisits a land that has suffered in a war. In some aspects, Itwaru's *Body Rites* is similar to Waqas Khwaja's more recent *No One Waits for the Train* (2007), which recreates the gruesome scenes of the 1947 partition of the Indian subcontinent into India and Pakistan.

In "fresh water pain" the speaker evokes memories of indenture in the Caribbean, of crossing salt water only to find fresh water and servitude in a foreign land: "an indentured present I want and do not want / and have become" (*Body Rites* 22). There is irony in what the speaker has been and is becoming as an indentured servant in the British Empire, losing the native tongue for broken English, an experience comparable to the experiences of Africans in the slavery era on ships in the Middle Passage. Itwaru even uses the term "middle passaged" in this poem.

Itwaru's focus on pain and suffering is intensified in nine poems titled "entombed survivals," where the final movement reiterates "no one returns" until the speaker seems at the end to return to an environment where searching (presumably for the entombed) has ended (*Body Rites* 54). The reader is left unsure as to whether the speaker has escaped alive or is free in spirit because he/she is dead. In "drought," the imagery is of a Caribbean scene stricken as if with "the seventh plague": "out of the fields of sugarcane blades and scorpions / I have come to this" (*Body Rites* 59). The drought is almost symbolic of the poverty of the soul in North American life. In "visit," the speaker visits his Caribbean home to remember a simpler way of life now lost amid political turmoil: "that was another world where jamoons and semitoos / were forever ripe" (*Body Rites* 60).

The closing poems of this volume bear the book's title "Body Rites." These "rites" are a series of "chants," thirteen in all. From the poetry of war, destruction, loss, suffering, and pain, the poet turns to erotic poems, presumably from a male speaker addressed to a female listener. The final poem ends with the imagery of sexual union as the joining of the minds as well as the bodies of the speaker and his loved one: "being in you being out of you / you being in me in every wave" (*Body Rites* 82).

In the poems of Sasenarine Persaud, there are similarities to David Dabydeen and Arnold Itwaru in memories of Guyana and experiences as an immigrant in Canada. Persaud is a poet and fiction writer who is now living in the United States. Persaud's poetry is transnational in that he publishes in different countries. According to the poet's official Web page, Sasenarine Persaud was born in Guyana, lived for several years in Canada, and currently resides in Tampa, Florida ("Sasenarine Persaud"). His awards include: the Arthur Schomburg Award (New York) for his contribution to Caribbean Literature and his pioneering of Yogic Realism; the K.M. Hunter Foundation Award (Toronto) for his fiction; two Canada Council awards for poetry; grants for fiction and poetry from the Ontario Arts Council; and fellowships and scholarships from the University of Miami and Boston University" ("Sasenarine Persaud"). Persaud's poetry collections include *Between the Dash and the Comma* (1989), *Demerary Telepathy* (1989), *A Surf of Sparrows' Songs* (1996), *The Hungry Sailor* (2000), *The Wintering Kundalini* (2002), *A Writer Like You* (2002), and *In a Boston Night* (2008).

Two of Persaud's collections of poetry are closely examined in this chapter as representative samples of his poetic method. These volumes are *A Surf of Sparrows' Songs* and *The Wintering Kundalini*. Persaud's poetry is frequently filled with allusions to Hindu mythology as well as social customs prevalent in the Indo-Caribbean community in Guyana. India appears as an ancestral homeland, far away and permanently associated with Hindu mythology and classical Indian literature. Persaud's poems are sprinkled with Hindi and Sanskrit words that effectively "foreignize" everyday North American images and experiences. In Persaud's poetry, the speaker or persona is easily recognized as the voice of the poet himself. The settings of the poems can vary from Guyana to Miami and Coral Gables in Florida to Toronto in Canada. However, the psyche of the speaker is recognizably Indo-Caribbean, with a philosophical frame of reference that is rooted in Hinduism. Despite their artistic quality, the ethnic elements in Persaud's hybridized poetry make the poems less accessible without glossaries. This type of linguistic "foreignizing" or "exoticizing" is also observed in the poetry of Fiji-born Australian poet Sudesh Mishra. In contrast to the poets of the South Asian diaspora, who often tend to "foreignize" their images by interspersing words from South Asian languages, the use of South Asian vocabulary in English-language poetry is much more restrained in the poems published from the Indian subcontinent.

The volume titled *A Surf of Sparrows' Songs* is subtitled "a poemanjali." "Anjali" is a Sanskrit derivative word meaning "offerings to God," which recalls Indian Nobel laureate Rabindranath Tagore's *Gitanjali*, or song-offerings. This volume contains many different love poems, varying from the sensitive and emotive to the bluntly erotic. In the opening poem of the volume, "The Indian Fig Trees at Coral Gables," the speaker reflects upon a Florida landscape and thinks of the tree under which the Buddha became enlightened in the remote past of ancient Indian history (*A Surf of Sparrows' Songs* 1). In the erotic poem "Another Atlantic Seashore" the speaker states that "our souls lap at each other over sandbars / that breakers would slam skin" (*A Surf of Sparrows' Songs* 4). In "Puja Performed on Another Shore, South Miami Beach" (*A Surf of Sparrows' Songs* 6) the speaker envisions a Hindu religious service performed on the beach, and a romantic mood is captured in "I want to touch your fingersoul / as the coconut fronds touch" in the poem "In the Cultural Centre Courtyard, Miami" (*A Surf of Sparrow's Songs* 11). And in "No Summer Camp, Farewell," the speaker, who was raised in the tropics, does not remember summer camps and the change of seasons common to North America: "no summer camp farewells having come / from eternal tropic's formless" (*A Surf of Sparrows' Songs* 58). The final poem of *A Surf of Sparrows' Songs* is "Column Seven Diwali," in which the speaker celebrates his love in the context of the Hindu festival of lights: "only spirit passes body we are flame / a thousand lamps lit a thousand years" (*A Surf of Sparrows' Songs* 89).

Sasenarine Persaud's *The Wintering Kundalini* (2002) is also steeped in the Hindu philosophical tradition. In Hindu treatises on yoga, the "Kundalini" is seen as a serpent or cobra coiled at the base of the human spine, representing "evolutionary energy" that is awakened through the practice of yoga and meditation (Saraswati 16). In "Audience with God," the Hindu speaker suggests the destructive capability of the human race: "Aadmi [man] made pins, knives, guns/rockets, robots, bombs, cars" (*The Wintering Kundalini* 10). The speaker in "Spring, Toronto" is an immigrant from the Caribbean who marvels at the change of seasons in Canada: "This Canadian spring unimaginable to tropical eyes: A hundred shades of green" (*The Wintering Kundalini* 28). In "Cobra: The Wintering Kundalini," the speaker describes dressing in layers during the Canadian winter while seeking out his lover (*The Wintering Kundalini* 62–63). While the allusions to Hindu philosophy, mythology, and religious practices make Persaud a powerful voice for bicultural diasporic South Asians in North America and the Caribbean, the frequent need for the reader to consult the glossary makes the reading experience somewhat challenging.

All the South Asian poetry from Canada discussed in this chapter explores the sense of place, of unhomeliness, of self-definition, dislocation, and loss, and creates permanent artifacts of hybridity with elements of both Western and Eastern cultures. In displaying these characteristics, South Asian Canadian poetry has close similarities with the English-language poetry of diasporic South Asians in the United States, the United Kingdom, Fiji, and Australia.

WORKS CITED

"Arnold Itwaru." literaturealive.ca. Accessed 9 April 2012.
Bahri, Deepika. "Michael Ondaatje." Postcolonial Studies, Emory University. www.english. emory.edu/Bahri/Ondaat.html. Accessed 9 April 2012.
"Caribbean Voices." www.caribvoice.org/Poetry/cdabydeen. Accessed 15 February 2009.
Crusz, Rienzi. Beatitudes of Ice. Toronto: TSAR, 1995. Print.
_____. Insurgent Rain: Selected Poems 1974–1996. Toronto: TSAR, 1997. Print.
_____. Lord of the Mountain: The Sardiel Poems. Toronto: TSAR, 1999. Print.
"Cyril Dabydeen." http://peepaltreepress.com/author_display.asp?au_id=13. Web. 7 April 2012.
Dabydeen, Cyril. Born in Amazonia. Buffalo: Mosaic Press, 1995. Print.
_____. Stoning the Wind. Toronto: TSAR, 1994. Print.
"Four Poems by Cyril Dabydeen." http://english.chass.ncsu.edu/jouvert/v5i1/daby2.htm. Accessed 15 February 2009.
Itwaru, Arnold Harrichand. Body Rites: Beyond the Darkening. Toronto: TSAR, 1991. Print.
Ondaatje, Michael. Handwriting. New York: Random House, 2000. Print.
Persaud, Sasenarine. A Surf of Sparrows' Songs. Toronto: TSAR, 1996. Print.
_____. The Wintering Kundalini. Leeds, UK: Peepal Tree, 2002. Print.
"Rienzi Crusz." www.lib.uwaterloo.ca/discipline/SpecColl/archives/crusz.html. Accessed 9 April 2012.
Saraswati, Swami Satyananda. Asana Pranayama Mudra Bandha. Munger, Bihar, India: Yoga Publications Trust, 2004. Print.
"Sasenarine Persaud." mysite.verizon.net/kshatek. Accessed 9 April 2012.

SEVEN

Strangers in a Strange Land[1]: South Asian Immigrant Poets in the United States

South Asian poets writing in the United States in the last hundred years have returned to some common concerns, such as the effects of exile upon the artist's psyche, memories of the homeland, feelings of marginalization in American society, inner conflict, and the anxiety of existence. Many of these poems capture the South Asian immigrant's anxiety in being caught between East and West in the land of his/her adoption. Indo-Caribbean poet Ramabai Espinet's term, "a nowhere place," may be viewed as a trope of the world inhabited by the speakers/personae of the poems composed in the New World by diasporic South Asian poets. Recognizable elements of postcolonial writing, such as hybridity, are evident in many of the poems. The exile's nostalgia for the lost homeland is at times displayed through South Asian landscapes that have recognizable elements of pastoralism. Often there is the "foreignizing" of images of everyday life in North America as seen through the immigrant's lens. In contrast, there are also attempts to foreignize or "domesticate" images of everyday scenes in South Asia that surface in the poet-speaker's memory.

Some well-known South Asian poets who have lived and published in America include A.K. Ramanujan, Shiv K. Kumar (who returned to India), G.S. Sharat Chandra, Meena Alexander, Chitra Divakaruni, Sujata Bhatt, Agha Shahid Ali, and Zulfikar Ghose. Other diasporic South Asian poets in the United States include Darius Cooper, Waqas Ahmed Khwaja, and Syed K.M. Hassan (the deceased co-author of this study). In their choices of poetic methodology, these poets often show a preference for the confessional mode, often adapting the confessional mode to capture the fractured self of the artist in exile in all its complexity of emotion. The women poets often explore their inner dilemmas in terms of female sexuality, traditionally a taboo subject in South Asian cultures; some of these poets are discussed in chapters nine and ten. Also, it is important to note that the majority of these poets are academicians immersed not only in creative writing but in literary research as well. All of the South Asian American poets discussed here come from educated, middle-class backgrounds in their countries of origin, and in their migration to the New World, they have moved into professional employment. The anger and radical politics that are visible in the poetry published in South Asia in the last hundred years is much less apparent in South Asian American poetry.

A.K. Ramanujan

The earliest South Asian poet of note in America is A.K. Ramanujan (1929–1993). Modernist influences are apparent throughout his writings. The late Ramanujan was a professor of Dravidian linguistics at the University of Chicago. Attipat Krishnaswami Ramanujan was born in Mysore, India, in 1929, receiving his B.A. and M.A. in English language and literature from the University of Mysore. He received a graduate diploma in theoretical linguistics from Deccan University in Poona in 1958, and arrived in the United States in 1959. In 1962, Ramanujan became an assistant professor at the University of Chicago, where he worked for many years and developed the program in South Asian studies. In 1963, Ramanujan received his Ph.D. in linguistics from Indiana University. He received the national honor of "Padma Sri" from the Indian government in 1976, and the MacArthur Prize Fellowship in 1983. Ramanujan was a scholar and a bilingual writer who published works in both English and Kannada (the native language of his ancestors). His published works include scholarly articles and translations.

Scholars and literary anthologies continue to classify Ramanujan as an "Indian" poet rather than an Asian American poet, perhaps because more studies of Ramanujan's poetry have been published from India than from the United States. The poetry of Ramanujan illustrates the fact that while citizenship can change in the global society of our times, the past self and Old World values of the South Asian immigrant poets, juxtaposed with the culture and values of New World societies, often give rise to anxiety (*angst*) and self-division as these artists face their own marginalization in America.

The earliest and most extended exploration of the subjects of exile and resulting inner conflicts appears in the writings of Ramanujan. In his online article, Rajeev Patke presents an almost itemized textual analysis of what he titles "The Ambivalence of Poetic Self-Exile: The Case of A.K. Ramanujan." According to Patke, the diasporic condition is a form of translation (1). He interprets "translation" in three ways: one, the person travels away from a place viewed as home, and hence experiences a sense of loss; two, translation involves changing or adapting to another use; three, translation is a transfer of property (Patke 1). Patke writes, "This is the sense in which the diasporic as migrant or exile conflates loss and gain, the elegiac and the recuperative, by figuring the self as the bearer of a legacy, which belongs ... to the acts of mind in which pastness and futurity have their being, as gain-in-loss" (1). Bruce King discusses the poetry of Ramanujan, Shiv Kumar, Sharat Chandra, and Vikram Seth in the same chapter of *Modern Poetry In English* (2001), suggesting that "no doubt the greater opportunities (especially at universities) outside India have contributed to their exile" (209). According to King, "Indian expatriate poets do not write from the position of a distinct foreign community, such as the exiled black or West Indian novelists, but their writing reflects the perspective of someone between two cultures" (209). He also states that these immigrant poets "look back on India with nostalgia, satirically celebrating their liberation or asserting their biculturalism, but they also look skeptically and wryly on their new homeland as outsiders" (King 209).

The observations of both Patke and King are valuable because they show that the complex effects of exile on South Asian poets in America have been of interest to scholars for some time. Lyrical poetry is clearly the preferred form among South Asian American poets. This body of hybridized lyrical poetry has a very strong affinity with the confessional mode of modern and postmodern American poetry, while the imagery and experiences in these poems evoke memories of life in South Asia. The present study suggests that these motifs of exile and loss emerge clearly in the confessional mode often used by these poets. The adaptation of the confessional mode is effective in capturing the fractured self of the artist as the experience of exile merges into the type of alienation that is a recurring motif of postmodern poetry in North America. The self of the poet is often juxtaposed with experiences of the phenomenal world, telescoping past and present, temporal as well as spatial dimensions of the artist's experiences. This is the postmodern poet's depiction of Heidegger's *Dasein* (being-in-the-world). And the diasporic South Asian poet's world is between two continents and two cultures, or perhaps more than two continents and more than two cultures.

It is rewarding to focus on the poetics of Ramanujan while drawing comparisons with Kumar and Sharat Chandra. Ramanujan had a long writing career and produced a considerable body of poems. According to Bruce King, the existing body of criticism on Ramanujan's poetry has been misleading in its emphasis on roots (215). King finds that in Ramanujan's poems, "an organic world in process, changing, or growing, but continuous, is closer to the vision of Ramanujan's poetry" (215–16). King also compares Ramanujan's poetry to that of the early T.S. Eliot and Jules Laforgue (210).

Ramanujan wrote and lectured on a number of subjects in literature and culture in his lifetime. According to Jahan Ramazani, "At the heart of Ramanujan's poetry are ironic, if plangent, meditations on transfer and loss between East and West, on survivals and disappearances between past and present" (*The Hybrid Muse* 77). Major areas of interest for Ramanujan were folklore, Hindu and Buddhist philosophical concepts, Indian classical literature, and Hindu religious poetry from the Middle Ages focusing on the Bhakti movement. His poetry is dynamic and his subjects and style changed many times over his entire career. Ramanujan wrote *The Striders* (1966), *Relations* (1971), and *Second Sight* (1986), with *The Black Hen* published posthumously in *The Collected Poems* (1995). In the preface to *The Collected Poems*, Krittika Ramanujan notes that at his death the poet left 148 poems on three computer disks that were subsequently edited and arranged by Molly Daniels (xv). Krittika Ramanujan comments that "Ramanujan worked on these poems off and on for years, as was his habit. He often joked that these poems were like babies, they dirtied themselves and he had to clean them up" (*Collected Poems* xv).

Ramanujan's well-known poem "River" presents a memory poem that describes the drying up of a river in southern India in the hot dry season, to be followed by the floods during the monsoon season. The poem is about the making of poetry where the old and new poets only record the images of the river in the rainy season, "of the floods" (*Collected Poems* 38). Then there is Ramanujan's persona, who was there for a single day during the floods (*Collected Poems* 39). The Hindu religious poets of old are referenced in the names of the cows "Gopi" and "Brinda." Ramanujan's speaker suggests that the old and new poets did not mention the presence of tragedy, but his emphasis differs in cataloging the victims of the flood — namely, the cows Gopi and Brinda, as well as "one pregnant woman / expecting identical twins" (*Collected Poems* 39). Almost throughout his career, Ramanujan's poetic personae juxtaposed images of America with images of India, often incongruously, even with the tone of a confession. This is seen in "Breaded Fish," where a wife or girlfriend serves the speaker breaded fish, even placing one in his mouth, and he can neither eat nor sit as a memory of a woman lying dead on a beach surfaces: "length of woman, dead / on the beach in a yard of cloth" (*Collected Poems* 7). In the poem "Still Life," what seems to be a romantic lunch date is followed by a grotesque image of reality: "and I saw the half-eaten sandwich" (*Collected Poems* 712).

In the poem "This Pair," the speaker satirizes the predicament of new parents with a baby. Parenting and babies are positive images in America as well as India. However, in this poem, "this fertile shabby pair / faintly smell already of unwashed hair" (*Collected Poems* 13). Similarly, instead of the attractive imagery associated with newborn babies, there comes the idea of neonatal jaundice, a common condition of newborn infants, in "On the Very Possible Jaundice of an Unborn Daughter": "how can my daughter / help those singing yellow" (*Collected Poems* 14). In "Still Another for Mother," the speaker or persona is literally a stranger in a strange land: "she will not let me rest / as I slowly cease to be the town's brown stranger and guest" (*Collected Poems* 15). He imagines the setting of a domestic dispute between a middle-aged couple whose home he passes, concluding that merely walking on is polite, as if nothing has happened and he has not observed the conflict. Essentially an outsider, the speaker recalls the past in another land: "silent house, given on her marriage day to my father, for a dowry" (*Collected Poems* 16). The word "dowry" invokes a custom from Ramanujan's Indian past: dowries were once required in many parts of India, although now banned by law.

Similarly, "Lines to a Granny" is a poem full of nostalgia and Old World memories: "tell me again in the dark about the wandering prince" (*Collected Poems* 17). In the poem titled "On Memory," the poet's bicultural and perhaps fragmented self surfaces in images of Indian and Western culture: "nursery rhymes / on Tipu Sultan or Jack and Jill" (*Collected Poems* 21). The poem titled "Christmas" contains a juxtaposition of the speaker's two worlds. The tone is confessional with images of entrapment, as in "limed": "And I am limed / on branches as bare as roots" (*Collected Poems* 32). "Conventions of Despair" is again in the confessional mode: "But, sorry, I cannot unlearn / conventions of despair" (*Collected Poems* 34).

In such poems as "Some Relations" or "Middle Age," Ramanujan's work contains recurring images of deprivation as well as the meaninglessness of existence in the late twentieth century. In "Middle Age," the deprivation is global: "I hold them close from famine to famine / looking for mothers and penguin mens" (*Collected Poems* 167). Thus the fragmentation of the artist's psyche and internal landscape is a part of the postmodern diasporic South Asian poet's condition.

Shiv K. Kumar

Shiv K. Kumar's American experiences mark a short period in his writing career. He is permanently based in India and well established as a poet and scholar. Kumar is fairly well known in India for his poetry in English. Kumar's Indian poetry has been discussed in chapter three, and contains recurring motifs of dislocation and anger. Bruce King suggests that the best of Kumar's writing is set in India, and that Kumar's favorite mode is satire (120–21). "Days in New York" is one of Kumar's few poems about living in America. The tone of the poem is very angry, a reminder that Asians are a less visible minority in American popular culture, as the speaker is mistaken for a Puerto Rican, Jamaican, or Native American. Neither Hispanic nor black nor Native American, the speaker explains to the person questioning him that he is "a brown Indian from the land of Gandhi" (Kumar, Varnamala). He becomes entirely unimportant as his questioner promptly leaves. Kumar's speaker begins with a negative critique of American society by stating that he lives "in a garbage can." The speaker also has his own transgressions to confess: "I open each morning my neighbor's *Times* / whisked away from his door" (Kumar, Varnamala).

G.S. Sharat Chandra

The late G.S. Sharat Chandra (1935–2000) published both poetry and fiction. Sharat Chandra was born in India, and earned a law degree from the Osgoode Law School in Toronto in 1966. He arrived in the United States in the 1960s, wishing to become a writer. He received an M.F.A. from the University of Iowa Writers Workshop in 1968. For most of his career, Sharat Chandra was a professor of creative writing and English (1983–2000) at the University of Missouri–Kansas City. He was the recipient of a Fulbright Fellowship and an NEA Fellowship in Creative Writing. He published ten books, including translations from Sanskrit and English into the Indian language Kannada. At the time of his death from a brain aneurysm in 2000, he had been married to his wife Jane for about thirty-eight years. The couple had three children. G.S. Sharat Chandra's poetry has some similarities to the work of Shiv K. Kumar. Bruce King suggests that the personae in his poems are mostly insecure (219). Sharat Chandra's poems set in India are quite negative, depicting corruption, injustice, and poverty. Like Kumar, Sharat Chandra depicts exile as being part of the human condition, of *Dasein* or being-in-the-world. Sharat Chandra may be viewed as a South Asian American poet whose writings continued to flow and change, both in style and themes, until his sudden demise in 2000.

In "Shortchanged Lives," there is the "yuppie" American voice of Mrs. Gentry juxtaposed with that of the Indian speaker. Mrs. Gentry's three-week visit to India gave her the lasting impression of a "Dreadfully poor place": "[I] saw a dead boy in the street" (Sharat Chandra, "Shortchanged"). The speaker realizes that the tremendous disparities that have always been a part of Indian life are difficult to explain to those unaccustomed to Indian culture or to the philosophical beliefs of Eastern religions. The speaker suggests that for suffering individuals, death is a release from the pain of life on earth (according to traditional beliefs). These beliefs in heaven (swarga) may be the ultimate hallucination for the starving and the forsaken. While there is anger and satire directed at social injustice, there is also the implication that both the New and the Old World are inadequate in different ways.

In the recurring confessions of self-division and alienation in the poems of A.K. Ramanujan, Shiv K. Kumar, and G.S. Sharat Chandra, the world of the postmodern South Asian poet is one of long-term exile, where exile becomes symbolic of the human condition itself. The world inhabited by the poet-speaker is an imaginary space between East and West, a "nowhere place." The critic Ashok Bery has cited Bruce King's comparison of A.K. Ramanujan's work to a "house of mirrors" (155).

The fragmentation of the self, alienation, anxiety, and dislocation are all recognizably modernist elements that are apparent in G.S. Sharat Chandra's poetry. Sharat Chandra's collection of poems titled *Family of Mirrors* (1993) is analyzed in this chapter. This book was a nominee for the 1993 Pulitzer Prize. The title page of *Family of Mirrors* displays the letters of the title and the poet's name reversed. This volume of poetry is dedicated to the poet's son and to the "loving memory of Isaac Bashevis Singer." The reference to Singer suggests the poet's interest in his work (Singer was an immigrant writer who composed in Yiddish and then in English). Many of the poems in this volume were presumably published in poetry journals in North America.

Family of Mirrors is divided into five sections. In the first section of this volume, the first poem, "Runaway Sister," appears on a left-side page instead of a right-side page, reinforcing the idea of reversed or mirror images. The mirror image that is so central to A.K. Ramanujan's poetry runs through Sharat Chandra's poetry as an image of the South Asian immigrant's quest for self-identity, an identifiable modernist motif in poetry. The runaway sister is the speaker's sister in a memory poem set in Southern India in the mid-twentieth century. The sister is a young woman in love with acting who has failed her school examinations. She packs her tin suitcase, ready to leave for Bombay (now Mumbai), the center of India's motion picture industry. However, her dreams do not materialize as she settles into the role of the middle-class Indian housewife: "she won a certificate in acting, / married our neighbor the insurance salesman" (*Family of Mirrors* 10). In "Facts of Life," the speaker remembers his late father, who "died of a malignancy" despite his healthy lifestyle: "My father, teetotaler, vegetarian / took two baths a day" (*Family of Mirrors* 11). "The Hamper" is another memory of the speaker's early childhood, one of being held and loved by his mother: "nose in my belly her quick kisses / wandering over my shirtless body" (*Family of Mirrors* 13). The old laundry hamper made of mahogany and wire mesh becomes associated with memories of childhood games played by the poet/speaker's siblings. The stress and strain of expatriate life surface in "Mount Pleasant, USA," where the title is ironic:

"of promises in my exile / the cage I carry is the cage I made" (*Family of Mirrors* 14). The speaker emphasizes that the exile is self-imposed. However, in Iowa, the male speaker dreams of his aging mother in Nanjangud in southern India. Many of the poems in *Family of Mirrors* appear to have autobiographical content, such as "My Daughter's New Dog," in which the speaker is a loving father who tolerates the activities of his daughter's new puppy: "I don't like to be licked / by a pup in the morning" (*Family of Mirrors* 15).

In the second section of *Family of Mirrors,* Sharat Chandra presents poems for different voices, several of which are "fables." Familiar images are defamiliarized, even mythologized, in poems such as "Fable of the Talker," "Fable of a Three Year Old," "Fable of the Coarse Rose," and "Fable of Hearts." In "Children," the speaker addresses his partner as both observe their children growing up: "they now seek others / with no thought for you and me" (*Family of Mirrors* 25). The thoughtlessness and egocentric attitudes of adolescence are encapsulated in these lines. In "Fable of Hearts" (*Family of Mirrors* 24) the child speaker talks about drawings of hearts that the mother sticks to the refrigerator — a touching and familiar image of domesticity. "Fable of the Coarse Rose" has elements of parody that critique traditional images of love poetry. Here there is a rose that has a "spanking hand" in a decentered world where "it became ludicrous to speak to strangers / of one's experiences with rose slaps" (*Family of Mirrors* 23). There is a recognizable tone of misogyny in this fable. In "Fable of a Three Year Old," the speaker, a small child, has a morbid fear of dead bodies coming out of graves: "One night I saw a dead body eating / the chocolate cake my Mom had made for my birthday" (*Family of Mirrors* 21). The child tells another imaginary entity, the toothfairy, of the nightmare. The toothfairy then repairs the cake and dismisses the dead body. The nightmare quality of this poem in the familiar setting of an American home is intensified by Sharat Chandra's use of a child speaker. In the piece titled "This Poem," images of violence appear while the speaker focuses on the ruthlessness of human beings on this earth: "This poem is my mouth in splinters / chew it well brother" (*Family of Mirrors* 18). The act of poetic utterance itself splinters the speaker's mouth.

The third section of *Family of Mirrors* is about experiences with different cultures. "Hawaiian Zen Fleas" (*Family of Mirrors* 28–29) combines images of meditation and sexuality in a most startling combination of incongruous elements. The irony is reminiscent of English metaphysical poetry, such as John Donne's "The Flea," a reminder that Sharat Chandra was a professor of English: "wisdom is coming, / you see the fleas clear as Bodhisatva" (*Family of Mirrors* 29). "Chinaman's Hat, North Shore, Oahu" combines elements of mythology with reminders of the history of early Chinese American immigrants in Hawaii. The mirror-image poem of the dead Chinese immigrant's hat is that of gum-chewing American tourists in China leaving others "hob-bling with American gum / stuck in their soles" (*Family of Mirrors* 32). In "Honey, Its Sugarless," this annoying everyday image from the streets and parking lots of North America — thoughtlessly spat-out gum that sticks to the unwary pedestrian's shoes — suggests that the tourists have taken their bad habits with them in their foreign travels. The poem "Confusion" captures the poet-speaker's need for solitude while writing in order to focus better: "who keeps saying I want to be alone / because I am writing a poem about confusion" (*Family of Mirrors* 33).

"Identities" is about traveling from one country to another and using one's passport, stamped with many different visas. This poem contains a pre-monition of death, a final surrender of identity: "Someday I'll take my dupli-cate selves, / give up my face" (*Family of Mirrors* 34). In "Ars Poetica" (the title borrowed from Latin literary theorist Horace), there is a striking image of the financial limitations of supporting a family as a poet and college pro-fessor, when after "four years of teaching and paying necessary bills," the speaker's "wife bought a jordache / and a leather bag," minor but touching images of conspicuous consumption and social status in America (*Family of Mirrors* 35).

The fourth section of *Family of Mirrors* contains poems on the subject of love in which the tone of the speaker ranges from sincerity to half-serious-ness to irony and sarcasm. In "Love Rites," the male speaker's reflection on an unstable relationship begins with cutting his finger while slicing cucumbers to prepare a salad for his woman friend, and concludes with "She's wooed by others / would you be my valentine" (*Family of Mirrors* 39). "Lovers" is a poem about parting or "a check-out time," signifying the transience of love: "I'll drive home, / you'll be a passenger on a jet" (*Family of Mirrors* 40).

"Love Poem" (*Family of Mirrors* 41) is a brief reflection on love, separation, and writing poetry. Sharat Chandra's ability to capture deep thoughts in metaphor is evident in a definition of the poetic image: "the art of rescuing / the paramount in the fleeting" (*Family of Mirrors* 41). The "Love Song of Rasheed the Mad Cap" is a parody with a speaker who has a Middle Eastern accent and imagery that is evocative of the *Thousand and One Nights* (*Family of Mirrors* 43–44). "Until Sold Do Us Part" satirizes the materialism of North American life, where a divorcing couple, Joanna and George, are painting and landscaping their home for sale as they get divorced: "marriages may come apart / but a house keeps its equity" (*Family of Mirrors* 44). "Moths" is a poem in couplets where images of erotic moments mingle with sad memories, such as "I remember my father / grown thin as a cat with cancer" (*Family of Mirrors* 49).

The fifth and final section of *Family of Mirrors* contains several poems where the images and metaphors clearly show modernist influences, as in the image of the wife of a man across the street cooking dinner: "The bird is in the oven, / she switches on the television" (*Family of Mirrors* 55). The central image of this volume of poetry appears in the closing lines of "Vacancies": "I've anchored bone / to a family of mirrors" (*Family of Mirrors* 59).

Several poems in this last section are about the poet's art and self-identity, and the persona is a thinly disguised version of Sharat Chandra himself. The art of the poet is described in these lines: "I've written words, pushed them far, / pulled them from an orbiting leap" (*Family of Mirrors* 60). "Screws and Hinges" is an unusual piece that imagines the screws in door hinges coming to life, their moods changing from laughter and romance to subordination: "hinged to the obedience / of opening and closing" (*Family of Mirrors* 61). "Voyages" juxtaposes images of sleep and dreaming with the death of many passengers in an airplane crash: "the dismembered hurtle down / into the dark laps of the sea" (*Family of Mirrors* 62).

"Nightmare" (*Family of Mirrors* 66) depicts a speaker waking up from a terrifying dream. In "Van Gogh's Ear" (*Family of Mirrors* 72), the speaker juxtaposes images of Van Gogh's sufferings in life, such as cutting off his own ear, with the auctioning of his paintings at Sotheby's in London. The underlying message is that gifted artists are often not recognized when they are alive. "Shopping with Akhmatova" (*Family of Mirrors* 74) contains allusions to an Ukrainian poet, just as "Islands" alludes to W.B. Yeats's poetry in the phrase "Byzantiums of real estate" (*Family of Mirrors* 76).

The last three poems of *Family of Mirrors* are recognizably autobiographical. "Canyons Poet" is filled with self-irony, as the poet-speaker has to fill in for a "visiting" poet whose visit does not materialize: "Whose not visiting has made my poetry prosperous / My tenure talked about" (*Family of Mirrors* 80). "Still Kicking in America" describes the poet-speaker's permanent "foreignization" as a South Asian immigrant in America: "You speak such good English? / How long have you been here?" (*Family of Mirrors* 81). The final poem of the volume is titled "Swansong," as the speaker views "the black neck of a swan / drooping on the windowsill" (*Family of Mirrors* 83).

Agha Shahid Ali

Like G.S. Sharat Chandra, Agha Shahid Ali died at a time when his poetry was flourishing. Ali was born in India in 1949, and he died in 2001. He preferred to identify himself as an American poet and a Kashmiri poet (his family was originally from Kashmir). He earned a Ph.D. in English from Pennsylvania State University in 1984 and an M.F.A. from the University of

Arizona in 1985. He published *The Half-Inch Himalayas* (1987), *Rooms Are Never Finished* (2001), *The Country Without a Post Office* (1997), *The Beloved Witness: Selected Poems* (1992), *A Nostalgist's Map of America* (1991), *A Walk Through the Yellow Pages* (1987), *In Memory of Begum Akhtar and Other Poems* (1979), and *Bone Sculpture* (1972). Ali also published *T.S. Eliot as Editor* (1986), a translation titled *The Rebel's Silhouette: Selected Poems* by Faiz Ahmed Faiz (1992), and an edited collection titled *Ravishing Disunities: Real Ghazals in English* (2000).

Agha Shahid Ali's biography published in *The Half-Inch Himalayas* states that "Ali received fellowships from the Pennsylvania Council on the Arts, the Bread Loaf Writers' Conference, the Ingram-Merrill Foundation, the New York Foundation for the Arts, and the Guggenheim Foundation and was awarded a Pushcart Prize. He held teaching positions at the University of Dehli, Penn State, SUNY Binghamton, Princeton University, University of Massachusetts at Amherst, Hamilton College, Baruch College, University of Utah, and Warren Wilson College" (58).

In this chapter, several poems from *The Half-Inch Himalayas* are discussed as examples of Ali's recurring themes and motifs. Many of the poems in this volume are steeped in imagery of Ali's early life in northern India, for Ali had a lasting interest in the Islamic cultural traditions of this region. Many of his poems are set in the old city of Delhi and contain moments of nostalgia.

The opening poem of this volume is "Postcard from Kashmir," in which memories of his ancestral homeland surface upon seeing a postcard with a scene from Kashmir in his mailbox: "I always loved neatness / Now I hold / the half-inch Himalayas in my hand" (*The Half-Inch Himalayas* 1). This brief lyric overflows with spontaneity and love of Kashmir and its Himalayan scenes. This postcard opens the remaining poems of this book, which are chiefly memory poems, divided into four separate groups.

The first group of lyrics is impressionistic, with memories of Delhi and family members set up like snapshots from a family album. In "A Lost Memory of Delhi" the speaker (the poet) is on a bus ride into the past: "I pass my parents / strolling by the Jamuna River" (*The Half-Inch Himalayas* 5). In "A Dream of Glass Bangles," the speaker remembers the cold winters of Kashmir, closing with a startling image of a widow following the old north Indian custom of smashing her glass bangles immediately after the death of her husband: "a widow smashing the rivers / on her arms" (*The Half-Inch Himalayas* 7). In "Snowmen," the poet-speaker creates a myth of his snowman ancestor who came to Kashmir from Samarkand in Central Asia: "even if I'm the last snowman,/ that I'll ride into spring" (*The Half-Inch Himalayas* 8). In "Cracked Portraits," the speaker-poet reflects on old family portraits of his great-grandfather and grandfather. "Prayer Rug" is addressed to his grandmother who visits Mecca, and describes the chores of women completed "between the days' / five calls to prayer" in traditional Muslim households. In this first section of *The Half-Inch Himalayas* there appears a frequently anthologized poem titled "The Dacca Gauzes," which encapsulates the oppressive history of British colonialism in South Asia: "In history we learned: the hands of weavers were amputated" (*The Half-Inch Himalayas* 13). The fine muslins of Bengal were replaced by fabric from British cotton mills under colonial rule as the colonizers sought to destroy the ancient South Asian cotton textile industry where weavers spun the finest muslin and silk fabrics.

The second section of *The Half-Inch Himalayas* contains images of people and places from Ali's early life. The speaker-poet remembers a Delhi butcher who could quote the famous Urdu poets Mirza Ghalib and Mir in "Butcher"; this poem reminds readers of Ali's lifelong love of Urdu lyrics known as "ghazals." A four-line poem captures the sorry image of the impoverished fortune-teller in "The Fate of the Astrologer Sitting on the Pavement Outside the Delhi Railway Station." After seeing the classic Russian film, Kozintsev's *King Lear*, in a music theater in Chandni Chowk (now a busy inner-city shopping area in the old city of Delhi), the speaker reflects with nostalgia on the past glories of the Mughal empire destroyed by British colonizers: "I think of Zafar, poet and emperor, being led through the street" (*The Half-Inch Himalayas* 25). (The last Mughal emperor Bahadur Shah wrote poetry under the pen name of "Zafar.")

The painful memories of colonial history also surface in "Chandni Chowk, Delhi": "Can you rise away this city that lasts / like blood on the bitten tongue?" (*The Half-Inch Himalayas* 26). The poems "In Memory of Begum Akhtar" (*The Half-Inch Himalayas* 28–29) and "Homage to Faiz Ahmed Faiz" (*The Half-Inch Himalayas* 30–33) are elegies commemorating legendary Indian ghazal singer Begum Akhtar and famous Urdu poet Faiz Ahmed Faiz. Ali translated many Urdu ghazals into English, as well as poems by Faiz Ahmed Faiz.

In the third section of *The Half-Inch Himalayas*, the brief lyrics are set in America, Agha Shahid Ali's land of adoption. He has a recurring nightmare of "A Wrong Turn": "In my dream I'm always / in a massacred town" (*The Half-Inch Himalayas* 37). In "Vacating an Apartment," the speaker imagines that a couple has rented his apartment after his departure (or death): "The landlord gives them my autopsy; / they sign the lease" (*The Half-Inch Himalayas* 39). "The Previous Occupant" presents the opposite scenario, with the speaker-poet moving into an apartment and trying to imagine what the previous occupant (a native of Chile) was like. The speaker finds his presence everywhere: "my body casts his shadow everywhere / He'll never, never, move out of here" (*The Half-Inch Himalayas* 41). Ali uses two-line free-verse stanzas effectively in capturing street scenes, such as those in "Philadelphia, 2:00 AM" (*The Half-Inch Himalayas* 44) and "The Jogger on Riverside Drive, 5 AM" (*The Half-Inch Himalayas* 45). The brief poem "Stationery," which closes this section, is a love poem in which the speaker requests "The world is full of paper / Write to me" (*The Half-Inch Himalayas* 48).

The fourth and last section of *Half-Inch Himalayas* returns to memories of South Asia, as seen in "Survivor," which reconstructs the fate of a lost mountain climber whose spirit inhabits her old home, now occupied by another person: "He is breathless to tell her tales / in which I was never found" (*The Half-Inch Himalayas* 51). Thus time and again, Ali returns to the imagery of shadowy spirits who inhabit the homes of the living.

Nostalgic memories of Ali's youth in Delhi surface in "I Dream It Is Afternoon When I Return to Delhi" (*The Half-Inch Himalayas* 52–53). There are recurring elements of vision in Ali's poetry, expressed in his images of the past and of deceased loved ones. "I Dream It Is Afternoon When I Return to Delhi" is a dream vision of a return to the poet-speaker's past. In the context of this repeated wish to return to his South Asian past, Ali is recognizably a poet of exile, of "unhomeliness."

In the closing poem of *The Half-Inch Himalayas*, titled "Houses," the sense of loss, exile, and "unhomeliness" surfaces yet again: "I am thirteen thousand miles from home / I comb the moon out of the night" (*The Half-Inch Himalayas* 57). Another recurring motif in Agha Shahid Ali's poetry is the poet's premonition of his own early death, as in the lyric "In the Mountains," where the speaker imagines a strange being in the mountains (presumably the Himalayas): "farther and farther into the year / he waits for news of my death" (*The Half-Inch Himalayas* 56).

Zulfikar Ghose

Despite his numerous publications, the art of Zulfikar Ghose has received limited attention from critics, perhaps because Ghose's work is difficult to categorize. To some extent, Ghose's British affiliations, as well as his refusal to identify with any specific movement in postmodern poetry, have resulted in his poems not receiving the kind of critical attention that they deserve in contemporary scholarship on South Asian literature.

Zulfikar Ghose is a Pakistani American writer who has written books of poetry, short stories, novels, biographies, and literary criticism. Ghose was born in Sialkot in 1935; his family migrated to England in 1952. After completing his education at Keele University, Ghose worked for the *Observer* as a sportswriter. He has lived in the United States since 1969 and has worked at the University of Texas, Austin. Ghose's poems tend to fall into three categories:

1. Landscape poetry with British descent lines and images of his beloved London, which has been a mecca for postcolonial artists since World War II.
2. Poems with memories of the past, containing images of South Asia where the speaker "foreignizes" commonplace images of South Asian life, creating a sense of nostalgia for a land left behind in early life.
3. Poems with a sense of history that provides the poet-speaker with a sense of time and historic moments.

In several poems the above themes overlap, demonstrating Ghose's unique methodology.

In this chapter, the poems discussed come from Ghose's *Selected Poems*, which includes poems from earlier collections: *The Loss of India* (1964), *Jets from Orange* (1967), *The Violent West* (1972), and *A Memory of Asia* (1984). The appendix of *Selected Poems* contains Zulfikar Ghose's interview with Bruce Meyers that basically contains Ghose's poetic manifesto. Ghose states that he "developed an obsession with places, with landscapes" (*Selected Poems* 100). Ghose has stronger ties with the United Kingdom than with South Asia. However, despite his feeling of being free in Texas, he confirms the sense of his "unhomeliness." Ghose also concedes to various influences such as Proust and Wittgenstein (*Selected Poems* 103). With regard to the process of composing poetry, Ghose states:

> All I have when I am writing a poem are the words that have been put down on the page. I do not know where they come from. They suddenly appear there, and the only question is which ones do I want to keep and are there any others I want to add? I don't have ideas. I don't have a programme. I don't have an ideology [*Selected Poems* 105].

Most of the discussion in the Bruce Meyers interview turns to Ghose's early publications with contemporary British poetry. To some extent, Zulfikar Ghose's writing forms a bridge between diasporic South Asian poetry from Britain and diasporic South Asian poetry from North America.

Zulfikar Ghose's poetry contains imagery and motifs from three continents (Asia, Europe, and North America). Ghose makes frequent use of landscape poems. The poet's early life in South Asia, his education in the United Kingdom, and his entry into the circles of modern and postmodern poets in Britain during his youth have given him strong affiliations to the British tradition in poetry. Although most of his teaching and publishing career has been as a South Asian immigrant in the United States, Ghose's writings present clear instances of hybridity, the sense of exile and loss that permeates the writings of most "twice migrant" South Asian writers. Bhabha's "unhomeliness" provides an umbrella for analyzing Ghose's poetry. For Ghose, the loss of the early "home" in South Asia, the acquisition of a second "home" and secondary culture in England, and the subsequent relocation to America leaves the speaker/persona in many of his poems without a sense of location. For example, in the poem "A Private Lot," the speaker (a stand-in for the poet himself) visits a private lot with a Texas realtor who tries to persuade him to buy the lot to build "a home I would not want to leave" (*Selected Poems* 34). The closing line is ironic in the context of the poet's many relocations.

Like Agha Shahid Ali, Zulfikar Ghose's poetry recaptures scenes of daily life in South Asia and memories of early life and family members. As mentioned, Ghose displays a special affinity for landscape poems. Similar to Ali, the imagery of airplanes recurs in Ghose's writing. The airplane as a symbol of contemporary global society, of the relocations and dislocation of the South Asian diaspora, carries a special meaning. In poems such as "The Body's Independence" (*Selected Poems* 3–4), "The Loss of India" (*Selected Poems* 5–6), "The Mystique of Roots" (*Selected Poems* 7–8), "Flying Over India" (*Selected Poems* 9), and "This Landscape, These People" (*Selected Poems* 10–12), memories of the poet's early life are used to bring to life poems from South Asia: "The tall grass the monsoons left in the mountains / was aflame like corn in the setting August sun" ("Loss of India," *Selected Poems* 5). There is a clear sense of history in such poems as "This Landscape, These People"—"India halted: as suddenly as a dog, / barking, hangs out his tongue, stifles his cry" (*Selected Poems* 11)—and "The Body's Independence"—"India was at civil war, / the crow excreted where he pleased" (*Selected Poems* 4). The poet-speaker remembers his early biology lessons in "Bombay's Don Bosco High School," up until the time he fell ill of a kidney ailment and became very thin and weak. He also remembers his recovery from the illness.

Autobiographical elements are present in Ghose's landscape poems set in England, where he realizes his condition of exile: "To this country I have come / Stranger or an inhabitant, this is my home" ("This Landscape, These People," *Selected Poems* 12). Ghose also has many poems on his early life in South Asia, complete with memories of family members, such as "The Attack on Sialkot" (*Selected Poems* 15–16) and "The Picnic in Jammu" (*Selected Poems* 17–18). In his images of this former home, Ghose "foreignizes" images of daily life in South Asia while trying to depict images from Britain as familiar. Ghose's poems at times depict images of his favorite place, London, as in "Kew Bridge": "Dogs are bounding on Kew Green, chasing / a ball and bringing it back. I survive" (*Selected Poems* 28). In the brief lyric "The Alien," the poet-speaker, an immigrant in England, perceives that "With, a look, the

English transplant me / elsewhere, though their civil tolerance" (*Selected Poems* 13).

In the second phase of his immigrant experiences — living in Texas in the United States — Ghose writes of American landscapes, as seen in "On Owning Property in the U.S.A.": "such are the country's contradictions and / such the ambiguity of all dreams" (*Selected Poems* 33). In the landscape poem "It's Your Land, Boss," the speaker realizes his own transient condition and that he must be prepared to leave one day: "I must go / towards horizons which the jet liners cross" (*Selected Poems* 39). The immigrant experience thus becomes a metaphor for the finite human experience on earth. Ultimately, the poet-speaker in Ghose's poetry is compelled to look into the inner recesses of his own mind: "I sink into that darkness which is an unseen light, / my memory is made of opaque transparencies" ("The Oceans," *Selected Poems* 70).

Syed K.M. Hassan

The poetry of Zulfikar Ghose was much admired by the late Syed K.M. Hassan (1953–2009), who had begun to conduct research for this study before his sudden and untimely death in April 2009. Hassan was born and raised in Bangladesh, coming to the United States in 1984. He received his B.A. and M.A. in English from the University of Dhaka, as well as an M.A. in history. He received his Ph.D. in English from Purdue University. He worked as an English professor in Bangladesh and the United States. At the time of his death he was a tenured professor of English at Claflin University in Orangeburg, South Carolina. He is survived by his wife and three daughters. Hassan was very familiar with poetic forms in Bengali and Urdu. His area of doctoral study was modern British poetry with a focus on the poetry of W.B. Yeats and the poetry of resistance. For Hassan, poetry and ideology were to some extent inseparable. Syed Hassan never viewed himself as an American. He liked to describe himself as a "citizen of the world" (after the letters of eighteenth-century British writer Oliver Goldsmith), by which he referred to the diasporic condition of many South Asian writers and artists. Syed Hassan viewed poetry as a transnational literary genre.

Syed Hassan began (and later continued) to publish his poetry with Writers Workshop in Kolkata, India, because he viewed the work of the late Purushottam Lal as very significant for the recognition and preservation of South Asian artists writing in English. Syed Hassan published *Between Barbed Wires* (1977), *Inner Edge* (1987), *Ashes and Sparks* (1989), *Rhymes for Muslim Children* (1992), and *Burning the Olive Branch* (1995), as well as several articles, and served as the U.S. correspondent for *Holiday*, an English-language weekly with a large circulation in Bangladesh. Hassan's poetry was recognized in literary circles in his native Bangladesh. He left behind several unfinished manuscripts. The poems discussed here are from his *Collected Poems* (2003), the volume selected for the author by Hassan himself as representative of his work.

Like Ali and Ghose, Hassan's poetry is filled with imagery of historic moments in South Asia as well as literary allusions to English classics. His deep concern for political turmoil in Bangladesh is a recurring motif, as seeb in "Cry Bangladesh Cry": "Your prolific gods are falling one by one / Mujib, Taj, Manzur, Zia" (*Collected Poems* 56). Hassan's concern with social justice also recurs in his poem "Cobra Eggs": "The east dies by robbing the rich / The west thrives by robbing the poor" (*Collected Poems* 81). In "Democrazy" Hassan criticizes the United States: "It is outrageous to have Freedom / Of Speech, in the land of the deaf" (*Collected Poems* 119). He was also very sympathetic to the cause of the displaced Palestinians, as in "Dreams of Bet She'an": "Driven out of my hometown at four / For forty years in half a dozen cities" (*Collected Poems* 115).

In many of Hassan's poems the quest for self-identity is evident. In "Whole Man in Fire" the speaker asks, "Was not the whole man on fire / a test big enough to last millennia?" (*Collected Poems* 124). In "The Wrong Divide" the speaker alludes to certain ethnic stereotypes in South Asia: "Taking me for being somebody else / A Bengali not to be trusted in trade" (*Collected Poems* 43). In "Dacca 1971," during Bangladesh's year of liberation, the speaker senses his own alienation: "Perhaps I am the only beast / Imprisoned within this monstrous zoo" (*Collected Poems* 26). The quest for self-identity in Hassan's poems is ultimately a quest for truth. In the brief lyric "Whoever Is Afraid of Madness" (the closing piece of Hassan's *Collected Poems*), the speaker states that "Whoever is afraid of madness / is afraid of the truth" (*Selected Poems* 125). These lines contain a premonition of this poet's last months, spent vainly trying to recover from the effects of a stroke. Ill and unsure whether he would ever be able to write again, Syed Hassan recited the lines of the mad King Lear in his last telephone conversation with the author of this study.

Waqas Khwaja

Like the other diasporic South Asian poets discussed in this chapter, Pakistani American poet Waqas Khwaja is a college professor in the United States. Born in Pakistan, Khwaja has been a practicing lawyer and a visiting professor of law in Pakistan. He wrote columns for *The Frontier Post* and *The*

News International before migrating to the United States in 1994. He received a Ph.D. from Emory University and is a professor of English at Agnes Scott College in Decatur, Georgia. Khwaja has published two collections of poetry: *Six Geese from a Tomb at Medum* (1987) and *Mariam's Lament* (1992). His *Writers and Landscapes* (1991) is a literary travelogue. He has also published two anthologies of Pakistani literature titled *Mornings in the Wilderness* (1988) and *Short Stories from Pakistani* (1991).

In this chapter, poems from Khwaja's third collection, *No One Waits for the Train* (2007), are discussed as examples of his poetic method. The cover of this collection has a photograph of train tracks in a sepia tint. The train of Khwaja's opening poem is a symbol of an existential journey into nothingness. Readers are reminded of the "death trains" of 1947, when trains full of massacred passengers pulled into stations in the newly formed West Pakistan. The woman waiting for the train that never comes is a symbol of unfulfilled wishes: "She mutters to herself in agitation / Watching for a railway train" (*No One Waits for the Train* 13).

Waqas Khwaja is an artist in love with words. He is innovative in technique in that his poems provide a bridge between contemporary poetry in English and the poetic genres, forms, and literary devices in South Asian vernacular languages such as Hindi and Urdu.

In *No One Waits for the Train*, Khwaja presents recurring allusions to Baba Farid, Bulle Shah, Kabir, and Nanak, traditional literary figures in Urdu, Punjabi, and Hindi vernacular literature. Khwaja's poems frequently use settings of political turmoil and violent episodes in South Asian history, such as the partition of the subcontinent into India and the two nations that originally made one Pakistan in 1947, as in the speaker's account of being the sole survivor on a death train in the poem "I Tell This Without Embellishment": "Their hoard of women's breasts / And hacked limbs of infants and children" (*No One Waits for the Train* 59). In the above lines, and elsewhere too, Khwaja tends to dwell upon macabre and deathly images that give his poems a surrealistic quality. The speaker of this collection has an inner compulsion to give an account of the massacres. One wonders to what extent the speaker's voice depicts a psyche permanently scarred by witnessing the massacres. Likenesses may be perceived in the writings of survivors of the Nazi Holocaust and in the poems of South Asian Canadian poet Arnold Itwaru, in whose *Body Rites* the speaker describes scenes of a land ravaged by war and destruction.

The emerging picture of life in South Asia in Khwaja's *No One Waits for the Train* is one of continued political instability, especially in the context of contemporary political and social issues in Khwaja's native Pakistan. One can recognize this depiction of scenes of violence by Khwaja as a postcolonial worldview. One recalls Franz Fanon's observations on the meaningless violence of postcolonial societies (*The Wretched of the Earth* 89, 123). In the poem "My Inside Is Empty," Khwaja's speaker laments, "The lost ghosts of stragglers / People who have lost their way" (*No One Waits for the Train* 81). In his allusions to the well-known literary artists of the past, the speaker-poet expresses nostalgia for an older and simpler way of life in South Asia: "Just before sunset, the family took / Their spinach and rice together" ("Beyond the Wooded Slope," *No One Waits for the Train* 18).

Yet, in the midst of the violence, pain, and suffering depicted in Khwaja's poems, there are moments of beauty and lyricism in images of a past time when poetry was celebrated, as in "I Bide My Time": "with wandering kabir / and meera singing in the streets" (*No One Waits for the Train* 78). Like Agha Shahid Ali, Khwaja celebrates the beauty of his ancestors' home in Kashmir. Kashmir's landscape comes to life in the poem "The River People," in which Dal Lake is described "with its acres of lilies and water chestnuts / its fertile floating gardens" (*No One Waits for the Train* 31). However, these moments of epiphany are all fleeting. Overall, the picture of life in South Asia that emerges in *No One Waits for the Train* is one of a decadent civilization and a world gone awry.

Darius Cooper

Like the other poets discussed in this chapter, Darius Cooper, a native of Mumbai in India, received his early education in India and came to the United States for doctoral study. Having completed his Ph.D. at the University of Southern California, Cooper is a professor at Mesa College, San Diego, where he teaches courses on literature and film. His poems have appeared in journals in India and the United States.

Only one of Cooper's poems is discussed here because Cooper's work as a first-generation South Asian immigrant poet deserves recognition. This poem appears in Vilas Sarang's anthology *Indian English Poetry Since 1950: An Anthology*. Cooper's "A Crude Definition of Family" creates an unforgettable image of a poor couple and their son, whom they love. This family may be homeless or living in very unhygienic conditions, encapsulated in the words "Even lice are welcome in this square / to share happiness" (Sarang 151). This unforgettable image of human emotions amid extreme poverty and squalor is probably set in the slums of Cooper's native Mumbai, a megalopolis with high-rise buildings in close proximity to extremely unsanitary slums.

Thus, in this chapter, the diasporic South Asian poets discussed use their formal academic training to create complex poems that present the dual experiences of both immigration and postcoloniality. Hybridization, unhomeliness, and alienation are common threads that run through the poetry of A.K. Ramanujan, Shiv K. Kumar, G.S. Sharat Chandra, Agha Shahid Ali, Zulfikar Ghose, Syed Hassan, and Waqas Khwaja.

NOTE

1. The title of this chapter is inspired by Robert A. Heinlein's popular science fiction novel, *Stranger in a Strange Land* (New York: Avon, 1961).

WORKS CITED

Ali, Agha Shahid. *The Half-Inch Himalayas.* Middletown, CT: Wesleyan, 1987. Print.
Bery, Ashok. *Cultural Translation and Postcolonial Poetry.* Basingstoke, UK: Palgrave Macmillan, 2007. Print.
Fanon, Franz. *The Wretched of the Earth.* New York: Grove, 1963. Print.
Ghose, Zulfikar. *Selected Poems.* Karachi: Oxford University Press, 1991.
Hassan, Syed K.M. *Collected Poems of Syed Khwaja Moinul Hassan.* Kolkata: Writers Workshop, 2003. Print.
Heinlein, Robert A. *Stranger in a Strange Land.* New York: Avon, 1961. Print.
Khwaja, Waqas. *No One Waits for the Train.* Belgium: Alhambra, 2007. Print.
King, Bruce. *Modern Indian Poetry in English.* New Delhi: Oxford University Press, 2001. Print.
Kumar, Shiv Kumar. "Days in New York." Varnamala: Indian-English Poetry. www.geocities.com. Accessed 11 February 2005.
Patke, Rajeev. "The Ambivalence of Poetic Self-Exile: The Case of A.K. Ramanujan." http://english.chass.ncsu.edu/jouvert/v5i2/rspatk.htm. Accessed 23 August 2010.
Ramanujan, A.K. *The Collected Poems of A.K. Ramanujan.* Delhi: Oxford University Press, 1995. Print.
Ramazani, Jahan. *The Hybrid Muse: Postcolonial Poetry in English.* Chicago: University of Chicago Press, 2001. Print.
Sarang, Vilas. *Indian English Poetry Since 1950: An Anthology.* New Delhi: Orient Longman, 1990. Print.
Sharat Chandra, G.S. *Family of Mirrors.* Kansas City, Missouri: BkMk Press, Umkc, 1993. Print.
_____. "Shortchanged Lives." http://indianenglishpoet.blogspot.com. Accessed 11 February 2005.

EIGHT

"But here are the meanings": The Voices of Contemporary South Asian American Male Poets

The dominant patterns of self-reflexivity, hybridization, and exploring memories, as well as examining cross-cultural and social justice issues that have been discussed in the poetry of an earlier generation of South Asian male poets in North America, continue to appear in the poems of nineteen contemporary South Asian male poets analyzed in this chapter. Vijay Seshadri's phrase "But here are the meanings" encapsulates the complexity of this body of poetry. Like the earlier poets, several of these contemporary South Asian male poets are educators or in professions that allow them to engage in the literary arts. A few are in healthcare or engineering-related careers. This growth of South Asian poetry in the last two decades is significant because it shows that South Asians are finding their own niche in the American literary scene. Only one of the nineteen poets analyzed in this chapter has returned to India to write. Some of the poets are truly transnational in that they have lived in more than one country and their transnational experiences emerge in their poems without visible foreignization. Several use American imagery as that of the country that they identify with most closely.

This chapter analyzes the samples of poetry anthologized in *Indivisible* (Banerjee et al. 2010) as representative of the poetry of Mohammed Faisal Hadi, Vijay Seshadri, Vikas Menon, Amarnath Ravva, Srikanth Reddy, Vivek Jain, Ro Gunetilleke, Amitava Kumar, Sachin B. Patel, Ravi Chandra, Ralph Nazareth, Faisal Mohyuddin, Homraj Acharya, Kazim Ali, Ravi Shankar, Vinay Dharwadkar, Aryanil Mukherjee, Indran Amirthanayagam, and Jeet Thayil. These poets are grouped according to similarities in theme and poetic methodology, although there is some overlapping between the groups. Hence subtopic headings have not been used in this chapter.

Self-reflexivity and the ironies of the human condition recur in the poetry of Vijay Seshadri, Amarnath Ravva, Ravi Chandra, and Srikanth Reddy. Vijay Seshadri (born in 1954) came to America at the age of five, and teaches at Sarah Lawrence College. Seshadri is the recipient of several awards for poetry (*Indivisible* 30). He earned an A.B. degree from Oberlin College, and an M.F.A. from Columbia University. His published collections of poetry include *Wild Kingdom* (1996) and *The Long Meadow* (2004). In the title of this chapter, Seshadri's poem "The Disappearance" is quoted: "bamboo-tough and thickly clustered, / The myths are somewhere else, but here are the meanings" (*Indivisible* 31). This poem is about the many roles that the speaker has played in life, which the speaker looks back upon as if viewing a series of snapshots. The self-reflexivity in Seshadri's poem is significant because most of the contemporary poets discussed in this chapter reflect upon self-identity in the environment they live in.

Seshadri's poems present unique uses of "you" and "I." The commonplace and often overused second-person pronoun of familiar American speech is cleverly used by Seshadri to desconstruct the speaker and the listener in some of his poems, such as "Elegy." The speaker of "Elegy" is instructing the listener about a man who is dead leaving pages of unsolved equations in an abandoned old town. This "elegy" fuses the listener with the dead man, for in the elegy's third and final stanza the reader makes the connection that this elegy is for the lives of common people: "until his death becomes your death. / You will restore his confiscated minutes to him one by one" (*Indivisible* 32). One recalls modernist poems such as W.H. Auden's "The Unknown Citizen." This preoccupation with death recurs in Seshadri's "The Dream I Didn't Have," where the speaker is dead on an autopsy table and the police officer gives the coroner a form to sign, and the speaker reflects, "I felt along my length his long riverine incision / Outside it was Chicago" (*Indivisible* 33). The macabre element in this poem is striking, as is the intensity of emotion encapsulated in the piece titled "Memoir." In "Memoir," the recollections are of experiences of shame, embarrassment, and guilt, of mistakes made in communicating with other human beings. The opening lines state the speaker's position on the hidden stories of people's lives: "Orwell says somewhere that no one ever writes the real story of their life / The real story of a life is the story of its humiliations" (*Indivisible* 33).

Images of contemporary American life that are evocative of the decentered world of the postmodern artist appear in the poems of Amarnath Ravva. Ravva was born in New York, and holds a B.A. in comparative literature from the University of California, Berkeley, and an M.F.A. in writing and integrated media from the California Institute of the Arts (*Indivisible* 69). In Ravva's poem "I am Burning a Pig in My Room, Apollinaire," the speaker addresses a person who is wounded in the head from a war (*Indivisible* 69). In the middle of the poem, the reader realizes that this poem is about the memory of the person who died of the head wound and an injection: "but you're / the stiff in the photo" (*Indivisible* 70).

In "Bear Scat Flat," the speaker describes a setting where a bear-skin rug is a central image that reminds readers of violent endings. The speaker looks at his female companion Liz: "over the table the bear the rug / between us" (*Indivisible* 73). The poem titled "the spectacle of a few trees in spring, off the 5" is a memory poem by a male speaker who remembers his youth in Los Angeles. The speaker is at a rest stop/rest area off the highway with his companion, watching birds mate (*Indivisible* 74). The speaker describes the landscape around Los Angeles from his younger days before the urbanization extended to the hills (*Indivisible* 75). He remembers being with a girl and thinking about sex. Then he is older and meets a woman who is a painter with whom he goes to clubs, and he remembers, "Back then we learned the city / by having sex in the car, watched" (*Indivisible* 75). The rite of passage that the speaker remembers is recognizably American.

The voices of diverse people emerge in the personae depicted by Ravi Chandra, who states, "I find affinity with people of many diasporas in the San Francisco Bay area while being rooted as a South Asian American" (*Indivisible* 137). Chandra attended Stanford Medical School and "he practices psychiatry at a community mental health clinic" serving "an Asian and Russian immigrant population." He has been successful with slam poetry (*Indivisible* 137).

In the poem "Cleanup on Aisle #3," the speaker ponders why every type of person has a counterpart in a type of food (in America) when it comes to stereotyping ethnic groups. The speaker admits to spending hours in the aisles of a supermarket trying to find his counterpart in food. He realizes that his search is "Existential Hunger" by concluding "it's what's inside that counts" (*Indivisible* 138). In "The Old Man Speaks," the speaker is a physician tending to Mr. Wise in room 243. This patient was injured by either a falling tree or a tree limb, and is being treated for cracked ribs and a collapsed lung. The doctor tries to make conversation by asking what kind of a tree was involved in the accident. The closing of the poem is the irony of the patient's answer: "Apple, he whispers. It / was *beautiful*" (*Indivisible* 139).

Self-reflexivity and the ironies of the human condition are emerging themes in the poetry of Srikanth Reddy, an award-winning South Asian American poet serving as an assistant professor of English at the University of Chicago. Born in Chicago, Reddy is a graduate of the Iowa Writers' Workshop and the doctoral program in English at Harvard University (*Indivisible* 80). In the poem "Jungle Book," the speaker remembers that as they were in the jungle, he queried his friend about the nature of sadness. The poem takes on a mythical aspect as the friend hands him a jackfruit and asks him to break open a seed. The interior of the seed has a new plant that grows and puts out jackfruit blossoms. Then comes sadness as the blossoms fall: "but when I said your name they blew everywhere" (*Indivisible* 81). The sadness may be interpreted as one of lost love.

In "Scarecrow Elegy" Reddy's speaker takes a page of poetry, walks into a sugarcane field, and inserts the page into the upraised hand of the scarecrow (*Indivisible* 81). The ink is bleached out by the sun, a white rectangle among the sickles of the sugarcane cutters, and the poem acquires a new significance: "worksongs rising / over it all. So then I said the poem aloud, my version" (*Indivisible* 82). Hybridization is present in Reddy's work through the central images of the jackfruit and sugarcane.

In the poem "Fundamentals of Esperanto," the speaker lectures on the rules of Esperanto, the history of Esperanto, moving into his own memories, and his journeys in real life and in his readings (*Indivisible* 84–86). The speaker would like to develop the use of Esperanto to counteract the widespread use of computer languages and "mutating patois." By composing an epic in Esperanto, the speaker hopes that future generations "may dwell in this song / and find comfort in its true texture frame" (*Indivisible* 86). Reddy's prose poem "Corruption" is also about words, ink, writing, and the glowing body of a cuttlefish soon after it dies: "phosphorescence reaches its greatest intensity a few days after death, then / ebbs away as the body decays. You can read by this light" (*Indivisible* 87).

Hybridity, immigrants' points of view, and self-reflexivity appear in the poetry of Kazim Ali, Faisal Mohyuddin, Mohammad Faisal Hadi, and Ralph Nazareth. Award-winning writer Kazim Ali teaches at Oberlin College and in the University of Southern Maine's Stonecoast M.F.A. program. Kazim Ali's family is from southern India (*Indivisible* 191). His poems present speakers who examine aspects of the self, as in "The River's Address," where the "river-citizen" follows the course of the river and the poem is the speech of the river itself. The river becomes a source of renewal, of inspiration, of exploring the inner self: "River-chases, compass-worn, here the source spills to the sea, / and here the waters wend from the seas back to the source" (*Indivisible* 191). The poem "Thicket" is about fathers, sons, God the Father, and human beings as his children. The father begins as a believer but at the closing of the poem the situation has changed: "Neither one of them seeking to see Him, / not saying His name, not asking to be saved" (*Indivisible* 192).

The poem titled "Event" presents a persona or speaker who presents an aspect of the poet himself. The "event" in the poem is perhaps a visit to a museum with a companion named Catherine, whose comments on paintings appear in italics at the beginning and end of the poem. The poem contains references to tombs and Egyptian artifacts, and closes with Catherine's line, *"There is no door, no way to get in"* (*Indivisible* 193). The message of this closing line applies to the poem itself, where the "event" itself cannot be placed by the reader.

In contrast to the absence of specific locations in the postmodern poems of Kazim Ali, Faisal Mohyuddin's poems are about places, people, and memories. Mohyuddin states, "Being a Pakistani Punjabi Muslim Midwestern American has infused and confused my existence since 1978" (*Indivisible* 148). Mohyuddin holds a B.A. from Carleton College and an M.S. in education from Northwestern University, and is working on an M.F.A. in fiction writing at Columbia College, Chicago. He is also an award-winning poet who teaches English at Highland Park High School (*Indivisible* 148).

Faisal Mohyuddin's elegy "Ayodhya" takes on the subject of religious conflict, religious hatred, and communal violence in the Indian subcontinent. The subtitle of the poem states that it was composed after the Babri Masjid massacre at Ayodhya, India, in 1992. This elegy is for the speaker's childhood friend Husham. The two friends grew up in Ayodhya, going to school and playing together. Husham was a Muslim and the speaker is a Hindu, for the city of Ayodhya had people of different religions. The speaker remembers one incident in his family's history in which his uncle cursed at his father for bringing his Muslim friend into their Hindu Brahmin home. The speaker's father was a close friend of the deceased Husham's father and used to address him as "Bhaiya" (brother) (*Indivisible* 150). Husham was a teacher and writer whose Pakistani-born wife Jamila often urged him to emigrate to Pakistan from India. The speaker imagines Husham at his old wooden desk hiding behind a wall of books at the time of the riot in which he lost his life. The speaker smashed his statues of Hindu deities upon learning of his friend's death. Every year, the speaker visits Husham's grave, and remembers the Hindu and Urdu songs they sang together in their boyhood, leaving their hometown with a bleak realization: "This is a city still devoid of faith, a city wounded / and bleeding, a city once ours to trust, once ours to pass on" (*Indivisible* 154). In this poem, Mohyuddin has created a brilliant piece with a lasting message about the need for religious tolerance and harmony in the Indian subcontinent.

The message of tolerance and the need for South Asian immigrants to accept America's diversity also appears in Mohyuddin's "Blood Harmonies," where a young man, a Muslim American, remembers his mother's attempts to keep her five children from socializing with non–Muslims: "in blood harmony, she would say, meaning / brother and sister, Muslim and Muslim, blood and blood" (*Indivisible* 154). The young male speaker badly wants to get acquainted with a girl he has seen but his mother's views permanently affect his social life (*Indivisible* 155). Mohyuddin's criticism of the sub-culture of South Asian immigrants in America is brought to life through the confusion of the speaker in "Blood Harmonies." Humor directed at the attempts of both women and men to find a perfect partner surfaces in Mohyuddin's piece titled "Poem Inspired by a Note Found Scrawled onto the Inside Cover of *One Day at a Time in Al-Anon* Sitting on a Bookshelf at Café Ambrosia, Evanston, Illinois." The speaker is male and he imagines the writer of the note to be a woman who has gone down to a frog pond (literally). The "note" at the beginning of the poem reads, "When my prince charming does come along / I'll be down at the pond kissing frogs" (*Indivisible* 155). In this poem, the fantasies of both the speaker and the woman who wrote the "note" are presented with humor.

For Chicago-born Mohammed Faisal Hadi, the lives of immigrants and the experience of being raised Muslim are preferred poetic subjects. Like Mohyuddin, Hadi is a public school teacher. Hadi is also "involved with Asian American art groups and immigrant community projects" in the Chicago region (*Indivisible* 12). He is a graduate of the University of Illinois at Urbana–Champaign (*Indivisible* 12). In the poem "Public Benefits," the speaker describes the predicament of newly arrived immigrants coping with bureaucracy and getting familiar with Social Security, American supermarkets, and utility companies; at the same time "we stack the evidence, / are asked to repeat ourselves" (*Indivisible* 15).

In addition to showing empathy for newly arrived immigrants, Hadi also depicts the inner dilemmas of Muslim women and men observing Islamic traditions. In the brief poem "Fatima," the speaker seeks to create the point of view of a Muslim woman who goes from fear to isolation until all her groceries are used up (*Indivisible* 13). Then she ventures out, head covered, to see the world outside: "the laundry the church the / bank the masjid the police" (*Indivisible* 14). The speaker empathizes with his uncle who fails to slaughter a goat at the Eid festival in the poem titled "My Uncle, Failing to Slaughter the Goat of his 12th Eid" (*Indivisible* 12–13). The uncle is ridiculed by his observers and appears to walk into another world: "You turn the pommel in your hand, upending fates. You walk backwards into a new land" (*Indivisible* 13).

Transnational experiences and history emerge in the poems of Ralph Nazareth, who emigrated from India. Nazareth studied at Bombay University in India, then earned his doctorate in English literature from SUNY at Stony Brook (*Indivisible* 140). He is a professor at Nassau Community College and managing editor of Yuganta Press in Stamford, Connecticut (*Indivisible* 140).

Nazareth's poem "A Question for Vaclav Havel" presents a speaker who describes an unexpected (and imaginary) interview with the former Czech president and writer Vaclav Havel. The speaker thinks of Havel's plays and describes him as a "former absurdist." Suddenly, the conversation turns to pottery, and the poem closes with an echo of T.S. Eliot's *Prufrock*, with a play on the word "pot" from the earlier reference to pottery but with the underlying connotation of "pot": "Then rising and grasping me by the arm, he says, breaking into a grin, 'Let us go then, you and I, and throw a pot!'" (*Indivisible* 141). In "Red Eye" the speaker is sitting on an airplane flying east next to a man who reads a document in Farsi. The speaker describes his fellow passenger as having the profile of Cyrus the Great, and reading while the other passengers sleep: "travelers all, stewards of the earth, we dream red-eyed / He alone keeps vigil with the lines which were unmoving" (*Indivisible* 141). Historical analogies also appear in Nazareth's poem "Horse Play," in which a four-year-old boy is engaged in playing horses with his father, who has read to his son about Alexander the Great's horse Bucephalus. The child plays Alexander and the father/speaker notes that "I took him up in my arms / this fallen fond imperator" (*Indivisible* 142). This poem captures a happy moment in the life of a father and his son.

Hybridization, transnationalism, and immigrant perspectives are presented in the poems of Sachin B. Patel, Vivek Jain, Ro Gunetilleke, and Indran Amirthanayagam. Sachin B. Patel was born in Gujarat, India, and came to the United States at the young age of four. Patel received his undergraduate degree in English from Carleton College in Minnesota, and practices internal and critical care medicine in North Carolina. According to Patel, "Through ten childhood migrations, it was living and working in a 'Patel Motel' that rooted my Desiamericanism" (*Indivisible* 111). In the poem "In the Business of Erasing History," the speaker describes the daily routines of a motel where guests leave, rooms are cleaned, and the next set of guests enters. The speaker imagines the scenes that have taken place in the rooms where the cleaning erases history: "We are in the business / of spraying, removing, scrubbing, and vacuuming — erasing" (*Indivisible* 112).

In the poem "The Blacktop Gospels" the speaker remembers his childhood, when he was ashamed of his South Asian ethnicity and his mother speaking Gujarati to him. He imagined telling his classmates that his father was a famous cardiologist "when in reality he / manned / the decaying bullet-holed 7-Eleven on Dekalb Pike" (*Indivisible* 113). The speaker assimilates better with diverse children in school as he becomes absorbed in basketball and finds common interests with his peers (*Indivisible* 114–16). The identity of the athlete in school seems to be more significant than ethnic identity. This poem by Patel encapsulates common experiences of the children of South Asian first-generation immigrants growing up in America.

Vivek Jain was born in Bhopal, India, in 1980, and spent his early life in Appalachia. Jain earned his undergraduate degree in biochemistry from the University of Virginia, and is a resident physician. He finds the search for self-knowledge to be a "lifelong endeavor" (*Indivisible* 96). Vivek Jain's poetry uses hybrid themes and images from India, as seen in the two poems "Ananda's Story" and "December, 1984," which re-create the scenes of the Bhopal Gas tragedy of December 1984, one of the world's worst industrial disasters at a Union Carbide plant in Bhopal. In "Anand's Story" there is a play on the meaning of the word "Anand," which means "joy" in the Hindi language. When the toxic gases escape over the city of Bhopal, killing several thousand people, Anand (the poem's speaker) wanders away into the hills. The images of this poem remind readers that the dark cloud of gas was followed by the smoke of mass cremations of the dead. This disaster was made by human beings: "god didn't make me / I wasn't his to make" (*Indivisible* 97). In "December, 1984," the speaker recalls that his own brother suffered and died. He imagines his brother being cremated on a mass pyre: "as woodpiles' flames confuse brown / skin for bark. He is displaced" (*Indivisible* 98). The poem closes with the terrifying image of lines of funeral pyres blazing on the shores of the River Narmada on a December night (*Indivisible* 98).

In "Poem for a Would-be Revolutionary, My Father," the speaker remembers that his aunt told them his father was arrested, beaten with bamboo sticks, and put in prison under the government of the late Indian prime minister Indira Gandhi. This poem needs annotation for the contemporary reader because the speaker is referring to infamous statutes and oppressive acts of Indira Gandhi's regime.

Sri Lankan–born poet Ro Gunetilleke also writes of the unrest and tragedies of South Asia. Gunetilleke states that "I lived through the 1983 communal riots in Colombo Sri Lanka and shed my national identity" (*Indivisible* 99). Gunetilleke lives in California and publishes both poems and short stories. In the poem "Lost Column," the speaker composes an elegy for a man who was kidnapped along with his satchel of writings, and then murdered in the forest: "they erased you / word by word" (*Indivisible* 100). In "Spirited Away," there is a play on "spirit," or alcohol, in which the speaker remembers sitting in his grandfather's lap in Sri Lanka, listening to a Marconi shortwave radio. The grandfather is drinking the strong drink called "coconut arrack" and sitting by the light of a gas lamp. The radio's antenna is a hairpin held by the child speaker in the year 1956 (*Indivisible* 100–101). The radio brings bad news: "Fires burn / Jaffna to Colombo" (*Indivisible* 101). The child then bends the hairpin antenna to get another radio station while the grandfather closes the window and finishes his drink (*Indivisible* 101). This narrative poem is very effective in illuminating scenes of family life in rural Sri Lanka in the 1950s. The radio preceded the television in bringing news and entertainment from different countries to people in the rural communities of South Asia.

Indran Amirthanayagam lived in Sri Lanka until the age of eight and in London until age fourteen, then moved to Hawaii (*Indivisible* 209). He is an award-winning poet writing in three languages — English, Spanish, and French. Amirthanayagam works as a U.S. diplomat, and has published poetry collections titled *The Elephants of Reckoning* (1993), *Ceylon R.I.P* (2001), *El Infierno de los Pajaros* (2001), *El Hombre Que Recoge Nidos* (2005), and *The Splintered Face: Tsunami Poems* (2008).

In "Runner," "Girl Dressed," and "The City, with Elephants," the speakers present numerous Sri Lankan images, suggesting the poet's ties to his early years and his family ancestry. In "Runner," the speaker remembers his admiration for a young Sri Lankan who did well in the 1972 Olympic Games in Munich (*Indivisible* 209–10). The speaker views an old snapshot of the young man in Munich, and wonders what became of him: "Perhaps he's an accountant / or clerk, some cog in an office" (*Indivisible* 210).

"Girl Dressed" presents images of a young girl dressed in her Sunday best on the seashore "by fisher huts, thatched / with fronds" (*Indivisible* 211). The setting is tropical (presumably Sri Lankan) and the girl wears her Sunday dress because she has no other clothing, for it is "two weeks now / after the waves raged" her home and her neighborhood (*Indivisible* 210). In the poem "The City, with Elephants," the elephant is reminiscent of Rienzi Crusz's use of elephant imagery in his poems. For Amirthanayagam, the elephant symbolizes everyday life in a Sri Lankan setting: "The elephants of reckoning / are lean and hungry" (*Indivisible* 212–13).

Hybrid imagery and themes of South Asian life and experiences surface in the writings of expatriate Nepali poet Homraj Acharya. Acharya describes himself as "a rural Nepali and an urban Washingtonian, with a buffalo-riding past and a Metro-riding present" (*Indivisible* 176). Acharya works as a public policy analyst in Washington, D.C., and writes in both English and Nepali. He is a graduate of the University of Colorado at Boulder and American University, and has published one translation, *The Principal's Secret* (1997); two collections of poetry, *Jecvit Kankal* (1999) and *Alubarima Deuta* (2003); and a novel, *Nirdosh Kaidi* (1995).

In "The Silk-Cotton Tree," the speaker remembers his boyhood and the tall silk-cotton tree that he once climbed. The tree is its own world, a home to beetles, to vultures, to bees, and to thieves who wait and watch (*Indivisible* 176–77). The flowers of the silk-cotton and its saplings can be fed to the farmer's buffalo, while the fluff (or silk-cotton) of the seed pods can be used like cotton wool, generating a myth: "It is said that a pillow made of silk-cotton / will talk to you at night" (*Indivisible* 177). Under the tree is a hollow where the villagers set up a shrine to perform religious rites and a goat sacrifice (*Indivisible* 178).

If the scene under the flowering silk-cotton tree encapsulates the images of life in a rural Nepali setting, Acharya's poem "The Kerosene Stove" tells the story of a male school teacher in the city, possibly Nepal's capital of Kathmandu (inferred from the allusions to Kathmandu newspapers) (*Indivisible* 179). The kerosene stove is moved around in the teacher's tiny dwelling. It was his wife's marriage dowry, and is used regularly to cook meals and boil water for the tea that is made several times daily by the thrifty Nepali housewife. The husband has several academic credentials — B.A., B.Ed., M.A., certificate from the Kwality Computer Institute, certificate from the Fluorescent Language Institute, M.Ed., and L.L.B. (law degree) (*Indivisible* 179). This overqualified individual does not have suitable employment and is looking for a better life. This poem satirizes the chronic problems with inadequate employment in Nepal, where a significant proportion of the population seeks work in India and in countries all over the world. The character in "The Kerosene Stove" is an adjunct professor in socioeconomics and anthropology from 6 A.M. to 8 A.M. at a college campus, and "from 9 a.m. to 5 p.m. a teacher of English / at the Celestial Stars Secondary School" (*Indivisible* 179). Every day, he reads ads in local newspapers looking for a new job. Then he comes to the realization that all his dreams are futile and all jobs are daily repetitions of certain tasks (*Indivisible* 180).

The transnational and hybrid qualities of South Asian poetry in English are best illustrated by the work and career of contemporary poet Jeet Thayil, who is the recipient of American and European grants and has lived in India from 2004. Thayil states "I am a Malayali, Hongkonger, Bombayman, and New Yorker (not American), and my nation is the Republic of English" (*Indivisible* 234). Thayil was born in the state of Kerala in India in 1959 (Thayil, *Bloodaxe Book* 226). He was educated in Hong Kong, New York, and Bombay, and has published *These Errors Are Correct* (2008) and *English* (2004) (*Indivisible* 234). He has also edited the landmark collection of canonical and contemporary poets titled *The Bloodaxe Book of Contemporary Indian Poets* (2008). Thayil finds connections and continuities in almost two centuries' worth of South Asian Indian poetry in English spread over multiple continents (*Bloodaxe Book* 23). Thayil has moved toward a wide range of formal arrangements in his recent poetry (*Bloodaxe Book* 226).

In the fourteen-line poem titled "September 10, 2001" (the day before the 9/11 terrorist attack on New York), the speaker describes the experience of utter loneliness and silence, when the speaker longs to step out into the street and stop "a man without hope" or "a woman bent double" and tell them "that each of us walks with the same / impossible burden" (*Indivisible* 234). In the excerpt from "Premonition," the speaker has a dream of a Sunday in summer spent with his lost love: "I reached for you, but you weren't there. / Someone looked at me with pity and fear" (*Indivisible* 235). In the second movement of the excerpt, the male speaker remembers the words of his dead wife: "and our old argument still burns. / *How soon will you forget me if I die?*" (*Indivisible* 235).

Sources of medieval Indian history are used for Thayil's "Letter from a Mughal Emperor, 2006," in which the speaker views India as a temporary home: "A hundred years or a day, in the end you'll leave this place" (*Indivisible* 237). In "Flight," travelers return to their original home in the Indian subcontinent after having lived in other lands. They realize that their homeland has changed, and that the feeling of home is not limited to a geographical location: "I make my home with you, in transit. / The continent drops away and reappears" (*Indivisible* 239). This poem captures the essence of unhomeliness of the diasporean's transnational experience.

Hybridization, anxiety, alienation, and unhomeliness also appear in the poems of Vikas Menon, Amitava Kumar, Aryanil Mukherjee, Ravi Shankar, and Vinay Dharwadkar. Vikas Menon has strong affinities with the culture of Kerala in India, although he was born in Ohio and raised in Pennsylvania. Menon received his M.F.A. in poetry from Brooklyn College and his M.A. in literature from St. Louis University, and he lives in New York City. He is employed as a grant writer for a health and human services agency, and is active in literary organizations (*Indivisible* 38). In the poem "Radha," the speaker ponders about Radha, the beloved of Krishna, imagining intimate moments with Radha in a contemporary setting. The object of the speaker's exotic fantasy may be an actual woman he is looking at on the subway train rise as he reflects on various ancient Hindu myths. The American present and the ancient Indian allusions blend as the speaker observes, "I feel her narrow stare, / she, who had strapped his sweatsoaked body" (*Indivisible* 39).

Menon's brief poem "Drown" contains startling images of drowning and the frailty of the human body: "He will arrive like us: / spitting water from his mouth" (*Indivisible* 40). The speaker suggests that even a god is negatively affected underwater. In "Urdu Funk: The Gentle Art of Subtitles," the speaker satirizes love poetry from South Asia with veiled women, secret lovers, and engaged fathers. The speaker in this poem is a man who does not wish to be involved in such a stereotypical South Asian family drama: "don't develop an affair with / me, this is the dust of the storm in you" (*Indivisible* 41). This scenario is not uniquely South Asian but rather a situation rooted in patriarchal family structure, as seen in the plots of *Romeo and Juliet* and

Westside Story. Menon's speaker rejects the romantic scenario as well as the culture in which the scenario is rooted. Thus Menon's poetry re-examines some of the received traditions of South Asian poetry in Indian vernacular languages.

Surrealist imagery appears in the postmodern poems of engineering mathematician Aryanil Mukherjee, who writes poetry in English and Bengali. Mukherjee was raised in Kolkata, India, and lives in Cincinnati, Ohio (*Indivisible* 205). He edits a Bengali/Bangla literary magazine, and is an English-Bangla bi-directional translator with eight books of poetry and poetics, including *Kabitaar anyakonakhaane / Another Place for Poetry* (2010), *chaturangik / SQUARES* (co-author Pat Clifford, 2009), *Sunaamir Ek Bachhar Par / One Year After the Tsunami* (2008), *late night correspondence* (2008), *Hawamorager Man / Weathercock Mind* (2004), and *Khelaar Naam Sabujayan / Greening Games* (2000). Mukherjee offers an explanation for his method: "Resisting the largely monoglotic nature of American poetry, I continue to work in two languages, in between and around" (*Indivisible* 205). In this choice of dual languages for poetic composition, Mukherjee's work is a reminder of the beginnings of South Asian poetry in Kolkata and the many decades in which poets wrote in both Bangla and English. The Indian subcontinent continues to produce bilingual poets.

Aryanil Mukherjee's poetry contains both American and South Asian images. In the brief poem "after promise," the setting is clearly American, a park where, in a light breeze, the speaker contemplates diversity: "Lincoln park — too crowded this afternoon / The leaves are dead, instead flags of a million countries flutter" (*Indivisible* 206). In the poem "treeforms :: the touch of language," the poet has sets of vertical and horizontal lines in the left margin of the page. The speaker ponders over various images from everyday life, over lines and curves, trying to make meaning from them: "broken down the ant-lines on the wall / from here to childhood" (*Indivisible* 206). Mukherjee often uses double colons for the titles of his poems, as in the nightmarish "memory writings::picnic," in which a group of people are cooking outdoors at a picnic in the forest. There is clearly a play on the Bengali/Bangla word for "picnic" ("banbhojan"), which literally means "forest feast," when two green monsters come down from the trees and eat a woman named Sharmi: "wok upturned on the grill a picnic reversed / forest feasting on human limbs" (*Indivisible* 207). The reader is left wondering about the actual relationship of the speaker to the woman named Sharmi.

In contrast to the surrealistic fantasy world created by Aryanil Mukherjee, the poetry of Amitava Kumar piles layer upon layer of hybrid images to examine social justice issues across cultures. Kumar is a professor of English at Vassar College and has published *Husband of a Fanatic* (2005), *Bombay–Lon-*

don–New York (2002), *Passport Photos* (2000), the novel *Home Products* (2007), and a work on the global war on terror titled *A Foreigner Carrying in the Crook of His Arm a Tiny Bomb* (2010).

In the long poem "Mistaken Identity," Kumar's speaker narrates almost endless lists of South Asian stories, including many violent ones, that can all be ascribed to mistaken identities. This poem is entirely heteroglossic, and the speaker questions the validity of the act of naming itself. Because naming and identification are inadequate, the poem does not have a closure: "The poem about mistaken identity is in a sense not about names at all: / its just about declaring that it is never enough. For if it were enough..." (*Indivisible* 105).

In "Against Nostalgia," the speaker is a diasporic Indian reflecting back on past images of his own history, his family's history, and his reading of accounts of ancient India by the Greek writer Megasthenes (*Indivisible* 106–10). The poem has a refrain-like line from an old popular song: "Those were the days." In rejecting the concept of nostalgia, the speaker immerses himself in these nostaligic waves to understand that one cannot go back to the land one has left behind. Perhaps the only way to preserve those moments lost in time is in one's poetry: "What will come back during evenings / like this one to haunt you are the poems" (*Indivisible* 110).

For Ravi Shankar, an associate professor and the poet-in-residence at Central Connecticut State University, "language's mystical inflections" are highly significant (*Indivisible* 198). Shankar is the founding editor of *Drunken Boat*, an international online journal of the arts. His published works include *Instrumentality* (2004), a collection of poems (*Indivisible* 198). He is also coeditor of *Language for a New Century: Contemporary Poetry from Asia, the Middle-East and Beyond* (2008).

Ravi Shankar's "The Flock's Reply to the Passionate Shepherd" is a parody of sixteenth-century English poet Christopher Marlowe's classic love poem "The Passionate Shepherd to His Love." In Shankar's poem, the sheep turn on their shepherd, an anticlimactic scenario, and accuse him of wasting time wooing his "nymph," whom they consider "a tease." The sheep are attached to their shepherd and invite him to join them in play: "If such delights your mind, might move / Then live with us and be our love" (*Indivisible* 199).

In the poem "Before Sunrise, San Francisco," the speaker is sitting in a bar drinking and thinking about the past, sleepless, noting, "The only eyes on you are two / Pimentos stuffed into olives" (*Indivisible* 200). This surrealistic image quietly emphasizes the speaker's loneliness. Similar arrangements of discordant images set the tone of Ravi Shankar's "Return to Mumbai," where the speaker presents images of the megapolis and its crowded suburbs:

"Bombay no longer, the island / Circumscribed by water exhausts" (*Indivisible* 201).

Well established as a critic and editor of Indian poetry in English, Vinay Dharwadkar is also a poet. Dharwadkar was born in Pune, India, and educated at Delhi University and the University of Chicago. He is a professor of Indian languages and literatures at the University of Wisconsin, Madison. Dharwadkar has also translated modern Hindi, Marathi, Urdi, and Punjabi poetry (*Indivisible* 202). His work appears in the volume *Sunday at the Lodi Gardens* (1994). He has edited *The Oxford Anthology of Modern Indian Poetry* (1995), *The Collected Poems of A.K. Ramanujan* (1995), *The Collected Essays of A.K. Ramanujan* (1999), and *Cosmopolitan Geographies: New Locations in Literature and Culture* (2001).

In Dharwadkar's memory poem "Thirty Years Ago, in a Suburb of Bombay," the speaker remembers an episode from his childhood when he played a game of marbles with the one-armed boy next door. The one-armed boy was older than the speaker and highly skilled at playing with marbles. The speaker lost a jarful of marbles, and lay at night remembering his loss "of the jarful of small bright possessions I hadn't / told my mother I'd lost in someone else's game" (*Indivisible* 204). In "Draft of Excavations" the poet presents a series of images of a medieval Indian city that has been excavated: "below the stench of slums / a blueprint history" (*Indivisible* 203).

Dharwadkar's poems end on images and scenes from everyday life with unique and memorable qualities. In "Houseflies," the flies describe their mating scene: "as we mate in every facet / of our big domed eyes" (Thayil, *Bloodaxe Book* 89). In a brief poem titled "Words and Things," the speaker ponders the act of using words and naming objects, concluding that "words forget themselves / and move among the things you cannot name" (*Bloodaxe Book* 90). In "Life Cycles," the speaker contemplates farmers working in a rural area in India: "all the work is done by hand: bare bodies, / bare heads, bare hands. Trees blur into the sky" (*Bloodaxe Book* 91). Scenes from the interior of a family's home appear in "Walking Toward the Horizon," in which familiar images of disorder and daily life are presented without the actual presence of the house's owners. The two rooms being described create scenes like two still-life paintings. Outside the home, the scene changes to a city street with "newspapers in vending machines, a woman walking; / a patch of blue; and a horizon, out of sight somewhere" (*Bloodaxe Book* 90).

It is important to recognize the continuities of themes and imagery that exist in the work of the older generation of male South Asian poets in America and that of the contemporary poets discussed in this chapter. There are also similarities between the poets discussed in this chapter and the contemporary poets from the Indian subcontinent discussed in chapter four.

WORKS CITED

Banerjee, Neelanjana, et al., eds. *Indivisible: An Anthology of Contemporary South Asian American Poetry*. Fayetteville: University of Arkansas Press, 2010. Print.

Thayil, Jeet, ed. *The Bloodaxe Book of Contemporary Indian Poets*. Highgreen, Northumberland, UK: Bloodaxe Books, 2008. Print.

NINE

"Other" Histories:
South Asian Women Poets in
North America and the Caribbean

The inner landscape of South Asian women poets in North America and the Caribbean often depicts the two dilemmas of being an artist in exile and of being a female artist. The poetry of Meena Alexander, Sujata Bhatt, Chitra Divakaruni, Mahadai Das, and Ramabai Espinet opens up perspectives on women's processes of self-discovery, of defining their existence not only in South Asian society but globally as well. In the lyrics of these women poets, there emerges a tremendous ambivalence, or an apparent dichotomy, between the woman artist as a thinker and her female body.

Female sexuality has generally been a taboo subject in South Asia in colonial and post-colonial times. And although ancient and medieval poetry in the classical and vernacular languages of South Asia contains significant amounts of erotic imagery and symbolism, such materials diminished significantly in South Asian poetry starting in the nineteenth century. This decline is presumably traceable to the colonial domination of India by Victorian England. The earlier tradition of erotic as well as mystical poetry was mainly composed by male poets. The poetry of South Asian women poets flowered from the late nineteenth century onward as more educational opportunities became available for women. However, the poetry of South Asian women writers in the late nineteenth and early twentieth centuries, whether in English or in vernacular languages, continued to express love and sexuality in platonic and even somewhat prudish terms well into the twentieth century. Some well-known South Asian women poets who dwell on platonic love include Toru Dutt, Sarojini Naidu, the Hindi-language writer Mahadevi Varma, the Bengali poet Nabanita Deb Sen, and others. The traditional imagery of South Asian women poets is evocative of emotion rather than sexuality. Somehow, custom and tradition steer propriety of linguistic expression away from examining the life of the woman's body.

Without getting tangled in the discussions of biological determinism that are permanently connected with the oppressive history of women, especially in South Asian cultures, it is important to remember that the American feminist poet Adrienne Rich, in her innovative collection *The Dream of a Common Language* (1978), showed readers several decades ago that women's poetry basically lacked a "received" tradition of poetic language that reiterated the condition of being a woman. In exploring the history of South Asian women as "others," contemporary diasporic Indian poets explore the possibilities of creating a poetic language that is universally adaptable to expressing the condition of being a woman, and of the poet as an artist who possesses a woman's body.

In the Caribbean, there are relatively few Indo-Caribbean female poets. The late Mahadai Das is the most widely recognized poet in this group. The lack of literary publication from Indo-Caribbean women is ascribed to "the dubious 'protection' of a traditional, domestic role" by Caribbean literary critics such as Denise de Caires Narain (169).

The poems of Meena Alexander, Chitra Divakaruni, and Sujata Bhatt present various aspects of women's processes of self-discovery. There emerges a dichotomy between the artist as a thinker, a figure of wisdom with whom the poet identifies, and the poet whose psyche resides within a woman's body, which is an object of sexual desire and a medium for childbearing. There are underlying analogies between the birth of poems and the birthing of babies. These discoveries made by the postmodern woman artist who seemingly inhabits two disparate worlds — either one of intellectual pursuits and artistic expression or one of the traditional role of finding a partner, childbearing, and raising a family — are not unique to South Asian women poets. The life and writings of the late Sylvia Plath contain comparable themes and imagery. In order to be successful as scholars and writers, generations of women have had to walk away from the choice of bearing and raising children.

In the context of readers in South Asia, in the everyday life and popular culture of South Asian peoples, motherhood is admired but female sexuality is a taboo subject. However, in the postmodern context, the veil appears to be lifting in contemporary women's poetry published in South Asian regional languages as well as in the lyrics of diasporic South Asian women poets. The present focus is upon the denotation and connotation of erotic imagery in poems by Alexander, Divakaruni, and Bhatt. The discovery of oneself as a sexual being is part of the mature poet's discovery of selfhood and self-knowledge, of uncovering one's sensual existence in the phenomenal world.

Meena Alexander began her poetic career in India, where she was born and educated. Later Alexander emigrated to the United States and became based in New York. She was educated in Khartoum, Sudan, and Nottingham, England (Bahri). After obtaining her Ph.D. from Nottingham University, she taught at Delhi University, Central Institute of Hyderabad, and Hyderabad University. In 1979, Alexander and her husband moved to New York City, where they raised their son and daughter (Bahri). Currently she is a distinguished professor of English at Hunter College and the Graduate Center of the City University of New York. Alexander's poetry suggests that the images of her ancestral roots in the Indian state of Kerala continue to influence her poetry.

Meena Alexander's perspectives on women's sexuality include images of the lover, of pregnancy and childbirth, and of love and death. Alexander depicts sex as both birth and death, as beginning and ending. Motherhood in Alexander's poems can be painful and brutal. In her autobiography *Fault Lines* (1993), Alexander writes:

> But even there, I wonder. Everything that comes to me is hyphenated. A woman poet, a woman poet of color, a South Indian woman poet who makes up lines in English, a post-colonial language, as she waits for the red lights to change on Broadway. A Third World woman poet, who takes as her right the inner city of Manhattan, making up poems about the hellhole of the subway line [193].

In "House of a Thousand Doors," the speaker describes the condition of being a woman in a small town in Alexander's native state of Kerala, perhaps a memory of her grandmother: "She kneels at each / of the thousand doors in turn paying her dues" (Haq 11). The speaker describes the kneeling, praying woman as a "poor forked thing," a phrase that is a recognizable allusion to Shakespeare's *King Lear* as an echo of the human being's condition on earth: "Thou art the thing itself: unaccommodated man is no more but such a poor, bare, fork'd animal as thou art" (III.iv.106–8).

In "South of the Nilgiris," published in the collection titled *River and Bridge* (1996), the speaker, who is pregnant, dreams of a dialogue with her six-year-old son: "He pointed at my belly / watermelon swollen" (7). The speaker even mentions the disfiguring stretch marks of pregnancy. The son replies in her dream that he is happy not to have been born female because he will not have to bear a child. While the son laughs and plays, the mother feels the unborn fetus (her daughter) move under her ribs (*River and Bridge* 7). In "Passion," childbirth is re-created in the context of "passion" as pain or suffering, returning the word to its Latin root: "After childbirth / the tenth month's passion" (8). The woman in labor screams repeatedly like a "raw, ungoverned thing" (*River and Bridge* 8). The last movement of "Passion" realistically depicts the old rural Indian practice of placing women on a mat on the floor during labor and delivery. The woman's mouth is stuffed with rags, and she is pulled down from her bed to the floor (*River and Bridge* 10–11). Alexander's use of graphic details makes labor and delivery a raw experience.

In "Toxic Petals," Alexander connects a romantic episode with the urge to create poetry. Sensuality is linked to intellectual creativity. In the act of lovemaking, the female speaker feels that she is "chock full of poems" and a veritable four-armed goddess of South Asian mythology (*River and Bridge* 13–14). The speaker-poet also discovers her inner connection with her maternal grandmother (*River and Bridge* 14). In "Skin Song," Alexander describes in graphic detail the crowning of the infant's head in childbirth: "the head / of the too-big-child tore the mother's tender skin" (*River and Bridge* 19). In the fourth movement of "Skin Song," the speaker describes an adolescent girl's first discovery of her biological difference as she learns to cope with menstrual bleeding (*River and Bridge* 20–21). Elsewhere, Alexander's poetic images of love quote Faiz Ahmed Faiz, which in translation reads, "Beloved, do not ask me for that love again" (46). Poetry and sensual desire mingle in images of the lover reading to the speaker in bed of "a poet who must crawl to god's gate" (*River and Bridge* 47).

Elsewhere in Alexander's impassioned poetry, nostalgia is a recurring mood. In the slim volume *Night-Scene, The Garden* (1992), the poems are written for two or three voices. This mode of composition suggests that these poems were written to be performed in a dramatic style. There seem to be images drawn from the poet's visits to Kerala as a child. The setting is Tiru-villa, a small town in Kerala in southwestern India. The speakers seem to be a mother and a daughter, two adult women who are describing the house and garden of their childhood, and a happier time that is past: "Father had this house built right / roof pitched to the silver lightning rod above" (*Night-Scene* 8).

The loss of the house and garden through litigation, and its subsequent recovery through more litigation, is vividly described (*Night-Scene* 9–10). Lengthy lawsuits over disputed ancestral homes and land are not unusual in India. The voice of the mother continues to describe her love for her child: "I'd hug you tight and think child, my child, my only child" (*Night-Scene* 14).

The mother's narrative poems describe the mad Aunt Chonna, a boating trip, and sarees hung outside to dry. In the eighth poem, titled "Night-Scene," the speaker is the daughter, now remembering her mother and grandmother amid night scenes of her childhood, coming to the realization "that sweet hell in me / the poet rose" (*Night-Scene* 26). The symbolism of the garden, with the vivid images of life in a small Kerala town in the past, is evocative of a stage of youth and innocence, an Edenic phase of existence. But in the middle of this peaceful world, there is the painful image of birthing: "And the infant thrust past / her mother's bone" (*Night-Scene* 30).

There are recurring images in Alexander's poetry that refer to literary artists of diverse cultures. In "River and Bridge," the title poem of the volume of the same name, the speaker at "the Hudson's edge" perceives her own continuity with the poetic vision of the Greek writer Homer and the Sanskrit poet Vyasa. The poems "For Safdar Hashmi" and "Moloyashree" celebrate the contributions of Hashmi, a young Marxist playwright beaten to death on January 1, 1989, near Delhi while showcasing the play *Halla Bol*, and his wife Moloyashree, who continued to perform the play in support of the rights of striking workers. In "Paper Filled With Light," Alexander celebrates the work of Gujarati poet Uma Shankar Joshi (1911–1989), who was a follower of Mohandas Gandhi. The speaker appears to be in the Isamu Noguchi Garden Museum in New York City: "I am here in Isamu's garden, by an old warehouse, by a children's park, by the East River" (*River and Bridge* 43). Poetry, sculpting, and landscape architecture are all art forms in this poem by Alexander that provide commentaries on human life and experience.

Some of Alexander's literary allusions are not easily recognized by readers of English-language poetry and explanatory notes accompany relevant poems. For example, in the love poem "Asylum," the closing lines quote the Iraqi poet Badr Shakir el-Sayyab (1927–1964). Elsewhere, a female persona who packs her pots and pans and leaves home in New York cries out, "Like Mirabai" (*River and Bridge* 73), referring to a medieval Indian woman poet of the Bhakti movement. In "Raw Bird of Youth," Alexander celebrates the poetry of Kamala Das, a well-known modern woman poet from Kerala. The speaker perceives connections between her own experiences and Das's poetry: "I sense the sudden rush of lilac, mortality's noise. Kamala, in a brash wilderness where does love go?" (*River and Bridge* 79).

Alexander's collection titled *Illiterate Heart* (2002) presents recognizably female voices as the speakers of these poems. In search of poetic language to express women's perceptions of their sensory experiences, the speakers often turn to literary allusions. The opening poem of *Illiterate Heart* is titled "Provenance." In this poem, Alexander develops the idea of knowledge as "its own provenance," comparing the recesses of the mind to the ruins of the Indus Valley civilization at Mohenjo Daro. The speaker of this poem invites the reader into a world of writing: "With you I enter a space where verbs / have little extension, where syntax smolders" (*Illiterate Heart* 3). In "Port Sudan," allusions appear to be autobiographical, as the female speaker begins with a phone call from her father, who wants her to come from America to see him. The speaker-poet allows memories of her childhood in Sudan to surface, remembers a trip to upper Egypt, and celebrates the contributions of her father: "The same man loved his daughter so / he knew she needed knowledge" (*Illiterate Heart* 11). "Port Sudan" is followed by "Elegy for My Father," in which the speaker describes scenes from her memories of times spent with her father almost as if she were putting together a collage of pictures. Then the speaker-poet describes the funeral itself, where, as the oldest child, she had to cover the deceased father's face with a piece of "pale muslin" (*Illiterate Heart* 15). The last movement of this poem is a realistic expression of how moments of grief tend to recur after the loss of a parent: "The past makes sparks and fragments / pour in my eyes" (*Illiterate Heart* 15).

In "Glyphs" and "Valley," the speaker describes memories of outdoor experiences in a country setting shared with a male companion (*Illiterate Heart* 38–39). There are fleeting erotic images, such as "your shoulder blades bronze / as a parachute string" ("Valley," *Illiterate Heart* 39). In a similar style, the speaker in Alexander's "Man in a Red Shirt" begins with an erotic image of a woman who sees a man with a red cotton shirt open at the neck: "hairs on his chest / taut as the wind blew" (*Illiterate Heart* 43). The man is speaking to a group of poor people whom he is trying to unite while the woman listening to him is deeply moved by his appearance and his message (*Illiterate Heart* 43–44). "Translated Lives" presents a series of images of the diasporic South Asian experience of living in different continents, particularly from the viewpoint of an academic: "and the academies bow low: white shirts, threadbare elbows / scraped into arcane incandescence" (*Illiterate Heart* 46). This poem closes with the question of whether the past should be all-consuming.

Some of Alexander's poetry has a nightmarish quality, as seen in "Gold Horizon," where the speaker narrates a conversation with the spirit of a dead woman to whom she tries to describe the immigrant experience in New York. The dead woman seems to be based on a childhood memory from the poet's early years in India, and there is a vivid description of the dead woman's mutilated body: "feet cut at the ankles, / severed from her calves" (*Illiterate Heart* 48). The speaker describes wrestling with this spirit that is stripped to the skin (*Illiterate Heart* 49), giving this poem a macabre atmosphere.

In "Indian April" the speaker remembers the songs of a wandering minstrel in India who sang Hindu devotional lyrics and played on a tin can (*Illiterate Heart* 54–57). The speaker alludes to several rivers in three continents as part of past memories and appears to identify with the art of the minstrel: "You who sang America are flush now with death, / your poems — bits of your spine and skull" (*Illiterate Heart* 57).

The title poem of the volume is "Illiterate Heart," in which the speaker begins by recounting the experience of reading Joseph Conrad's *Heart of Darkness* at the age of nineteen: "I was Marlowe and Kurtz and still more / a black woman just visible at the shore" (*Illiterate Heart* 63). The poem is possibly autobiographical with memories of learning to read and reading Mohandas Gandhi's autobiography, the writings of Karl Marx, and the poetry of William Wordsworth. The speaker also remembers learning the Dravidian language Malayalam. Over the years, all of these reading experiences urge her to seek to define herself. It is ironic that in spite of being steeped in languages and reading, the heart remains "illiterate" (*Illiterate Heart* 68). The speaker-poet's closeness to her mother appears again in "Rites of Sense," where the speaker returns for a few weeks to visit aged parents in India. The elderly mother is exhausted from taking care of the weak and presumably ill father. The speaker massages her mother's feet, a traditional gesture of affection and respect for elders in South Asian culture: "In twilight as she lies on a mat / I rub my mother's feet with jasmine oil" (*Illiterate Heart* 72). In "Red Parapet," the poet as speaker remembers being with her sister as a six year old and watching a cobra shed its skin: "gazing as it leapt / clean out of its skin, up the red parapet" (*Illiterate Heart* 74).

The poems toward the end of *Illiterate Heart* present speakers who are Japanese. "Giving Names to Stones" contains memories of an internment camp (*Illiterate Heart* 78), while "Daffodils" alludes to "Kasuya Eiichi, poet of Japan" (*Illiterate Heart* 80). "Roadside Music" invokes a muse-like character who is Japanese: "She comes to me. Ono no Komachi / in a kimono of pale silk" (*Illiterate Heart* 81). "Water Table" contains allusions to farmers' revolts in colonial India: "streaked with indigo from the fields / of Champaran" (*Illiterate Heart* 83). Romantic memories surface in "Poem in Late October": "There is mist in the restaurants / where we used to lunch" (*Illiterate Heart* 84). "Diary of Dreams" brings up images of Gandhi and the Indian freedom movement (*Illiterate Heart* 86). The closing work of this volume is a fairly long autobiographical poem titled "Black River Walled Garden," which contains loosely connected images of the speaker's past: "In dreams come calling / migrant missing selves" (*Illiterate Heart* 99).

Like Meena Alexander, Sujata Bhatt is a diasporic South Asian artist who has lived in different continents. Bhatt was raised in Pune, India, and also in the United States, earning an M.F.A. from the Iowa Writers' Workshop (literature.britishcouncil.org). She has also lived in Canada and Germany, and is married to a German writer. Bhatt has translated poems from Gujarati into English as well as from German into English (literature.britishcouncil.org). She has published six collections of poems: *Brunizem* (1988), *Monkey Shadows* (1991), *The Stinking Rose* (1995), *Point No Point* (1997), *Augatora* (2000), *A Colour for Solitude* (2002), and *Pure Lizard* (2006). Bhatt has additionally won several poetry awards, including the Commonwealth Poetry Prize (Asia) in 1988, the Alice Hunt Bartlett Award in 1988, and the Cholmondeley Award in 1991 ("Sujata Bhatt"). In keeping with the theme of this chapter, only a selection of poems from *The Stinking Rose* have been analyzed. Much of Bhatt's poetry is allusive, containing multiple references to poets, artists and creative women. She uses epigraphs from Marie Curie, Margaret Atwood, and Adrienne Rich.

In *The Stinking Rose*, Sujata Bhatt approaches the theme of being female as well as an artist with unique insights. The "stinking rose" is actually another name for garlic. In the poem "Pelvis with Moon," the speaker reflects on the shape of the human pelvic bone: "She who feels the meaning of the sky, / Of the moon behind the pelvis bone" (*The Stinking Rose* 35). The imagery evokes women's strength and creativity in that the female pelvis is designed by nature for childbirth. Bhatt's use of the symbol of the garlic bud is a total reversal of the romantic symbolism of the rose. The images of this volume frequently suggest women's fertility and pregnancy. For example, in the lyric "What Does the Flower of Life Say, Frida Kahlo?" the central image is the fertilization of human ova, and this poem is addressed to the artist Frida Kahlo, making an obvious connection between artistic creativity and fertility. There is ambivalence in the attitudes toward women's existence and female sexuality. Bhatt's poems often suggest the ability of the woman poet to stand outside the bodily experience.

In the title poem of the book, "The Stinking Rose," garlic almost becomes an aphrodisiac. Garlic will sing to "your slippery muscles — will keep / your nipples and your legs from sleeping" (*The Stinking Rose* 39). It likewise becomes the symbol of woman's fertility as Bhatt cites a passage from the ancient Greek physician Hippocrates on an old Greek fertility test. The woman speaker of "It Has Not Rained for Months" awaits the moment of conception: "this clove of garlic deep inside me / where it burns" (*The Stinking Rose* 72). In "Old World Blood," the speaker examines the body-to-soul connection by stating that she needs to live more fully through the body, perhaps having a baby: "Then, would my body be able / to teach my soul something new?" (*The Stinking Rose* 92). The speaker in Bhatt's "Ophelia in Defence of the Queen" becomes an apologist for Gertrude's sexual and social transgression: "Prince Hamlet! I've had enough of your degrading the Queen's womb" (*The Stinking Rose* 93).

Bhatt's erotic imagery often depicts the unpleasant reality of women's lives in different settings. The speaker in "More Fears About the Moon" is afraid to conceive more babies as she vividly recalls suffering repeated miscarriages: "Fetus after fetus lost. / Can't you take me away" (*The Stinking Rose* 95). The closing poem of *The Stinking Rose* is "Frauenjournal," in which the speaker creates a collage from stories in the media where mothers kill and hurt their daughters. The culminating image is of a female genital mutilation (female circumcision): "makes sure that her seven year old daughter / has her clitoris sliced off" (*The Stinking Rose* 113).

While some of Bhatt's poetry celebrates the erotic, many other poems return to the painful reality of being a woman in a patriarchal environment. One such example is the brief lyric "Chutney," where the speaker presents an apparent ideological divide between South Asian homemakers in New Jersey who cook "perfect mango chutney" and the visiting South Asian woman scholar from Bombay (Mumbai) who goes to view Wallace Stevens' house and gazes upon it with "the eyes of the poorest Bombay woman / visiting a temple" (*The Stinking Rose* 29). While the homemakers pride themselves on the preservation of traditional South Asian cuisine, the presumably more educated woman scholar is an admirer of mainstream American literature. The implicit message is that both the homemakers and the scholar are confused in their priorities.

Chitra Banerjee Divakaruni is better known for her novels and short fiction than her poetry. Originally from Kolkata in India, she came to the United States to study and to earn her M.A. from Wright State University in Dayton, Ohio, as well as her Ph.D. from the University of California at Berkeley. She has taught at colleges in California and Texas and is the recipient of several awards for her fiction. She has actively participated in issues involving women from dysfunctional families ("Chitra Divakaruni"). Her collections of poetry include *The Reason for Nasturtiums* (1990), *Black Candle* (1991), and *Leaving Yuba City* (1997). In this chapter poems from the *Yuba City* collection are used as representative examples of Divakaruni's work.

Divakaruni's poetry addresses issues of male and female sexuality as well as social issues. The poems in *Leaving Yuba City* present both male and female viewpoints. Sometimes in these poems, sex is viewed as an age-old transaction. The emotions of women without men are depicted in swift brush strokes. In "The Nishi," the speaker remembers her mother's suicide after her father left: "her body hanging from the ceiling of the bedroom that was now hers alone" (*Leaving Yuba City* 5). Elsewhere, Divakaruni brings to life the discovery that schoolgirls in a girls-only convent school make regarding their attraction to boys at a chaperoned dance: "thinking of the slight tremble of boy-hands, / stubbed nails, lips fuzzy with new mustaches" (*Leaving Yuba City* 20). The poem "The Widow at Dawn" is a monologue of the widow's loneliness as she watches a cow with her calf: "palms against my flat belly, firmness of / unused breasts" (*Leaving Yuba City* 71). She wishes to scream her pain from the rooftop. The widow lives lonely and childless while she is praised by her relatives in the Indian extended family for all the help with housework and child care that she provides for them (*Leaving Yuba City* 72).

The prose poem titled "The Lost Love Words" contains the memories of a woman whose relationship has disintegrated. The speaker grieves for lost words of love: "you said these after the miscarriage, holding me close, after the doctor told us I couldn't have any more children" (*Leaving Yuba City* 77). In the poem "The Brides Come to Yuba City," women married by proxy to Sikh men residing in the United States finally get to see their unknown husbands. Divakaruni states, "Due to immigration restrictions, the wives of many of the original Sikhs who settled in Yuba City in the 1900s had to wait in India until the 1940s, when they were finally allowed entry to the United States" (*Leaving Yuba City* 103). She attempts to create the emotions of the women who fearfully wait for the consummation of their marriages to unknown men. An example of a Yuba City bride is Harvinder, married a year earlier to her husband's photograph. He is fifty-two and she is sixteen: "Tonight — like us all — / she will open her legs to him" (*Leaving Yuba City* 103).

Among the women poets of South Asian descent in the New World, the contributions of the Guyanese poet Mahadai Das (1954–2003) are significant in their images of women's lives, women's bodies, and histories. Das received her M.A. at Columbia University but could not complete her Ph.D. at the University of Chicago due to health problems ("Mahadai Das"). Her volumes of poetry include *I Want to Be a Poetess of My People* (1977), *My Finer Steel Will Grow* (1982), and *Bones* (1988). Mahadai Das's powerful images of female sexuality have been discussed in comparison to other Caribbean women poets by Denise de Caires Narain, who also compares Das to Sylvia Plath: "Many of the poems in *Bones* construct the figure of the woman as the very antithesis of the robust female figure 'astride' a green landscape ... instead, the images presented here are of a fragmented and dramatized body" (181).

In Das's "The Growing Tip," the growing tip does not cause a garden to grow but something frightening instead: "Oh she had things that grew / horns and tails, arms of different lengths" (Brown and McDonald, *The Heinemann Book of Caribbean Poetry* 71). The allusion to witchcraft is apparent, as is the reference to knowledge of "other histories" that women often possess but do not reveal in traditional and patriarchal environments. In Das's "Learner," the woman speaker identifies with powerful and destructive figures of Chinese and Hindu mythology: "I, oriental fire-dragon mother Kali / in China, wrap snakes around my neck" (*The Heinemann Book of Caribbean Poetry* 73). Mahadai Das's poetry often contains vivid imagery of the lost dreams of underprivileged people in the Caribbean: "Where are the golden horsemen? / They too are drowning" (*The Heinemann Book of Caribbean Poetry* 69). Her empathy extends to other continents as well: "At eighteen, Bushman fighting to control diamonds / in his glass head" (*The Heinemann Book of Caribbean Poetry* 73).

Like the late Mahadai Das, Indo-Caribbean poet Ramabai Espinet is an immigrant poet who relocated to North America. Espinet was born in 1948 in Trinidad and Tobago, was educated at York University in Ontario, Canada, and received a Ph.D. in English from the University of the West Indies, St. Augustine, Trinidad ("Ramabai Espinet"). She teaches at York University and Seneca College, in Toronto, Ontario, Canada. She has also published poetry, fiction, essays, and literary criticism. Her collection of poems *Nuclear Seasons* (1991) and her novel *The Swinging Bridge* (2003) have made her a powerful spokesperson for the lives of diasporic Indo-Caribbean women.

Of the five poets discussed in this chapter, Ramabai Espinet's themes and motifs are recognizably iconoclastic in their interpretation of women's experiences. Espinet's *Nuclear Seasons* contains three separate clusters of lyrics: "Hosay Night," "A Nowhere Place," and "Equitable Landings." Espinet's poems depict the marginalized experiences of Indo-Caribbeans in Canada. The voices of female immigrants, young girls, sex workers, widows, mothers, and indentured workers surface time and again in Espinet's poetry. The twice-migrant experiences of Indo-Caribbean women in Canada, with their dual colonization under British and Canadian cultural domination, as well as the overarching patriarchal domination of women in traditional South Asian culture, emerge in the voices of the women speakers of poems in *Nuclear Seasons* as these speakers quest for selfhood.

In the first poem, "Hosay Night," the speaker (an immigrant) looks back on Trinidad as a lost homeland: "This land is a home to me / Now homeless, a true refugee" (*Nuclear Seasons* 10). In "TAMANI: a cane-cutting woman," Ramabai Espinet presents compelling images of a woman cutting sugarcane: "At twilight she stood alone / Her shining cutlass green with grass" (*Nuclear Seasons* 11). "Bree and Me" presents a woman speaker who recalls lost and possibly forbidden love from her younger days in the Caribbean. Now the speaker is possibly in North America in a different society: "True in name and nature / Free to love you too" (*Nuclear Seasons* 18). Lost love recurs as a theme in "A Fishing Song" (*Nuclear Seasons* 23–24) and "For the Time Being" (*Nuclear Seasons* 25–26), while the images of fertility and creativity merge in Espinet's "Mama Glo" in a way similar to Sujata Bhatt's juxtaposition of these two themes: "I am fertile now / Rivers of creative memory" (*Nuclear Seasons* 27). Mama Glo is a mythical figure in Trinidad's folklore who combines characteristics of a woman and a water-snake (*Nuclear Seasons* 29).

Ramabai Espinet's "Orthodoxies" opens the second section of *Nuclear Seasons*, featuring a very angry speaker who defies political agendas and does not wish to become any category of "feminist," seeking "Only honesty in human relations / For us and others" (*Nuclear Seasons* 35). There is significant irony in the rugged honesty of this speaker who rejects the various labels

included in third-wave feminism and global feminism, seeking "only honesty."
"In the Jungle" emphasizes the speaker's inability to find a homeland: "I am
a stranger / Everywhere" (*Nuclear Seasons* 39). "For Patricia Deanna" is a brief
elegiac poem for a young pregnant Caribbean woman, an illegal alien in Canada, who fell from a balcony to her death when she tried to escape from immigration officers (*Nuclear Seasons* 45). The fear and alienation of the immigrant
woman is also voiced in "City Blues" in the lines "God what is the terror /
Which grips me to the core" (*Nuclear Seasons* 53). Amid all the sad and frightening experiences of the land of adoption, "a nowhere place," the poet-speaker
finds her muse: "I must bring / To birth — my word" (*Nuclear Seasons* 54).

The third section of *Nuclear Seasons*, titled "Equitable Landings," presents
aspects of women's history. "Afterbirth" captures the emotions of a woman
who has just given birth: "The day my sisters wrapped / And kept me and
my newborn" (*Nuclear Seasons* 58). The title poem of this collection ("Nuclear
Seasons") is an anti-war poem which suggests that mothers who have formerly
raised sons who grew up to wage wars will have to prepare their daughters for
"reclamation" (*Nuclear Seasons* 68). This powerful poem invokes the image
of Kali, a goddess of Hindu mythology who symbolizes the divine powers
that destroy evil to protect the good.

The poem "Merchant of Death" presents a woman speaker whose son
has just died in a war (*Nuclear Seasons* 63–67), while "Instruments of Love
and War" alludes to "Bombs are raining on Baghdad" (*Nuclear Seasons* 68),
suggesting that Espinet was opposed to the Gulf War of 1990–1991. It is interesting to note that anti-war sentiments directed at U.S. foreign policy have
been voiced by Canadian writers since the days of the Vietnam War, when
Americans who opposed the war often emigrated to Canada; one recent example of anti-war literature published by a Canadian writer is Lawrence Hill's
The Deserter's Tale (2007). Espinet's pacifist message is reiterated by the speaker
of "An Ageable Woman," a woman in the sugarcane fields who sings her song
"For healing and the earth / Delivered from falsehood" (*Nuclear Seasons* 81).
The final poem of *Nuclear Seasons*, "Lost Cargoes," brings a clearly environ-
mentalist theme in the story of the dead grandfather's message to posterity:
"Lighten the water, plant flowers / Gather the sea, lace the land" (*Nuclear
Seasons* 87).

This chapter thus seeks to show that South Asian women poets in North
America and the Caribbean have opened up a field of poetry that was formerly
not considered appropriate for women writers in the traditional cultures of
South Asia. The poets discussed here repeatedly re-examine the age-old roles
of women as lovers and mothers. To such inquiry at this time there is no closure but the distinct beginning of a poetic language that belongs to a female
tradition.

Works Cited

Alexander, Meena. *Fault Lines: A Memoir*. New York: Feminist Press at the City University of New York, 1993. Print.

_____. *Illiterate Heart*. Evanston, IL: TriQuarterly Books/Northwestern University Press, 2002. Print.

_____. *Night-Scene, The Garden*. New York: Red Dust, 1992. Print.

_____. *River and Bridge*. New York: TSAR, 1996. Print

Bahri, Deepika. "Meena Alexander." Postcolonial Studies, Emory University. www.english.emory.edu/Bahri/Alexander.html. Accessed 7 April 2012.

Bhatt, Sujata. *The Stinking Rose*. Manchester, UK: Carcanet Press, 1995. Print.

Brown, Stewart, and Ian McDonald. *The Heinemann Book of Caribbean Poetry*. New York: Heinemann, 1992. Print.

"Chitra Divakaruni." www.sawnet.org/books/authors.php?Divakaruni+Chitra+Banerjee. Accessed 7 April 2012.

de Caires Narain, Denise. *Contemporary Caribbean Women's Poetry: Making Style*. New York: Routledge, 2002. Print.

Divakaruni, Chitra. *Leaving Yuba City: New and Selected Poems*. New York: Anchor Books/Doubleday, 1997. Print.

Espinet, Ramabai. *Nuclear Seasons*. Toronto: Sister Vision Press, 1991. Print.

Haq, Kaiser. *Contemporary Indian Poetry*. Columbus: Ohio State University Press, 1990. Print.

"Mahadai Das." http://peepaltreepress.com/author_display.asp?au_id=15. Accessed 7 April 2012.

"Ramabai Espinet." literaturealive.ca. Accessed 9 April 2012.

Rich, Adrienne. *The Dream of a Common Language*. New York: W.W. Norton, 1978. Print.

Shakespeare, William. *King Lear*. In *The Complete Works of William Shakespeare*. Ed. David Bevington. New York: Longman, 2009. Print.

"Sujata Bhatt." British Council Literature. http://literature.britishcouncil.org/sujata-bhatt. Accessed 7 April 2012.

• TEN •

"Why I'm a poet": Contemporary South Asian Women's Poetry in the United States

With the exception of Mahadai Das, the women poets discussed in the previous chapter are all contemporary. This chapter discusses the writings of a selection of contemporary women poets of South Asian origin currently publishing in the United States as anthologized in the collection *Indivisible* (Banerjee et al., 2010). There are some similarities in themes and methodologies between the poets discussed in chapter nine and those discussed here. While *Indivisible* presents a number of talented women artists, its selection of poets, which seeks to be both "national" and "transnational," has led to significant omissions of contemporary women poets of South Asian origin. Sujata Bhatt and Ramabai Espinet are not included in this anthology because they are not in the United States.

Indivisible is a compilation by three contemporary women poets publishing in the United States. The theme of indivisibility, or taking a transnational approach to poets of South Asian ancestry publishing in the United States, brings into focus the common elements in the poetry composed by South Asian women. *Indivisible* anthologizes twenty-nine women poets. In addition to Divakaruni and Alexander, as well as the anthology's editors Neelanjana Banerjee, Summi Kaipa, and Pireeni Sundaralingam, these poets include Reetika Vazirani, Vandana Khanna, Maya Khosla, Tanuja Mehrotra, Bhanu Kapil, Minal Hajratwala, Sejal Shah, Mytili Jagannathan, Prageeta Sharma, Sasha Kamini Parmasad, Bushra Rehman, Shailja Patel, Aimee Nezhukumatathil, Dilruba Ahmed, Pramila Venkateswaran, Bhargavi C. Mandava, Reena Narayan, Purvi Shah, Monica Ferrell, Swati Rana, Subhasini Kaligotla, and Mona Ali. Many of the poems that appear in *Indivisible* were originally published in poetry journals.

While many of the poets examined in this chapter are relatively new to the American literary scene, and may or may not have the continued success of the well-established women poets discussed in chapter nine, it is necessary to examine this body of contemporary poetry by South Asian women in America because women poets arrived on the diasporic South Asian literary scene after male poets, and currently appear to have outpaced men in poetic productivity. The feminist movement in the United States is older and more established than in the Indian subcontinent. First- and second-generation women poets from South Asia have used the American literary environment to experiment with finding a niche for the voices of South Asian American women as artists, lovers, mothers, and everyday Americans aptly summed up in poet Shailja Patel's phrase "why I'm a poet." In this chapter, contemporary South Asian American women poets are grouped in small clusters according to their similarities in theme and method.

The common elements that connect the more recent women poets with established poets such as Alexander, Divakaruni, Bhatt, and Espinet are their recurring concern with the complexity of women's lives, intergenerational memories, and hybrid cultural experiences in North America. Three clusters may be identified:

(1) The point of view of women of South Asian descent is voiced by speakers in the contemporary poems of Reetika Vazirani, Tanuja Mehrotra, Minal Hajratwala, Neelanjana Banerjee, Reena Narayan, Purvi Shah, Monica Ferrell, and Mona Ali.
(2) Concerns with problems of race and the need for racial harmony surface in the poems of Vandana Khanna, Dilruba Ahmed, and Pireeni Sundaralingam.
(3) Hybridity, intergenerational differences, memories, landscapes, self-reflexivity, exile, and alienation recur in the poetry of the majority of contemporary South Asian American women poets, such as Maya Khosla, Bhanu Kapil, Summi Kaipa, Sejal Shah, Mytili Jagannathan, Prageeta Sharma, Sasha Kamini Parmasad, Bushra Rehman, Shailja Patel, Aimee Nezhukumatathil, Pramila Venkateswaran, Bhargavi C. Mandava, Swati Rana, and Subhasini Kaligotla.

Women's Concerns

Women's voices appear in the poems of Reetika Vazirani (1962–2003), who was the recipient of a Pushcart Prize and other awards. She earned her B.A. from Wellesley College and her M.F.A. from the University of Virginia (*Indivisible* 3). Her poetry collections include *White Elephants* (1996), *World Hotel* (2002), and *Radha Says* (2009).

Vazirani's poems use confessional techniques, with the women speakers examining their experiences and expressing a sense of irony, as seen in "It's a Young Country." In this poem, the woman speaker tries to reconcile herself to the real or imaginary unfaithfulness of her partner: "If you are seducing another / teach me to share you with humor" (*Indivisible* 4). Here the speaker struggles to find a New World solution to her jealousy. In the confessional piece titled "It's Me, I'm Not Home," the woman speaker fantasizes as to how she will feign sleep and not answer the phone when her partner (possibly unfaithful) calls: "It's late in the city and I'm asleep. / Please leave a message after the beep" (*Indivisible* 5). In contrast to the voices of women in troubled relationships, Vazirani's "Aerogram Punjab" presents a speaker who is writing to her brother while remembering their childhood. This South Asian speaker is pregnant and wonders if her baby is a boy or a girl, making a note of the usefulness of the Indian sari as women's clothing before, during, and after pregnancy: "sari never changes its size, our tailor's / discount. I have grown. What ails" (*Indivisible* 6).

Contemporary poet Tanuja Mehrotra holds a B.A. from Wellesley College, an M.A. in English from Tulane University, and an M.F.A. in creative writing from San Francisco State University. A recipient of poetry prizes, she has published in several poetry journals. Her poems use a hybridized form termed "threaded ghazals" (*Indivisible* 22). In "Manthara," the speaker describes the arts of the hunchbacked maid in the *Ramayana* who became the agent provocateur, instigating her mistress to prompt her husband to send the hero Rama into exile: "our life is just the hand we are dealt by God / but Manthara, fists clenched, rocks her imagined princess to sleep" (*Indivisible* 23). The use of the wise woman archetype combined with Hindu mythology creates a hybrid poem. Mehrotra's sestina titled "Nainital" also uses Indian names of places to describe a trip to an Indian city in the hills. In this poem the speaker remembers being a schoolgirl in India: "All in the past, what I loved of Lake Naini. / Impossible to see what it was or taste it even in a square of Cadbury chocolate" (*Indivisible* 25). Born in Cleveland, Ohio, and raised in the United States, Mehrotra foreignizes the speakers' voices in some of her poems.

In contrast, Mehrotra's "Song for New Orleans" combines prose passages with free verse, attempting to present the voice of a student in New Orleans: "professor maddy tells us a victorian scholar (in this very department, someone we know) purposely killed her corgi" (*Indivisible* 28). The frequent use of lowercase letters is in the modernist American tradition, as is the image of campus gossip encapsulated in the above lines. The ability to create both American and Indian voices suggests that this poet has appropriated both cultures successfully.

For performance poet Minal Hajratwala, the quest for self-identity is multifaceted: "Identity as platform, not label. My identities include Gujarati, queer, diasporan, San Franciscan, poet, performer, writing coach, editor, recovering journalist, and more" (*Indivisible* 46). A graduate of Stanford University, Hajratwala has published a work of nonfiction titled *Leaving India: My Family's Journey from Five Villages to Five Continents* (2009). In "Angerfish," the lesbian persona/speaker, whose name means "fish" ("minal"), expresses her early awareness of her lesbian sexuality even though she was raised in a traditional South Asian family: "as no one spoke then of cities / or queers" (*Indivisible* 48). This postmodern confessional poem ends with a surprising quotation from Buddhist scripture on the way anger and resentment can pile up and bind the self (*Indivisible* 50). In "Generica/America," the speaker satirizes American food and the behaviors of American women who may be on the antidepressant Prozac but present an exterior in which "we are always soft smiling / waxed lasered epilady'd" (*Indivisible* 52).

The satire on the condition of Indian American women deepens in Hajratwala's "Miss Indo America dreams," in which a young woman dreams of getting a Bollywood contract or a "rich anesthesiologist" for a partner so that she may rise above the reality of her community, with its strange oppositions: "beaten wives straight-A girls / immigrants with grease in their hair" (*Indivisible* 51). The anger and satire in Hajratwala's poetry makes her speakers unique as she exposes the hypocrisy and contradictions in the lives of South Asian Americans. The satirizing of pageants and the emptiness of women's lives are identifiably feminist concerns. Hajratwala depicts the Indian American women speakers who are willing participants in their own subordination. As a lesbian poet, Hajratwala's literary descent lines are traceable to generations of modern and postmodern lesbian poets in America.

The heterosexual woman's perspective emerges in the writings of Neelanjana Banerjee, one of the editors of the anthology *Indivisible*. Banerjee describes herself as "Midwestern-born, West Coast–transplanted, Bengali-speaking, South Asian American, person of color, Asian American feminist writer" (*Indivisible* 66). She received her M.F.A. in creative writing from San Francisco State University in 2007, and has worked as an editor and teaching artist (*Indivisible* 66). Banerjee writes both poetry and fiction.

Banerjee's poem "Cowgirl Series, I" is in the form of a dramatic dialogue with three brief scenes in which nineteenth-century American frontierswoman Calamity Jane (Martha Jane Cannary Burke), who is reported to have been infatuated with Wild Bill Hicock, meets the cowgirl Radha of Hindu mythology. Radha was a married woman who was the beloved of the prophet-king Krishna. The love of Radha and Krishna was the subject of Hindu mystical poetry during the medieval Bhakti movement in India (see chapter two). In the first movement Radha meets Calamity Jane, who is chewing tobacco. In the second movement, presumably Calamity Jane has listened to Radha's story, perhaps about Krishna's large following of "gopis" (cowgirls). Calamity Jane would leave Radha's lover among the Sioux Indians: "them people got their own gods, they won't / give a hoot about his blue ass" (*Indivisible* 67). The contrast between the pining lovelorn Radha and the tough-talking Calamity Jane provides a critique of both cultures because Radha and Jane are atypical representatives. In the closing movement of the poem, Radha continues to make chapattis (Indian bread) and her bangles tinkle, while Jane puts her boots on the porch railing and drinks whiskey as the day draws to an end (*Indivisible* 67). Indian love poetry depicts Radha as all emotion, and stories of Calamity Jane present her as a woman of action. This poem suggests that women's lives should strike a balance between emotion and action.

In Banerjee's "Priapos," the female speaker is in Greece at Ephesus viewing a statue of Aphrodite's son Priapos, born cursed to be ugly with a continuous erection. While the tour guide narrates the legend of Priapos and tourists take photographs, the speaker's male companion becomes sexually aroused: "You pull me behind a row of pillars, put your hand / under my skirt" (*Indivisible* 67). Yet, the same evening, the male partner gets drunk, is taken to their hotel by the speaker, begins to make love in bed and then passes out. The poem's closing brings an ironic observation that, over time, it is married women who have prayed to Priapos to bless their husbands with virility (*Indivisible* 68). Thus, in both "Cowgirl Series, I" and "Priapos," Banerjee presents a satirical view of women's relationships with men that are at times filled with disappointments.

Women's voices from the margins surface in the poetry of Purvi Shah, who holds an M.A. in English literature from Rutgers University and is the recipient of awards for her poetry (*Indivisible* 187). Shah was born in Ahmedabad, India, and lives in New York City, "where she recently served for more than seven years as the executive director at Sakhi for South Asian Women, a community-based anti–domestic violence organization" (*Indivisible* 187). Purvi Shah has published *Terrain Tracks* (2006), a book of poems.

Shah's poem "Made in India, Immigrant Song #3" is crafted as "a note from a New York City streetwalker" who is of South Asian descent, and who views herself as wearing a "Made in India" stamp like imported products from India. The image of the South Asian immigrant woman as a prostitute subverts the images of success that South Asian Americans prefer to project in the international media. The speaker views her own physical body from the outside: "the body's chamber is made / hole, the skin not smooth, circular" (*Indivisible* 188). This nameless prostitute in Shah's poem is yet another immigrant whose American dream has failed.

In the poem "Unhoming," the speaker describes the inner anxieties and loneliness in the life of a nameless housewife who cleans, cooks, and washes clothes day after day, and goes to bed tired from chores. However, instead of calmness and repose, the night "unveils your quieted fear" (*Indivisible* 189). It is almost as if the repetitive chores of the day are preferable to the night: "In day, you wifed. You create clink of cups, release comfort to *comfort*" (*Indivisible* 188). The partner or husband is absent from the poem, and this absence itself leaves questions open in the mind of the reader.

Just like the poems "Unhoming" and "Made in India, Immigrant Song #3," which begin and end almost abruptly, "Nature Ace POSTED" is a landscape poem about a place in the mountains that could be located anywhere in rural America. This location is an example of a place to which no one really belongs, described by Indo-Caribbean poet Ramabai Espinet as a "nowhere place." At the center of this poem is the journey of a red Taurus driving along Route 804. The reader assumes that this journey offers the view of nameless rural scenes as the mist comes in, and the air itself is "minted green every exhale. / Within the knell / of it all, mountains, hills" (*Indivisible* 190). The use of the word "knell" is ominous and heightens the tension of this poem's closing.

The inner anxieties and tensions of women speakers surface in the poetry of Monica Ferrell, who is an assistant professor of creative writing at Purchase College, New York. Ferrell's mother is Indian and her father is European American. She was born in New Delhi, India, and is a recipient of prizes for her poetry (*Indivisible* 194). She has also published a novel titled *The Answer Is Always Yes* (2008).

Ferrell's poem titled "Confessions of Beatrice D'Este" is a monologue ascribed to the Duchess of Milan, who lived during the Renaissance and died in childbirth.[1] Ferrell's speaker describes her wedding night, when her husband took her virginity and then fell asleep: "Watching him snore, at first I felt hurt" (*Indivisible* 195). At the beginning of this poem, the reader is aware that the speaker is recently deceased, having left behind all her fine possessions. The dead Beatrice D'Este is describing an out-of-body experience as she views her lifeless body: "when the doctors finally carried me / Wrapped in linen and sprinkled with camphor" (*Indivisible* 195).

If "Confessions of Beatrice D'Este" uses gothic elements, the poem "The Coin of Your Country" depicts a speaker who is equally confused and confusing. This speaker faces her own stormy emotions and violent impulses as she contemplates cutting up the shirts of her male companion: "When I take my scissors to your shirts" (*Indivisible* 195). The speaker believed her lover, who said that she was his love in German. When the relationship ends, the woman speaker goes home keeping a peaceful façade: "My pockets so rich with the coin of your country" (*Indivisible* 196). In the poem titled "In the

Binary Alleys of the Lion's Virus," the speaker also refers to the memory of a relationship in Germany: "A creature I greeted once in a dream: yes, at the crossroads of the hallowed grove / He kissed me — and must have slipped this curse between my lips" (*Indivisible* 196). The closing of this relationship between the woman speaker and the German-speaking man is presented in an unrhymed fourteen-line poem titled "Love, the Kunstkammer Version," where the man does not answer the speaker's letter, and she recovers her sense of selfhood: "Silence to my last letter, or that breath which stops / My saying what swims me too, unhurt and whole" (*Indivisible* 197).

Women's disappointments in their relationships with men also appear in the poems of Mona Ali, an economist who is currently an assistant professor at the State University of New York, New Paltz. Ali was born in Karachi, Pakistan, and is a dual citizen (*Indivisible* 220). In the poem "Noor" the speaker reflects on women's lives and the meanings of names. In the first stanza, a woman poet is mentioned as the mother of a newborn daughter named "Noor," an Arabic word for sunlight (*Indivisible* 220). In the second stanza, there appears the reader presumably of the book of poems: "The reader thinks, as her own marriage falls apart, / as a new year invites her into fresh starts of grief" (*Indivisible* 220). The reader thinks of her aunt named Noor (sunlight) who married her cousin Nayyar (moonlight), suggesting the differences between women and men. The traditional association of the sun as a masculine image and the moon as a feminine image is reversed in this poem.

Ali's poetic methodology is heteroglossic in that there are several incomplete stories within the poem "Noor," as seen in the final stanza, where the reader imagines love as a boat that comes into the sunlight with its sail shaped like a crescent moon. The symbolism of the crescent moon in this poem is a significant allusion to the Islamic practice of celebrating the festival of Eid-ul-Fitr with the sighting of the new moon that brings to an end the month of Ramadan, a month of fasting for Muslims. The new moon is viewed as a symbol of peace in Islamic culture. Thus, in this poem's closing, despite her own disappointments the reader is able to imagine love as a voyage to peace and light (*Indivisible* 220). The poem itself is in fourteen unrhymed lines with three incomplete stories.

Mona Ali's *zuihitsu* poem "The Wolf's Cry" is an experiment in jotting down random thoughts as they surface in the psyche of a contemporary Pakistani American woman speaker (*Indivisible* 221–24). The sprinkling of Urdu and Farsi words foreignizes the speaker's voice and suggests her bicultural perspective. The random impressionistic lines present transnational experiences such the sixteen emails in twelve hours of workaday life; the smell of the neighbor's cinnamon bread in America; the story of the girl Gabbeh, who runs away on her lover's horse; the European-born significant other who faced racism in Germany and thinks of converting to Christianity; and, finally, memories of a stormy relationship: "How you courted me in German, French, English, / How you cursed me in Arabic" (*Indivisible* 224).

Indo-Fijian immigrant poet Reena Narayan came to America as a child. She later earned her B.A. and MA. in English literature from California State University, and now teaches fourth grade (*Indivisible* 170). Narayan writes of her diasporic Indian heritage in "My Daughter," where the speaker addresses her five-year-old daughter clad in a blue dress, whom she views as a symbol of freedom full of childish questions. The freedom of childhood is contrasted by the speaker, the child's mother, who carries all the emotional burdens and unanswered questions that Indian women keep to themselves: "We do not ask questions / for fear of living in doubt" (*Indivisible* 171). The speaker notes the model of self-sacrifice that Hindu women have followed over centuries, praying for their children, husbands, and parents while forgetting themselves. Underlying this poem is the latent desire that the daughter will grow up free of the burden of tradition that has prevented South Asian women from becoming empowered.

Narayan's interest in evoking her Indo-Fijian family's multiple heritages appears in the poem that is titled "Tobacco Wrapped in *The Fiji Times*" (*Indivisible* 172–75). This long poem presents a speaker who is tending to her grandmother, an elderly Indo-Fijian woman who sits in a wheelchair, her legs paralyzed from a stroke for the past three years (*Indivisible* 172). The grandmother smokes a cigar rolled with the tobacco sent by a relative from Fiji. The grandmother gave away all her brightly colored Indian silk sarees one month after her stroke, and now wears only pants. The grandmother has received gifts wrapped in newspaper from the relative in Fiji. She takes the pages of the wrinkled newspaper and asks her granddaughter to read the names in the obituaries to find out if any of her old acquaintances have passed away. When her granddaughter asks if she knew any of those named in the obituaries, she responds, "*When you live in a small, small place for so long, / everyone is your relative*" (*Indivisible* 174). The poem ends with the grandmother sitting with the newspaper folded in her lap, smoking her cigar, thinking of those in faraway Fiji (*Indivisible* 175). This poem is an example of relocation for members of the old South Asian diaspora, as in the poems of Indo-Fijian poet Sudesh Mishra.

Racial Issues

The poetry of Vandana Khanna takes on themes of alienation, marginalization, and suffering as part of the experience of the first-generation immigrant from South Asia. Khanna's speakers describe these experiences in settings where first-generation immigrants try to make a living in America while seeking to preserve a traditional South Asian way of life. Vandana Khanna describes herself as "a Punjabi Virginian who spent childhood summers in Delhi, watched Bollywood films in the suburbs of D.C., and now makes a home in Hollywood" (*Indivisible* 7). Khanna received her M.F.A. from Indiana University in Bloomington. She has published *Train to Agra* (2000), *Homage to Vallejo* (2006), and *Asian American Poetry: The Next Generation* (2004) (*Indivisible* 7).

Khanna's poem "Blackwater Fever" contains autobiographical elements where the speaker has memories of the blistering heat of summers in northern India, contrasted with the reality of life in America in a different climate: "I'd awake to winter in D.C., find streets covered / in snow, the words of some ancient language blooming" (*Indivisible* 7). The mood and tone in the above lines is similar to poems describing memories of a past life in the writings of poets in Canada who have emigrated from Sri Lanka and Guyana. In "Hair," the speaker's memories take her back to the home of her childhood friend Anu, whose family members never cut their hair, indicating that they belonged to the Sikh religion. While the mother combs Anu's long hair, she warns her daughter of the dangers of interracial dating: "with each strand, a different story — of American boys / and dances, where skin touched, hair swayed" (*Indivisible* 9).

Violence and tragedy surface in "Dot Head" and "Echo," in which the speaker narrates painful memories. In "Dot Head" the speaker remembers apartments with smelly hallways and racial harassment that led to the speaker's brother getting a cut on his forehead that looked like the red mark or dot worn by their mother: "his bled down his face. A dot head, / a sand nigger" (*Indivisible* 9). This poem reminds readers that a gang that called itself "Dotbusters" spread messages of hate against Indian immigrants in the late 1980s in New Jersey. Sporadic gang attacks against Indian immigrants have continued for over twenty years. In "Echo" the speaker describes the scene of her father's death in a shabby hotel presumably where he worked. He has been murdered by two men who wanted money: "his body curls like the curve of a cheek, / a knife lies beside him, done with its work" (*Indivisible* 10). The child-speaker remembers the father's stories of Lahore (in Pakistan). The reader therefore assumes that the father left Lahore during the Hindu-Muslim riots to seek a new homeland. Escaping from the violence of the Old World, the father subsequently dies by violent crime in the New World. The child-speaker seeks to translate this experience into English but there is no way that poetry can transform the violent episode, with its underlying sadness and anger at the dead father's American dream turned into a nightmare with a tragic ending.

Like Vandana Khanna, Pireeni Sundaralingam, one of the editors of *Indivisible*, turns to themes of racial harmony in her poetry. Sundaralingam is quoted as stating, "Having witnessed ethnic violence in two countries, I find common ground with all those who work toward social unity" (*Indivisible* 231). Sundaralingam was born in Sri Lanka, and raised in both Sri Lanka and England. She currently lives in San Francisco, and has held scientific research posts at MIT and UCLA (*Indivisible* 231).

In the poem "Lot's Wives," the speaker reflects upon burning cities (possibly a scene of civil war): "Such death. The smell of justice / drifting on the burnt wind" (*Indivisible* 232). In the brief poem titled "Vermont, 1885," the speaker is W.A. Bentley, who "was the first to photograph a snowflake" (*Indivisible* 232). The poem begins with the description of snow-clad farms and a reference to the preacher's reminder of the day of judgment. Then, in the attic, the speaker takes a photograph of the snowflake, later suggesting that each snowflake has its own individual structure: "the snow disappears, is replaced / by a single, unique, six-pointed star" (*Indivisible* 232). The individual structure of each snowflake becomes a symbol for the acceptance of diversity.

The poem "Language Like Birds" presents the observations of a speaker, an expatriate with strong feelings about exile. To some extent, this poem encapsulates the quintessential experiences of the South Asian diasporean who seeks kindred spirits in foreign lands. Expatriates recognize the faces and physiques of those of their own race. They speak to new acquaintances in their native languages. Whether they are in Paris, Berlin, or New York, the words they associate with exile are "destiny," "family," and "fate": "These are the words that remain / when we find each other in foreign lands" (*Indivisible* 233). This expatriate speaker has a strong sense of loss that words cannot express. In this feeling of loss, of being exiled to a nowhere place, Sundaralingam's speaker reiterates the themes of exile and loss that recur in the poetry of both the old and the new South Asian diaspora. With the acquisition of foreign languages comes nostalgia for the vernacular South Asian language, which is no longer heard in the new country of adoption unless one meets a fellow immigrant who speaks the native tongue. And in some cases (as with the poets from Guyana and Trinidad), the native tongue is a *patois* rather than a language from South Asia.

Colonial history and racial oppression becomes the subject of Dilruba Ahmed's "The 18th Century Weavers of Muslin Whose Thumbs Were Chopped" (*Indivisible* 157). Ahmed is an educator who lives near Philadelphia. Her South Asian heritage is from Bangladesh. She has won awards for editing and writing. Ahmed received B.Phil. and M.A.T. degrees from the University of Pittsburgh, and her M.F.A. from Warren Wilson College (*Indivisible* 157).

Ahmed is also the co-editor of *Going Public with Our Teaching: An Anthology of Practice* (2005). In her poem on the muslin weavers whose thumbs were severed by the colonial English who tried to kill the muslin industry, Ahmed opens "after Agha Shahid Ali," evoking Ali's well-known poem on "The Dacca Gauzes," which reminds readers of the colonial atrocities against South Asian artisans. Dilruba Ahmed's speaker commemorates the weavers who suffered at the hands of those who spoke *ingrezi* (English) and "fashioned rice into cotton, made / slaves of them all" (*Indivisible* 157). The reader is reminded that in colonial times, the British cultivated cash crops on lands that once grew food crops in eastern India. While remembering this episode of colonial history, the speaker describes a country market or farmer's market in Bangladesh where rickshaws rattle on the streets and vendors sell oranges, green coconuts, pale cabbages, sugarcane, silk sarees, and jute rugs (*Indivisible* 158). Toward the end of the poem, the speaker addresses a child, and the reader realizes that this poem is actually a bedtime story for the younger generation (*Indivisible* 158).

Dilruba Ahmed's poem "Learning" presents a woman speaker describing how she and her partner are learning to dance. The speaker is wearing a brown silk blouse that she would not wear to teach first grade, and her partner is wearing the "navy cotton oxford" shirt that she bought him four years earlier (*Indivisible* 160). Learning to dance becomes an extended metaphor for living as a Muslim South Asian American in post–9/11 American society, where the speaker realizes that the letters on the nameplate "outside my office door — must be / a *Muslim, a maniac, a terrorist*" (*Indivisible* 161).

In the lyric "Invitation," the speaker invites her mother, who is deceased, to come out of her photograph on the dresser and journey with her back in time to the mother's youthful days in Bangladesh. The speaker, who lives in the United States, tries to imagine what her mother's life was like in a bygone era (*Indivisible* 161–63). Then, the speaker remembers that much time has gone by since she stopped writing to her mother, "sending crisp blue airmail / And my mother gone" (*Indivisible* 163). These lines encapsulate time and change. Before the days of Internet communication and reasonably priced international phone calls, South Asian expatriates had a letter-writing culture in which sending letters frequently and regularly to mothers back home was a duty.

Hybridity, Memories, Exile, Self-Identity

Bhanu Kapil's poetry approaches history from a unique perspective in "Humanimal, a project for future children" (*Indivisible* 35). Kapil states that

"I am a British (and newly U.S.) citizen, born to Indian (Punjabi) parents in the U.K. in 1968" (*Indivisible* 33). Kapil writes prose poems, and her published works include *The Vertical Interrogation of Strangers* (2001), *Incubation: A Space for Monsters* (2006), and *Humanimal, a Project for Future Children* (2009). She teaches writing at Naropa University, Colorado, and also in the low-residency M.F.A. program at Goddard College (*Indivisible* 35).

In *Humanimal,* Kapil's prose poems reconstruct a missionary's narrative of two feral children (wolf-children) found in Midnapur, West Bengal, India, in 1921. The two girls, Amala and Kamala, were placed in an orphanage. This unusual collection covers colonial history, the point of view of a feral child, the point of view of the missionary, and thinly disguised references to the poet's own father. The death of Amala, one of the feral children, is reconstructed from the missionary's narrative. The villagers come in large numbers to see the sick and dying child, who has memories of happy days with the wolf-mother who gave her milk. The sick girl refuses human food: "the dying girl as larval, perennially white, damp and fluttering in the darkness of the room" (*Indivisible* 36).

The poetry of Summi Kaipa, one of the editors of *Indivisible,* creates speakers whose prose poems are in the confessional mode. Kaipa has a doctorate in psychology, and an M.F.A. from the Iowa Writers' Workshop (*Indivisible* 41). She has published three chapbooks of poetry titled *The Epics* (1999), *I Beg You Be Still* (2003), and *The Language Parable* (2006).

Kaipa's prose poems are very allusive. In the excerpt from "A Personal Cinema," the speaker also refers to popular Bollywood actresses and actors of the 1970s and the Hindi hit songs of the 1970s. The speaker refers to the dated quality of the older film scripts, in which the physical and cultural distance between the continents seemed "insurmountable" (*Indivisible* 43). The speaker presents the attitudes of an older generation of South Asian immigrants with this observation: "Only the West can beget such exquisite womanly decadence, and I am filled with admiration and autobiography" (*Indivisible* 43). The excerpt is significant in that even in the twenty-first century, Indian films made in the subcontinent continue to depict women raised in Western cultures as decadent and sexually promiscuous.

In the excerpt from *The Epics,* the speaker's prose poems allude to characters and episodes in the Indian epics as well as to classics of literature in vernacular Indian languages. Kaipa's technique is in the confessional mode, as if memories were being recollected on the psychotherapist's couch, as well as heteroglossic. The allusions are stories within stories, with the central story being that of the female poet: "The girl poet catapulted public. The poet's brother was stumbling into the furniture and stealing the microphone" (*Indivisible* 45). Finally, the readings from the Indian epics become blended with images of everyday American life, suggesting the richness of the bicultural heritage of South Asian Americans, whose literary works are steeped in hybridity.

Memories, self-reflexivity, and the contemplation of generations — those in the Old World and those in the New World — are common elements in contemporary South Asian American poetry. In general, these intergenerational and transnational reflections recur in Asian American writing from the last half century. Award-winning poet Maya Khosla has "lived in Bangladesh, Burma, Bhutan, England, India, and several places in the United States, she now works as a consultant in biology and toxicology in California" (*Indivisible* 16). Khosla has published one collection of poetry titled *Keel Bone* (2003), a chapbook titled *Heart of the Tearing* (1996), and a collection of nonfiction titled *Web of Water* (1997).

In Khosla's monologue titled "Oppenheimer quotes *The Bhagavad Gita*," the speaker is the scientist J. Robert Oppenheimer, who is contemplating both his arrival as a refugee in the United States finding work as a physicist and the imaginary scenes of the first atomic bomb explosion as it begins to rain. The speaker has a moment of epiphany as he contemplates the effects of his scientific discoveries: "*Brighter than a thousand suns / I am become death, destroyer of the worlds*" (*Indivisible* 17).

In "Return to Grand Canyon," "Sequoia Sempervirens," and "Under Wolf-Paw," the speakers present recollections of moments and their associated landscapes that are frozen in time capsules. Two of the landscapes are in the western United States, and the poem "Under Wolf-Paw" could be set in almost any agricultural community. The "Return to Grand Canyon" is about the memories of words spoken by one who was close to the speaker. In this return, the speaker comes alone. The words are compared to juicy fruit of which all is eaten except the seed (*Indivisible* 18). It seems as if the speaker has brought the seeds, the core meaning of the words, to the canyon. The poem closes with the speaker becoming free of emotional baggage: "I empty my pockets into the great hush beneath" (*Indivisible* 19).

In "Sequoia Sempervirens" the poet uses the botanical name of the California redwood tree, known for its size and longevity. The speaker thinks of the sights and scenes witnessed by the trees that were living before the time of the Aztecs. For the speaker, the redwood trees suggest images of a community of women: "The sequoias form a country of giant women / in conference, wrapped in dark shawls" (*Indivisible* 19). Unlike "Return to Grand Canyon" and "Sequoia Sempervirens," "Under Wolf-Paw" presents a setting that is not easily identifiable. The speaker remembers a moment of saying farewell to someone living in a rural agricultural community (*Indivisible* 20–21). This individual offers farewell gifts to the speaker who is urged "to wake before the sky climbs, / and reach the border before light" (*Indivisible* 20).

The poems of Prageeta Sharma contain memories of generations and self-reflexivity. Sharma is an associate professor of English (poetry) and the director of the Creative Writing Program at the University of Montana in Missoula (*Indivisible* 88). She is an award-winning poet who has published three poetry collections: *Infamous Landscapes* (2007), *The Opening Question* (2004), and *Bliss to Fill* (2000).

In the brief poem titled "Paper," the speaker is possibly a writer who encounters her alter ego writing in her room: "This was how she found the unannounced guest, / writing with her pen at her desk" (*Indivisible* 89). The piece titled "Paper II" may be viewed as the story of a young South Asian American woman who becomes a poet (*Indivisible* 89). The parents, Madhu and Raju, were united in a traditional arranged marriage from which came their daughter, a poet. The poet has unsuccessful love affairs that take up her time, and she makes a confession to her parents: "She had certainly told them in a slow, / honest way, with a pre-planned epiphany — that she had lovers" (*Indivisible* 89). The contrast between the stable family life of the parents, whose marriage was arranged, and the unstable romantic relationships of the daughter suggest the differences between generations as well as Old World and New World cultures. In the closing lines of "Paper II," the poet realizes that disappointments can come up with both poetry and lovers (*Indivisible* 89).

In the brief piece "I Cannot Forget You," the speaker describes the scene of a couple breaking up their relationship. The actual setting appears to be a dining room, and the speaker remembers, "I speak out of turn. There is nothing / one can do when they behave poorly" (*Indivisible* 89). The poem "In Open Water, In Mathematical Star" captures a brief encounter "while it was your vodka that was clear. All who had been driving / pulled over to touch weather in rare bodily grain" (*Indivisible* 90). This poem is subtitled "After Breton," suggesting that the poet is influenced by surrealism in arranging imagery that seems disconnected and dreamlike.

Memories and fantasies surface in the poems of Bushra Rehman, who is of Pakistani ancestry. Rehman was born and raised in New York City and describes herself thus: "I am a Pakistani from Queens, New York City, with roots in North-West Frontier Province, underneath the waters of the Tarbela Dam" (*Indivisible* 117). Rehman has lived in Pakistan and Saudi Arabia. She has published the poetry collection titled *Marianna's Beauty Salon* (2001), and has co-edited *Colonize This! Young Women of Color on Today's Feminism* (2002) (*Indivisible* 117). Rehman's poetry explores untold stories of personal life, and the voices of her speakers re-create moments in their past loves with immediacy and intensity.

In the poem "Ami's Cassettes," the speaker finds her mother's cassette tapes from the 1980s. She remembers that her mother recorded the music from the television while she cleaned their home. When the speaker plays the tapes, she hears the music together with the background noise of babies crying, children fighting, and a child being spanked (*Indivisible* 117–18). The mother could not listen to her favorite music in peace and quiet: "The children wouldn't stop making noise / until my mother's own voice would break" (*Indivisible* 118). The speaker remembers the house with its orange carpets and plastic covers on sofas, as well as the sound of love songs and her mother crying (*Indivisible* 118). Underlying this memory poem is the suggestion that the love songs offered the mother an escape from the stress of her daily chores and childcare.

In the memory poem "At the Museum of Natural History," the speaker and her former lover stand looking at the skeleton of a Tyrannosaurus Rex. While they stand a few inches apart in the museum, hearing sounds made by children, they seem not to be afraid of proximity after their breakup (*Indivisible* 118–19). Then the speaker has a surrealistic vision of a time when they are both dead, imagining that if their skeletons are dug up and assembled, the bones of one may be mixed up with those of another. The poem closes with a memory of their former lovemaking: "that my fingers travelled all over / the empty space around your bones" (*Indivisible* 119). In the brief poem titled "The Difference," the speaker creates a surrealistic image of being moonstruck or carrying the moon in one's stomach, and writing late into the night: "Saying we know you, you're the one who / goes home alone and types in the dark" (*Indivisible* 119). The overarching image is of the artist as one whose imagination transforms everyday human experiences.

Hybridity, blending of cultures, and transnational allusions appear in the poetry of Aimee Nezhukumatathil, who was born in Chicago and serves as an associate professor of English at the State University of New York at Fredona. She is an award-winning writer who has published *At the Drive-In Volcano* (2007) and *Miracle Fruit* (2003), and has also received the Pushcart Prize (*Indivisible* 133). Nezhukumatathil states, "My mother is from the Philippines, and my father is from Kerala. They met in Chicago, where I was born, and I'm grateful to have this delicious blend of cultures informing my life and my work" (*Indivisible* 133). Her poem "The Mascot of Beavercreek High Breaks Her Silence" brings surprising memories of high school: "It was high school, after all. I was always cheering / for something. Still am. Something is always worth" (*Indivisible* 134). The closing of the poem plays on the words "cheer" and "worth," and ends on a positive note. Adolescent memories of a young (underage) Asian American female speaker who goes to a club with her friend Jill are presented in the poem "Mr. Mustard's Dance Club: Ladies Night," in which the two seventeen-year-old girls dance and do not drink: "We danced together, / (never with boys) never drank" (*Indivisible* 136). The young girls are left pondering a sexual innuendo in a statement made by a man at the club. Underlying the teenagers' simplistic view of the club is the world of the adult, with the insinuation of a sexual fetish regarding Asian American women. Thus Nezhukumatathil cleverly weaves in the complexity of growing up in America as an Asian American female.

In "Fishbone," the speaker is an Asian American child who faces her mother's preparation of a basket of fried smelt (*Indivisible* 134). The mother has taught her that if she feels a fishbone stuck in her throat, she should "roll some rice into a ball / And swallow it whole" (*Indivisible* 134). However, the child would prefer "normal food" like cereal, buttered toast and soft-boiled eggs (*Indivisible* 135). The mother also tapes a dime to a board each year as her child gets a year older and continues to speak of family traditions as they eat the fried fish (*Indivisible* 135).

In the poem "Last Aerogramme to You, With Lizard," Aimee Nezhukumatathil presents a speaker alone in Kovalam, Kerala, India, writing a last aerogramme. The beaches of Kovalam attract tourists, and the poet's father is originally from the state of Kerala in India. The phrase "With Lizard" in the poem's title is anticlimactic. However, as the poem unfolds, the core of the piece is unveiled as a story of the breakup of a relationship. The speaker is situated in a Kerala village on the seashore. The speaker mentions stray cats in the village, as well as local newspaper reports of village gangs entering huts armed with machetes to rob people of cash. The poem's opening is ominous as the speaker mentions finding a bat that had eaten bloody mosquitoes, a disturbing image of a food chain (*Indivisible* 135). As she writes her letter in an aerogramme, there are cats near the bed and a lone lizard, a gecko, moves over her wrist. Her eyes are wet with tears and she makes believe that the lizard is the reason for the tears: "way it skitters a loop around my wrist — exploring each elbow / makes me weep for you. My cheek is wet. A lizard makes it so" (*Indivisible* 136). This interesting use of the image of the lizard reminds readers of the reptilian image of the Tyrannosaurus Rex in Bushra Rehman's "At the Museum of Natural History," which is also about the breakup of a relationship.

For Indian immigrant poets Pramila Venkateswaran and Bhargavi C. Mandava, poetry is both hybridized and transnational. Pramila Venkateswaran teaches English and women's studies at Nassau Community College, New York. She describes herself as "a Tamilian Indian American living in New York, I write in English and translate modern Tamil poetry into English" (*Indivisible* 164). Venkateswaran has lived in the United States since 1982, and has published *Thirtha* (2002) and *Behind Dark Waters* (2008). Venkateswaran's poems "Draupadi's Dharma" and "Exile," anthologized in *Indivisible*, are both anti-war poems.

In the hybridized poem "Draupadi's Dharma," the speaker is Draupadi from the ancient Sanskrit epic, the *Mahabharata*. Draupadi addresses her husband Yudhisthira, wanting to know how long the war that he has begun in the name of justice will continue. Draupadi longs for the routines of women's lives in a time of peace. She says that "everywhere women yearn for the ordinary — / cook, clean, love, gossip, sleep" (*Indivisible* 165). Draupadi finds her husband's silence to be cold but she is firm in stating that she wants the war to end even though she was raped by the enemy at the beginning of the conflict.

In "Exile," the woman speaker addresses her absent friend Fauzia, remembering their girlhood in Kabul, Afghanistan, and the man she loved when she was young. Now all she sees are the trails of jet planes in the sky above a wartorn landscape. The poem has a surprise ending in the speaker's sudden realization: "Why is the house dark and where's everyone? / And, why don't I hear your voice, Fauzia?" (*Indivisible* 166). This ending offers at least two interpretations: one, the speaker was unconscious after a bombing episode and has regained consciousness to find that her family has either died or fled; two, the speaker is dead, and her condition is the permanent "exile" of the poem's title.

Like the poems of Venkateswaran, Bhargavi C. Mandava's poems bring transnational experiences. Mandava was born in Hyderabad, India, and raised in New York City. Mandava's poems have appeared in a number of journals, and she has published one novel, *Where the Oceans Meet* (1996). In the poem "Of Starry Silence," the speaker presents the narrative point of view of a fifteen-year-old male from Haiti who is found drowned in the Atlantic Ocean and washed ashore on the Miami coast: "All this / in between bites of mango and breadfruit" (*Indivisible* 167–68). The dead man has swum long distances in his attempt to escape from Haiti. His final escape is in death and this closing makes the poem very attractive. In contrast, the poem "Moonsweets" is a memory poem in which the speaker is an adult woman who recalls a visit to her grandmother's house. The speaker remembers her grandmother, who wore the white clothing of a Hindu widow, rolling moon-shaped sweets. The child brings the grandmother a red hibiscus flower that the child tucks behind the grandmother's ear (*Indivisible* 169). Shortly thereafter, the flower falls, slipping down the grandmother's back. However, the granddaughter is looking elsewhere at the sweets prepared by her grandmother: "as she eyes the silver canister / brimming with pale full moons" (*Indivisible* 169). The speaker remembers the expression of great concentration on her grandmother's face as she cooks: "she is not meditating — / she is cooking" (*Indivisible* 168).

Subhasini Kaligotla is a transnational poet from India who earned her M.F.A. in poetry from Columbia University, where she is currently a Ph.D.

candidate in art history (*Indivisible* 217). She has published her poetry in well-established journals, contributed to anthologies of contemporary Indian poetry, and served as editor of poetry journals. Kaligotla's poems are recognizably surrealistic.

In "Lepidoptera," the speaker views mounted insects in glass cases and compares their bodies to the tortured and elongated images of El Greco's paintings. The subtitle of this poem reads "after El Greco's *The Crucifixion with Two Donors*." The poem is addressed to a person who went into the shop on Valencia Street to look at "a scene of glass cases lined the walls, a phalanx of moths, but then you stepped in" (*Indivisible* 218). In the prose poem "Letter to New York," the speaker is a thinly disguised version of the poet herself. The speaker begins with the observation that everything in New York is hurried and one cannot be a flaneur. The speaker also starts hurrying along and the prose poem narrates random observations of New York City's street scenes (*Indivisible* 218). At the back of the speaker's mind is a romantic interest that she tries to overcome. The piece concludes with this observation: "your cabs are chrysanthemums again floating on the macadam. I am a fool to want you" (*Indivisible* 219). The image of commonplace American yellow cabs as flowers viewed from the windows of a tall building is quite unusual.

The speaker in "My Heart Belongs to Daddy" appears to be Sita, the heroine of the ancient Sanskrit epic, the *Ramayana*, who is the model of the faithful Hindu wife. In Kaligotla's subversive piece, Sita does not resist the advances of her kidnapper, King Ravan of Lanka (modern Sri Lanka). She has discarded all her jewelry on treetops so that tropical casuarinas look like modern-day Christmas trees (*Indivisible* 219). She prefers her island prison with the startling and subversive confession: "*I'm his woman now*" (*Indivisible* 219).

Transnational and hybrid imagery also appears in the poetry of Sasha Kamini Parmasad, who was born in Trinidad and raised in both Trinidad and New Delhi, India. Parmasad describes herself as follows: "A South Asian in New York, I am also a sixth generation Trinidadian, descendant of jahajees; I think of the Caribbean as my blood, India, my inherited bones" (*Indivisible* 91). Parmasad has lived in the United States from the late 1990s, receiving an undergraduate degree from Williams College, then an M.F.A. in creative writing from Columbia University in 2008 (*Indivisible* 91). Parmasad has received awards for her writing. She teaches creative writing, and is also an essayist and visual artist.

In the poem "Burning," a scene from a farm in Trinidad is depicted in clearly defined images of sight, sound, and smell. The noonday sun is as hot as the onions and garlic being fried by the grandmother in a black iron pot (*Indivisible* 91). A young girl stands at a window and watches her father capture a hog and slaughter it. The girl hears her grandmother singing as she cooks while the dying hog shrieks and becomes silent. The girl steps outside barefoot to see ants marching toward the hog's blood on the gravel: "and whisper, / Fetch me a hose" (*Indivisible* 92). The reader concludes that even if the blood is washed away, this scene will remain in the girl's memory.

In "Sugarcane Farmer," written "for Selina," Parmasad's speaker narrates a visit to an elderly woman who grows sugarcane. The speaker comes after a thirty-year absence. The old woman is a proud descendant of an Indian soldier who fought against the British in the Great Revolt of 1857: "talwar-bearing sepoy folded / into her, and she leaping" (*Indivisible* 93). Her sugarcane crop has failed, and she struggles with poverty and hunger. At age sixty-six, she welcomes her visitors with coconuts from a tree and does not mention that she lacks money for food or surgery. Her visitors make promises and leave and do not call her as she waits (*Indivisible* 94). This poem brings to life the stark reality of the extreme poverty of an old woman on a sugarcane farm in Trinidad and the reality of the departure of younger generations to seek a livelihood in other lands.

Similar to "Sugarcane Farmer," Parmasad's poem "The Old Man" features an elderly and wrinkled old man in rural Trinidad who has learned about the Tamil Tigers, a terrorist movement in Sri Lanka. The old man seems to have made connections between the bringing of indentured workers to the Caribbean and the bringing of Tamil workers to plantations in colonial Ceylon (Sri Lanka) under British rule. The old man fears that terrorism will destroy his island home: "It go take just one crazy coolie to / strap bombs to his heart" (*Indivisible* 95). The image of the suicide bomber created in the old man's *patois* is quite unforgettable.

The transnational performance poetry of Shailja Patel has won several awards. Patel is from Kenya and of South Asian descent. In her own words, "I am a radical Desi internationalist, pan–Africanist, feminist, and live in Nairobi and the San Francisco Bay Area" (*Indivisible* 120). Patel has won accolades in different countries for her performance poetry, and has published two poetry chapbooks: *Dreaming in Gujarati* and *Shilling Love*.

In "Shilling Love," the speaker narrates memories of growing up South Asian in Kenya with parents who work hard and save money, realizing that their immigrant life in Kenya is not stable (*Indivisible* 121). The children are urged to study hard so that they can be admitted to institutions of higher education in the United Kingdom. Then there are the memories of the 1982 military coup in Nairobi, when all the Asians were rounded up at gunpoint and expelled from Kenya (*Indivisible* 122). The speaker and her sister come with their parents to an international airport and, after many hours of interrogation, they are admitted into the United States (*Indivisible* 123–24). This poem's speaker vividly enacts the racial persecution of Asians in Kenya, and the homelessness of diasporic South Asians expelled from African countries who find refuge in the United States after a grueling interview with U.S. immigration personnel. The sufferings of the diasporic South Asian condition and, perhaps, the rejection faced across nations make the speaker become a poet (*Indivisible* 124). The "shilling love" of the title is reiterated in the refrain of currency exchange rates telling how many Kenyan shillings make an English pound each year from 1975 to 2000, the year the family enters the United States. The parents' entire savings is affected by the exchange rate until they arrive in the United States to be with their children. "Shilling Love" brings home the chilling truth of racial discrimination in Kenya: "never / be Kenyan enough / all my patriotic fervor / will never turn my skin / black / as yet another western country / drops a portcullis / of immigration" (*Indivisible* 122).

In "Love Poem for London," the speaker describes different nights in London at concerts and shows given by internationally famous performers from all over the world. At the center of this poem is a romantic relationship where the significant other is romantic and the speaker is interested in politics (*Indivisible* 125). The speaker's love for cultural richness and global diversity in London comes forth with the performance of William Shakespeare's *A Midsummer Night's Dream* by a Japanese theater company (*Indivisible* 125, 128), which is a central episode in this narrative. The end of the play leads to the romantic encounter described at the end of the poem: "I was electric you incandescent / my hair shot sparks your breath ignited" (*Indivisible* 126).

Sejal Shah is a South Asian American poet who was born and raised in Rochester, New York. Sejal Shah's poetry is filled with American imagery, and her connections to other continents are limited: "Though the daughter of Gujarati parents from Ahmedabad and Nairobi, I have been to India twice and Kenya never" (*Indivisible* 62). Shah received an undergraduate degree from Wellesley College, and her M.F.A. in fiction from the University of Massachusetts, Amherst. She works at Marymount Manhattan College as an assistant professor of English (*Indivisible* 62).

Sejal Shah's poetry presents women speakers who express themselves in the confessional mode regarding memories of relationships that may be in the speakers' past lives. For instance, in "Everybody's Greatest Hits," the speaker remembers dancing in her living room prior to the relationship coming apart: "Every word when leaving is about pointing. Pointing / is always about leaving. Lying is only leaving before you go" (*Indivisible* 62). With the impending separation, the speaker fantasizes about a wedding that will not take place and imagines speaking to a future daughter (*Indivisible* 62–63). In "Accordion," the speaker remembers her conversations with a significant other, of meetings in bars: "What I wanted was protection, was to see. To lean against / the bar, half-lit, and look into the half-lit places. To unfurl" (*Indivisible* 63). In the poem "Independence, Iowa," the speaker describes memories of a long drive with her partner through America's heartland. They pass cornfields and picturesque scenes, driving over bridges and stopping in small towns to savor the beauty of the American countryside: "You said: I'd like to hop trains some day. The world is full of things / we haven't done. Or said. In this corner of Iowa I feel far from every place else" (*Indivisible* 64).

Iowa-born Mytili Jagannathan teaches at the Community College of Philadelphia, and runs a consulting business, Itinerant Ink. She has published a poetry chapbook titled *Acts*, and holds a B.A. from Brandeis University and an M.A. from the University of Pennsylvania (*Indivisible* 77).

In the postmodern piece titled "nationalism redactor," Jagannathan uses lowercase letters and choppy phrases to suggest images of political unrest in the context of the Indian subcontinent. Jagannathan studied in Madurai, Tamil Nadu, India, for one year and is clearly well versed in the political and cultural issues of the Indian subcontinent. The repetition of the phrase "agitation and remorse" in this poem suggests the unrest within the psyche of the poem's speaker as the "camera solves resisting / bodies India day parade" (*Indivisible* 78).

Very similar to the images of agitation, crowds, and unrest in "nationalism redactor," in the brief poem "Dream Horse" the central image is one of destruction and violence. The title itself is ironic because the setting is one of darkness and rain where "in the forest of values / I disassembled a gun," as stated by the speaker (*Indivisible* 79). Here, too, the house becomes symbolic of turmoil and angst within the psyche of the poem's speaker/persona.

Transnational relocations have taken the contemporary poet Swati Rana from her birthplace in India to Canada, and then to the United States. Having attended Dartmouth College, Rana is a graduate student at the University of California, Berkeley. In addition to poetry, Rana has published short fiction about her extended family migrating across continents (*Indivisible* 214).

In the poem "Stopping for the Northern Lights," the speaker is driving on an interstate highway at nightfall, passing farms and barns. The speaker sees a black barn and imagines that a girl could have hanged herself from the rafters in such a place, and her lifeless body would be found at sunrise. The poem closes with an image of the eyes of the dead: "eyes are always open, / green and nightly" (*Indivisible* 215). Ironically, "Stopping for the Northern Lights" becomes an episode of the light going out of a girl's life. The memory poem "To Reveal" returns to the speaker's childhood, when her hair was in pigtails and she wore white bloomers. The girl is presumably playing with a boy. He is playing doctor using her toy stethoscope, asks the girl to reveal more than she is prepared for: "but I, too nervous even / to look, saw only where" (*Indivisible* 216).

As in the case of the many anthologies from the Indian subcontinent, a current collection of contemporary poetry is indicative of forms, influences, and recurring themes and motifs in South Asian American poetry viewed from the perspective of the editors. Due to the fact that several of the poets published in *Indivisible* are at an early stage of their writing careers, it is difficult to predict their future as poets.

NOTE

1. There was another Beatrice D'Este, Queen of Hungary, who lived in the thirteenth century and did not die young.

WORK CITED

Banerjee, Neelanjana, et al., eds. *Indivisible: An Anthology of Contemporary South Asian American Poetry*. Fayetteville: University of Arkansas Press, 2010. Print.

• ELEVEN •

Coda

The subject of this study is similar to many postmodern poems in that it defies the very idea of a conclusion or a closing; hence the musical term "coda" appears to be more appropriate for this closing chapter. The previous chapters have established that the almost two centuries of the English-language poetry of South Asians has its own hybridized and transnational tradition, with poetry collections being published from several countries located in different continents for an audience that seeks English-language publications. In the second decade of the twenty-first century, contemporary South Asian poetry in English continues to flourish both in the Indian subcontinent and amid the predominantly English-language culture of the South Asian diaspora in North America. It is difficult to predict the future of this growing body of poetry. It is even more difficult to predict the future for systematic critical studies of the major paradigms of South Asians' English-language poetry, as more and more collections are published by the poets of the diaspora. Several poets are also anthologists who are engaged in ground-breaking work in collecting and preserving South Asian English-language poetry. In addition to the decades of poetic preservation in the Indian subcontinent offered by the Writers Workshop in Kolkata and the Oxford University Press anthologies, the collections of Jeet Thayil titled *60 Indian Poets* (2008) and *The Bloodaxe Book of Contemporary Indian Poetry* (2008); Eunice de Souza's *Early Indian Poetry in English: An Anthology: 1829–1947* (2005); and the American anthology *Indivisible* (2010) should be recognized as important volumes that bring the work of South Asian poets writing in English to the attention of literary critics.

While English-language poetry now has its own niche in India despite an occasional negative review, and the Indian poets appear to be at ease incorporating South Asian words, allusions, and images into their poems, the "ethnic" aspect of South Asians' English-language poetry has both positive and negative attributes when discussed in the context of the poems of the South Asian diaspora. A question then arises regarding the future of "ethnic" allusions in the poetry of the South Asian diaspora. With second and third generations born and raised overseas, will the future poetry simply become part of the larger North American or British or Australian canvas? Or, as in the Caribbean and Fiji, will South Asian poets maintain an element of their ethnic heritage? Thus, there also arises a larger question of whether an "ethnic" element in poetry makes the writing less accessible to a culturally diverse audience. Or does the "ethnic" element actually increase the prospect of "selling" a manuscript to a publisher? For example, a basic question comes up as to what extent the "ethnic" elements, such as allusions, images, and loan words from South Asian languages, are really integral to sensory experiences presented by the speakers in a large number of contemporary diasporic South Asian poems.

In order to explore these questions, future critics may have to address the sociological aspects of South Asian immigration and cultural assimilation in different countries. The patterns of South Asian immigration and cultural assimilation are quite diverse because the immigrants are socio-economically stratified. The speakers' voices in the American anthology *Indivisible* are predominantly from the middle class and educated using the conventions of formal English, while Sudesh Mishra's Indo-Fijians in Australia contemplate being unemployed, and in the United Kingdom Daljit Nagra's Punjabi immigrant personae express their anti–Western ideas in broken English. A recurring motif in the poems of first-generation immigrant poets is nostalgia for the sights, sounds, and smells of the lost homeland and for loved ones left behind. With second-generation poets, the personae often compare the ethnic and "foreign" mannerisms, speech, and values of their parents' generation to their own.

It is important to note that in the English-language poetry of South Asians, women poets generally tend to create female voices and male poets mostly present male speakers. Androgynous speakers are infrequent. Only a few poems explore homosexual identities. However, for centuries, in the vernacular poetry in Indian languages, male poets created personae that were female. It may be theorized that due to its origins under colonial British literary influences and its continued use of Western models, flexibility in constructing gender identities was not given much consideration in the development of the English-language poetry of South Asians.

Recent works of scholarship, such as Jahan Ramazani's *The Hybrid Muse: Postcolonial Poetry in English* (2001) and Ramazani's *Transnational Poetics* (2009), and Rajeev Patke's *Postcolonial Poetry in English* (2006), have theorized on the poetics of postcolonial poetry in English from broadbased perspectives within the larger frame of postcolonial studies. The preceding chapters of this study focus upon the paradigms of almost two centuries of South Asian poetry in English, demonstrating continuities from the colonial into the postcolonial eras, and from late modernism to a rich medley of postmodern poems published from different continents by contemporary poets of South Asian descent. An example of the contemporary relevance of the English-language poetry of South Asian poets in the United States can be observed in Pramila Venkateswaran's article in the *Writer's Chronicle* (2011) titled "Recent Trends in South Asian American Poetry." The publication of this article is significant in that this journal is published by AWP (Association of Writers & Writing Programs) and is distributed to all creative writing professionals who are members of this organization. This article selectively presents the contributions of two generations of South Asian American poets from the last fifty years. Like the anthology *Indivisible*, Venkateswaran's article marks an attempt to find a niche for South Asian American poetry within the canon of contemporary American poetry. In the context of the critics and poets covered in the present study, it is interesting to note that Venkateswaran refers to Ramazani's discussion of poetics in his analysis of the late A.K. Ramanujan's poetry. Venkateswaran's article also makes references to the poems of Vijay Seshadri, Agha Shahid Ali, Chitra Divakaruni, Meena Alexander, Reetika Vazirani, Kazim Ali, Bhanu Kapil, Minal Hajratwala, Shailja Patel, Saleem Peeradina, and Ralph Nazareth. For a first-time introduction to South Asian American poetry, Venkateswaran's coverage is representative, also providing the following valuable observation:

> For the Indian American poet, while the marginal status of the immigrant can be a place of discovery, it is also a double-edged sword; as the writer's marginal status sharpens perception, it also stereotypes the writer as "immigrant" thus making him/her feel boxed in. We see recent first and second generation Indian American poets, like Vijay Seshadri, distancing themselves from the immigrant theme ... in Reetika Vazirani's poems, the immigrant theme is in the background ... some poets like Ralph Nazareth, Agha Shahid Ali, and Saleem Peeradina foreground the immigrant narrative presenting its poignancies and absurdities in such complex and profound ways [38].

In closing, it is perhaps appropriate to offer the projection that South Asian poetry in English will continue to flourish and perhaps branch out just as the English-language fiction of South Asians has blossomed and grown in the twenty-first century. The increase in the publication of poetry anthologies may be followed by an increase in scholarly articles and critical studies as this genre finally becomes well established after having suffered relative neglect for the first hundred years.

WORKS CITED

Banerjee, Neelanjana, et al., eds. *Indivisible: An Anthology of Contemporary South Asian American Poetry*. Fayetteville: University of Arkansas Press, 2010. Print.
de Souza, Eunice, ed. *Early Indian Poetry in English: An Anthology 1829–1947*. New Delhi: Oxford University Press, 2005. Print.

Patke, Rajeev. *Postcolonial Poetry in English*. Oxford: Oxford University Press, 2006. Print.

Ramazani, Jahan. *The Hybrid Muse: Postcolonial Poetry in English*. Chicago: University of Chicago Press, 2001. Print.

_____. *A Transnational Poetics*. Chicago: University of Chicago Press, 2009. Print.

Thayil, Jeet, ed. *The Bloodaxe Book of Contemporary Indian Poets*. Highgreen, Northumberland, UK: Bloodaxe Books, 2008. Print.

_____, ed. *60 Indian Poets*. New Delhi: Penguin India, 2008. Print.

Venkateswaran, Pramila. "Recent Trends in South Asian American Poetry." *The Writer's Chronicle* 43.5 (2011): 36–42. Print.

Bibliography

Alexander, Meena. *Fault Lines: A Memoir.* New York: Feminist Press at the City University of New York, 1993. Print.
_____. *Night-Scene, The Garden.* New York: Red Dust, 1992. Print.
_____. *River and Bridge.* New York: TSAR, 1996. Print.
_____. *Illiterate Heart.* Evanston, IL: TriQuarterly Books/Northwestern University Press, 2002. Print.
Ali, Agha Shahid. *The Half-Inch Himalayas.* Middletown, CT: Wesleyan, 1987. Print.
Alvi, Moniza. *Carrying My Wife.* Newcastle upon Tyne, UK: Bloodaxe Books, 2000. Print.
Banerjee, Neelanjana, et al., eds. *Indivisible: An Anthology of Contemporary South Asian American Poetry.* Fayetteville: University of Arkansas Press, 2010. Print.
Bery, Ashok. *Cultural Translation and Postcolonial Poetry.* Basingstoke, UK: Palgrave Macmillan, 2007. Print.
Bhabha, Homi K. "Culture's in Between." *Artforum* 32.1 (1993): 167–68, 211–12. Print.
_____. "Indo-Anglian Attitudes." *TLS: Times Literary Supplement* (February 3, 1978), 3958: 136. Print.
_____. "Indo-Anglian Attitudes," (Letter). *TLS: Times Literary Supplement* (April 21, 1978), 3968: 445. Print.
_____. *The Location of Culture.* London: New York: Routledge, 1994. Print.
Bhatt, Sujata. *The Stinking Rose.* Manchester, UK: Carcanet Press, 1995. Print.
"Biography of Sarojini Naidu." www.poemhunter.com/sarojini-naidu. Accessed 8 April 2012.
Bradley-Birt, F.B. *Twelve Men of Bengal in the Nineteenth Century.* Calcutta: S.K. Lahiri & Co., 1910. HathiTrust Digital Library. Accessed 8 April 2012.
Brians, Paul. *Modern South Asian Literature in English.* Westport, CT: Greenwood Press, 2003. Print.
Brown, Lloyd W. *West Indian Poetry.* Boston: Twayne, 1978. Print.
Brown, Stewart, and Ian McDonald. *The Heinemann Book of Caribbean Poetry.* New York: Heinemann, 1992. Print.
Burris, Sidney. *The Poetry of Resistance: Seamus Heaney and the Pastoral Tradition.* Athens: Ohio University Press, 1990. Print.
Crusz, Rienzi. *Beatitudes of Ice.* Toronto: TSAR, 1995. Print.
_____. *Insurgent Rain: Selected Poems 1974–1996.* Toronto: TSAR, 1997. Print.
_____. *Lord of the Mountain: The Sardiel Poems.* Toronto: TSAR, 1999. Print.
Dabydeen, Cyril. *Born in Amazonia.* Buffalo: Mosaic Press, 1995. Print.
_____. *Stoning the Wind.* Toronto: TSAR, 1994. Print.
Dabydeen, David. *Slave Song.* Leeds, UK: Peepal Tree, 2005. Print.

_____. *Turner: New and Selected Poems*. Leeds, UK: Peepal Tree, 2002. Print.

de Caires Narain, Denise. *Contemporary Caribbean Women's Poetry: Making Style*. New York: Routledge, 2002. Print.

de Souza, Eunice, ed. *Early Indian Poetry in English: An Anthology 1829–1947*. New Delhi: Oxford University Press, 2005. Print.

_____, ed. *Nine Indian Women Poets: An Anthology*. New Delhi: Oxford University Press, 1997.

Dharwadkar, Vinay. "Poetry of the Indian Subcontinent." In *A Companion to Twentieth Century Poetry*. Ed. Neil Roberts. Malden, MA: Blackwell, 2001: 264–80. Print.

Divakaruni, Chitra. *Leaving Yuba City: New and Selected Poems*. New York: Anchor Books/Doubleday, 1997. Print.

Du Bois, W.E.B. *The Souls of Black Folk*. 1903. Electronic Text Center: University of Virginia Library. Web. 8 April 2012.

Dwivedi, A.N. *Indian Poetry in English: A Literary History and Anthology*. Atlantic Highlands, NJ: Humanities Press, 1980. Print.

Espinet, Ramabai. *Nuclear Seasons*. Toronto: Sister Vision Press, 1991. Print.

Ferguson, Arthur B. *Clio Unbound: Perception of the Social and Cultural Past in Renaissance England*. Durham, NC: Duke University Press, 1979. Print.

Gandhi, Leela. *Postcolonial Theory: A Critical Introduction*. New York: Columbia University Press. 1998. Print.

Ghose, Zulfikar. *Selected Poems*. Karachi: Oxford University Press, 1991.

Goff, Barbara. *Classics and Colonialism*. London: Duckworth, 2005. Print.

Grant, Kevin, ed. *The Art of David Dabydeen*. Leeds, UK: Peepal Tree, 1997. Print.

Guerin, Wilfred L., et al. *A Handbook of Critical Approaches to Literature*. 6th ed. New York: Oxford University Press, 2011. Print.

Haq, Kaiser. *Contemporary Indian Poetry*. Columbus: Ohio State University Press, 1990. Print.

Hassan, Syed K.M. *Collected Poems of Syed Khwaja Moinul Hassan*. Kolkata: Writers Workshop, 2003. Print.

Hillis Miller, J. *Tropes, Parables, Performatives: Essays in Twentieth Century Literature*. Durham, NC: Duke University Press, 1991. Print.

"Kamalar baromasi." In East Bengal Ballet-Purbabanga-Gitika. sos_arsenic.net/loving-bengal/purbo.html. Accessed 20 February 2012.

Khwaja, Waqas. *No One Waits for the Train*. Belgium: Alhambra, 2007. Print.

King, Bruce. *Modern Indian Poetry in English*. New Delhi: Oxford University Press, 2001. Print.

Lahiri, K.C. *Indo-English Poetry in Bengal*. Kolkata: Writers Workshop, 1974. Print.

March, Richard, and Tambimuttu. *T.S. Eliot: A Symposium from Conrad Aiken*. London: Editions Poetry London, 1948. Print.

Mehrotra, Arvind Krishna. *The Oxford India Anthology of Twelve Modern Indian Poets*. Delhi: Oxford University Press, 1992. Print.

Mishra, Sudesh. *Diaspora and the Difficult Art of Dying*. Dunedin, New Zealand: University of Otago Press, 2002. Print.

Mishra, Vijay. *The Literature of the Indian Diaspora: Theorizing the Diasporic Imaginary*. London: Routledge, 2007. Print.

Munro, Doug. "In the Wake of the Leonidas: Reflections on Indo-Fijian Indenture Historiography." *The Journal of Pacific Studies* 24.1 (2005): 93–117. www.usp.ac.fj/jps/Doug-Munro.pdf. Accessed 8 April 2012.

Nair, K.R. Ramachandran. *Gathered Grace: An Anthology of Indian Verse in English*. New Delhi: Sterling, 1991. Print.

Ondaatje, Michael. *Handwriting*. New York: Random House, 2000. Print.

Parthasarathy, R. "Indo-Anglian Attitudes" (Letter). *TLS: Times Literary Supplement* (March 10, 1978), 3963: 285. Print.

_____, ed. *Ten Twentieth-Century Indian Poets*. Delhi: Oxford University Press, 1976. Print.

Patke, Rajeev. *Postcolonial Poetry in English*. Oxford: Oxford University Press, 2006. Print.

Paz, Octavio. *The Bow and the Lyre: The Poem, the Poetic Revelation, Poetry and History*. Austin: University of Texas Press, 1973. Print.

Persaud, Sasenarine. *A Surf of Sparrows' Songs*. Toronto: TSAR, 1996. Print.

_____. *The Wintering Kundalini*. Leeds, UK: Peepal Tree, 2002. Print.

Pirbhai, Mariam. *Mythologies of Migration, Vocabularies of Indenture: Novels of the South Asian Diaspora in Africa, the Caribbean, and Asia-Pacific*. Toronto: University of Toronto Press, 2009. Print.

Pocock, J.G.A. *Politics, Language, and Time: Essays on Political Thought and History*. New York: Athenaeum, 1971. Print.

Puttenham, Richard [George]. *The Arte of English Poesie* [Arber facsimile edition]. Kent, OH: Kent State University Press, 1970. Print.

Ramanujan, A.K. *The Collected Poems of A.K. Ramanujan*. Delhi: Oxford University Press, 1995. Print.

_____. *Uncollected Poems and Prose*. Ed. Molly Daniels-Ramanujan and Keith Harrison. New Delhi: Oxford University Press, 2001. Print.

Ramazani, Jahan. "Contemporary Postcolonial Poetry." In *A Companion to Twentieth Century Poetry*. Ed. Neil Roberts. Malden, MA: Blackwell, 2001: 596–609. Print.

_____. *The Hybrid Muse: Postcolonial Poetry in English*. Chicago: University of Chicago Press, 2001. Print.

_____. *A Transnational Poetics*. Chicago: University of Chicago Press, 2009. Print.

Said, Yunus, ed. *Pieces of Eight: Eight Poets from Pakistan*. Dhaka: Oxford University Press, 1971. Print.

Sarang, Vilas. *Indian English Poetry Since 1950: An Anthology*. New Delhi: Orient Longman, 1990. Print.

Sen, Sudeep. *Dali's Twisted Hands*. New York: Peepal Tree, 1994. Print.

Sharat Chandra, G.S. *Family of Mirrors*. Kansas City: BkMk Press, Umkc, 1993. Print.

Spear, Percival. *A History of India*. Vol. 2. New York: Penguin, 1978. Print.

Tambimuttu, J.M. *Out of This War: a Poem*. London: The Fortune Press, 1941. Print.

Thapar, Romila. *A History of India*. Vol. 1. New York: Penguin, 1966. Print.

Thayil, Jeet, ed. *The Bloodaxe Book of Contemporary Indian Poets*. Highgreen, Northumberland, UK: Bloodaxe Books, 2008. Print.

_____, ed. *60 Indian Poets*. New Delhi: Penguin India, 2008. Print.

Venkateswaran, Pramila. "Recent Trends in South Asian American Poetry." *The Writer's Chronicle* 43.5 (2011): 36–42. Print.

Verma, K.D. *The Indian Imagination: Critical Essays on Indian Writing in English*. New York: St. Martin's Press, 2000. Print.

Wong, Mitali, and Zia Hasan. *The Fiction of South Asians in North America and the Caribbean*. Jefferson, NC: McFarland, 2004. Print.

Index